MICROBES

MICROBES

Editor

Varun Shastri

ISHA

ISHA BOOKS

DELHI-110033

Microbes

ISBN: 81-8205-381-1

Rs. 690

Published in 2006 in India by
Isha Books
D-43, Prithviraj Road, Adarsh Nagar, Delhi-110033
E-mail : ishabooks@hotmail.com

Laser Typesetting at: Master Computers, Delhi
Printed at: Salasar Imaging System, Delhi

Preface

A microbe or microorganism is an organism that is microscopic. Microbes are often illustrated using single-celled, or unicellular organisms; however, some unicellular protists are visible to the naked eye, and some multicellular species are microscopic. The study of microbes is called microbiology. Microbes are found everywhere in nature. Even in hostile environments, like the poles, deserts, geysers, rocks, and the deep sea, some types of microorganisms have adapted to the extreme conditions and sustained colonies; these organisms are known as extremophiles. Microbes are used in brewing, baking, biotechnology, recycling of other organisms' remains and waste products, and many other processes. They can also be harmful as pathogens when, as parasites, they cause infections.

Microbes have an important place in all ecosystems and in most higher-order multicellular organisms. For mankind they are important because they participate in the earth's element cycles, and because of their use in the creation of certain types of food, medicines and biological weapons. An in-depth understanding about the structure, functions and applications these tiny organisms is essential for all who related to modern life sciences. The present book provides overall information about microbes in a simple style. Besides students and teachers of life sciences, microbiologists, researchers and budding scientists will also find this book of utmost use.

Editor

Conents

1

Fundamentals of Microbiology

Microbiology is the study of organisms that at some point in their life exist as single cell and contain a nucleic acid genome that can replicate. Many organisms fall into this definition including algae, fungi, protozoa, bacteia and archaea. Together these organisms have a profound impact on the biosphere, making up the majority of life both in number and total mass. Many illnesses are causing by infection with microbes and understanding these infections has lead to cures and better treatments.

The emergence of new infectious agents will spur continued interest in microbiology. Many more microbes grow harmlessly in the environment, taking advantage of chemicals and/or sunlight to grow. Research into microbes has also helped us understand the basic framework of life and revealed the basic fundamental rules that govern living systems. In the past microbes have been used in experiments to answer many scientific questions and they will continue to serve as excellent tools of inquiry in the future. A significant number of these discoveries have lead to important applications in many areas of human endeavor.

Despite the involvement of a small faction of microbes in disease, many other microbes actually enhance our well-being. The harmless microbes that live in our intestines and on our skin actually help us fight off disease. They actively antagonize other bacteria and take up space, preventing potential pathogens form gaining a foothold on our bodies. Indeed, like all large organisms, humans have entire communities of microorganisms in their digestive systems that contribute to their overall health.

Bacteria are very small. Yet despite their size they show a surprising degree of structural complexity. Learning the structure of a microbe helps in understanding how a microbe functions. To drive this point home, here are a few examples.

— Disease causing bacteria (pathogens) have various structures that enhance their ability to cause illness. One important property is the ability to attach to the intended victim. pili, a proteinaceous surface structure on bacteria, are critical in this process.

— Many bacteria are capable of movement in their environment either by flagella or gliding motility. In the case of flagella, bacteria have a long, flexible, spiral shaped structure, the flagellum, that helps to push the microbe through solution. Flagella also help in the detection of favorable or unfavorable conditions and move the bacterium in an appropriate direction.

— As a microbe grows it has to synthesize more of itself. Knowing what it is made of and how it is put together is critical to gain an understanding of the growth process.

— Microbes are also capable of exchanging genetic information by mating. This process involves another type of surface structure, the F-pilus.

— Bacteria will take steps to insure their survival. This can take the form of creating resting structures that allow the microbe to "sleep" during bad times. During abundant times, many microbes will store excess carbon, nitrogen, sulfur or phosphorous in inclusions in the cell.

Not only is structure important to understand functional relationships, it's also fascinating to observe what these little architects come up with.

Universal Structures in Bacteria

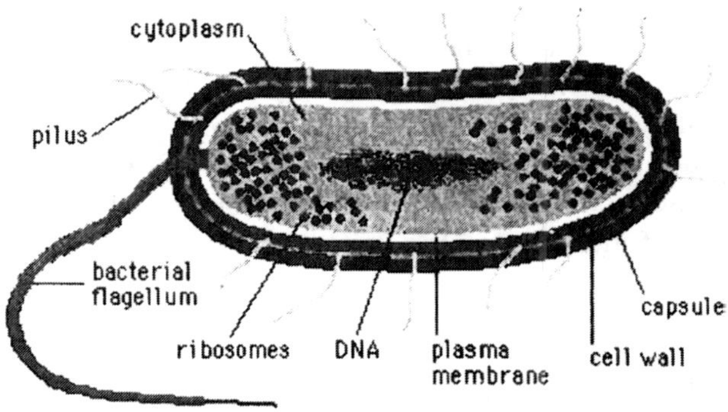

Figure 1: A cartoon of a general bacterium.

No one bacterium contains all these structures. Archaea and Bacteria share many structures, but significant differences. There are some universal structures that all bacteria have. The basic building blocks of life, DNA, RNA, and protein, are common to all organisms not just microbes. Also, all microbes have a cell membrane. Most bacteria have a cell wall, but not all.

Light, fluorescence, and electron microscopes are important of course. But so is bacterial genetics, molecular biology and biochemistry. Microscopes help scientists to visualize where these structures are located and how they are arranged spacially on the microbe. Bacterial genetics and molecular biology identify and analyze the genes necessary for the synthesis and regulation of these structures. Biochemistry permits the examination of each part separately and in the presence of the whole bacteria.

The powerful combination of these disciplines has presented a deep understanding of how a bacteria is put together, but there is still much to learn.

Cytoplasm

The cytoplasm or protoplasm is the portion of the cell that lies within the cytoplasmic membrane. The cytoplasmic matrix is defined as substances within the plasma membrane, excluding the genetic material. It is relatively featureless by electron microscope—although small granules can be seen. However, the cytoplasm carries out very important functions for the cell.

Characteristics of cytoplasm

- Gel-like consistency, with very different properties when compared to s solution made up in a test tube.
- Compartmentalization
  - The glycolysis enzymes are organized into a unit and degrade substrate in a assembly line fashion.
  - Many DNA synthesis enzymes congregate at the replication fork.
- Constituents
  - Proteins including enzymes
  - Vitamins
  - Ions
  - Nucleic acids and their precursors
  - Amino acids and their precursors
  - Sugars, carbohydrates and their derivatives
  - Fatty acids and their derivatives

The cytoplasm holds many cellular constituents, including the cell pool. It is within the cytoplasm that many of the functions for cell growth, metabolism and replication are carried out.

Specific regions of interest in the cytoplasm

— *Genetic regions*: The regions containing the hereditary information for the cell.

— *Proteins*: Found throughout the cell either as reaction catalysts or in various structures of the cell.

— *Ribosomes*: The protein synthesis machinery.

Nucleic Acids

Nucleics acids, Ribonucleic acid (RNA) and Deoxyribonucleic acid (DNA), serve as storage units for our hereditary information. DNA can be thought of as a large cookbook with recipes for making every protein in the cell. RNA helps the ribosome translate the information in DNA into protein.

The building blocks: Despite their importance in cellular function, nucleic acid structure is surprisingly simple. RNA and DNA are long polymers of only 4 nucleotides, adenine, guanine, cytosine and thymine (or uracil for RNA). The nucleotide structure can be broken down into 2 parts. The sugar-phosphate backbone and the base. All nucleotides share the sugar-phosphate backbone.

Nucleotide polymers are formed by linking the monomer units together using an oxygen on the phosphate, and a hydroxyl group on the sugar. A, T, G and C are capable of being linked together to form a long chain. The 3'-hydroxyl group on the ribose unit, reacts with the 5'-phosphate group on it's neighbor to form a chain.

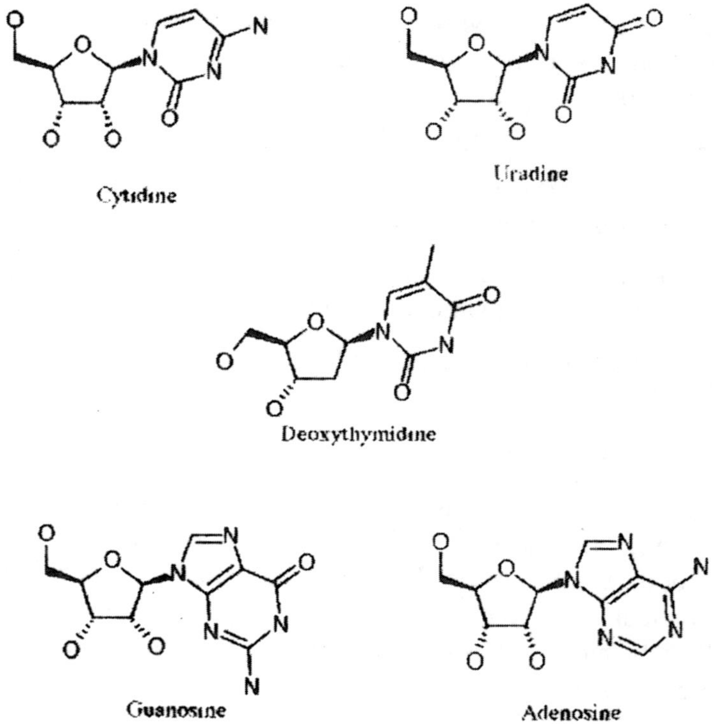

Figure 2: The structure of nucleotides.

The base on each nucleotide is different, but they still show similarities. adenine (A) and guanine (G) are purines, notice the two ring structure, with the differences in the molecules coming in the groups attached to the ring. Likewise, cytosine (C) and thymine (T) and uracil (U) are pyrimidines and share a similar structure, but differ in their side groups. (Figure 2).

Base Pairing: If two strands of nucleic acid are adjacent to one another. The bases along the polymer can interact with complementary bases in the other strand. As shown in Figure 3, adenine is capable of forming hydrogen bonds with thymine and cytosine can base pair with guanine. Adenine forms two hydrogen bonds with thymine, cytosine forms 3 with guanine. The G to C pair is 33% stronger than the A to T pair due to the extra hydrogen bond.

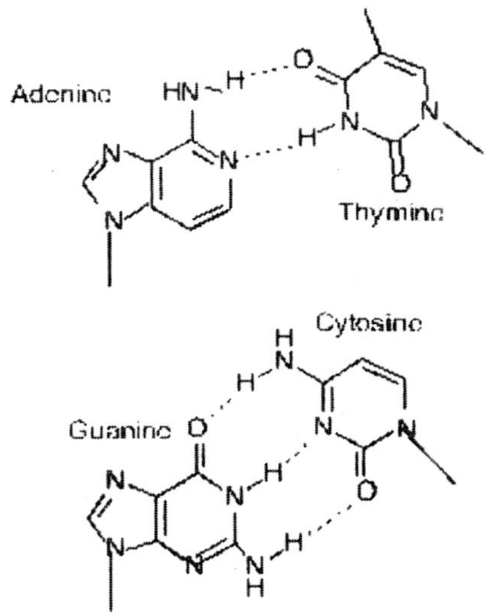

Figure 3: Base pairing between nucleic acids.

Cells contain two strands of DNA that are exact mirrors of each other. When correctly aligned, A can pair with T and G can pair with C. Because these strands are mirrors of each other, the amount of A is equal to the amount of T and the amount of C is equal to the amount of G in any double stranded DNA molecule. In solution, the two strands will usually find each other and form a double helix. This reaction is favorable because of the numerous hydrogen bonds that can be formed between the complementary bases.

The DNA molecule can stretch for millions of base pairs and the DNA sizes of organisms can vary greatly. However that the size of the DNA genome is not always a measure of how advanced an organism is, unless you think newts (genome size 19,000,000 kb) are more advanced than humans (genome size 3,500,000 kb).

```
—A–T–G–C–G–A–T–C–G–A–T–C–G–C–G–C–T–A–T–G–C–A—
 |  |  |  |  |  |  |  |  |  |  |  |  |  |  |  |  |  |  |  |  |  |
—T–A–C–G–C–T–A–G–C–T–A–G–C–G–C–G–A–T–A–C–G–T→
```

RNA is similar in structure to DNA, except that uracil (U) takes the place of thymine in the molecule and the ribose unit on each sugar contains a hydroxyl group. RNA serves 3 functions in ribosomes. These functions center around translating the genetic information in DNA into protein.

Genetic Rregions: Bacterial cells lack a membrane defined nucleus. However a descrete region in the bacterial cytoplasm seems to contain the genetic material and this nucleiod region can often be distinguished on EMs of cells. Most cells have only one main chromosome although a few species do have 2 or more.

Bacterial Chromosome

The bacterial chromosome consists of a single, circle of deoxyribonucleic acid. To learn more about basic nucleic acid stucture follow the link. DNA is double stranded- two strands line up antiparrallel to each other and the bases are linked together with hydrogen bonds. Due to the nature of these bonds the strands form a left handed double helix.

The entire molecule is a linear sequence of bases. The typical E. coli cell has 4.6 x 106 bases, this would make a strand of DNA 1400 m long, but E. coli is only 2-3 m long. The size of bacterial DNA is halved by the circular structure of the DNA, but much more is needed of course. A series of strategies are employed by microbes to compact the DNA, yet leave it accessible for its necessary functions.

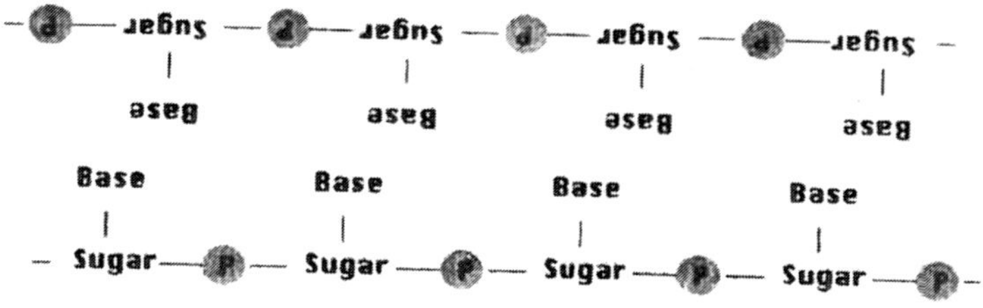

A schematic of the bonding of one DNA strand to another

The relaxed circular chromosome, with a diameter of appoximately 430 m, is first segregated into about 50 chromosomal domains by DNA-protein interactions with nucleotide binding proteins such as HU, IHF and H-NS. There is sufficient HU protein in the cell to bind the DNA every 300 to 400 bp and these protiens are thought to act in a fashion similar to the histones in eucaryotic organisms. An intact chromosome with its full complement of DNA binding proteins will result in a particle with a maximum diameter of 17m. The DNA is further compacted by twisting the DNA in each domain around itself, called supercoiling (Figure 4).

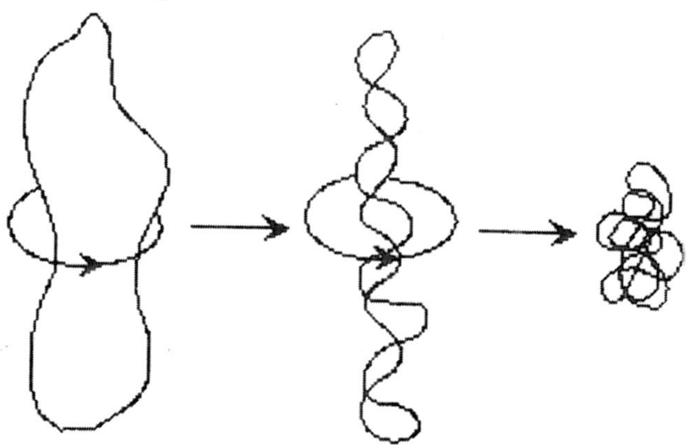

Figure 4: Supercoiling of DNA.

A collection of enzymes (one of the more notable being DNA gyrase) is responsible for winding the DNA. Imagine the DNA as a rubber band held at one end. DNA gyrase twists the DNA about itself causing it to fold over. By repeating this process many times the DNA is organized into a series of supercoiled regions. A fully supercoiled chrmosome will be about 1m in diameter and is small enough to fit inside a bacterium.

Function

Protein production: The single most important purpose of the genetic material of any cell is that it holds all the information necessary for a cell to carry out its many functions. The sequence of bases in the DNA contain this information or genetic code. You have all had this before, but just as a quick review the central dogma is...

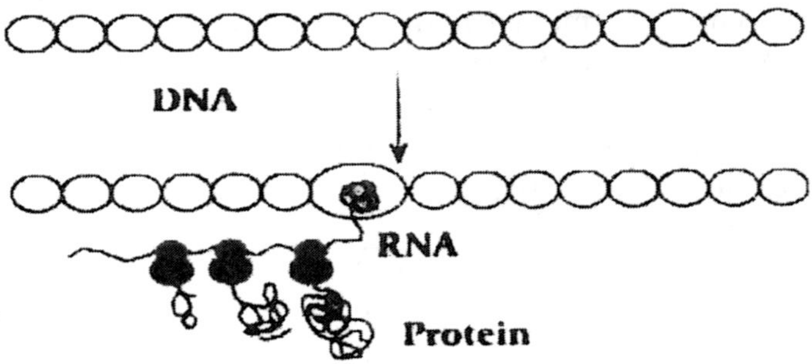

Figure 5: DNA is transcribed into RNA that is then translated into protein by the ribosome.

Replication: DNA must be able to replicate itself to pass on this genetic information. It must do this precisely. Remember structure dictates function. The process is surprisingly simple. Since DNA is double stranded, the two strands separate and each one serves as a template to make another complementary strand. This process is known as semiconservative replication. At each cell division, each cell gets one old strand and one new strand. Replication is accomplished by the coordinated efforts of many cellular enzymes.

One of the best understood enzymes is polymerase, which forms the phospodiester bond between the phosphate residue on the sugar of the incoming nucleotide and OH residue on the sugar of the growing DNA chain. Synthesis is always 5' ->3'. This enzyme can also proof read and correct any mistakes made along the way.

Because bacterial chromosomal DNA is supercoiled it makes replication a little trickier. For most bacterial chromosomes, replication of the circular DNA is bi-directional. This leads to a characteristic structure known as a theta structure.

Extrachromosomal Plasmids

Although bacterial cells have only one main chromosome, they may have other pieces of genetic material. These smaller pieces of DNA are known as plasmids and are defined as extrachromosomal pieces of DNA which are capable of autonomous (or regulated) replication. Structure of extrachromosomal plasmids is similar to chromosome. Covalently closed circular DNA although considerably smaller. In a few species linear plasmids have been found.

Often we refer to the size of a piece of DNA by the number of 1000s of base pairs (kilobases (kb)) Chromosomal DNA is typically about 4000 kb, plasmid DNA ranges from 1-200 kb. There may also be anywhere from 1-700 copies of a plasmid in a cell. The function of plasmids is not always known, but they are not normally essential to the host, although their presence generally gives the host some advantage.

Advantages plasmids bestow on the host

— Antibiotic resistance - Some plasmids code for proteins that degrade antibiotics-a big advantage for pathogens.

— Some encode for proteins which confer virulence factors on the host. For example- E. coli plasmid Ent P307 codes for an enterotoxin which makes E. coli pathogenic.

— Conjugative plasmids - These allow exchange of DNA between bacterial cells

Protein Structure

Proteins and peptides (small proteins) are essential to the cell. They serve two major functions in the cell. Some proteins are enzymes that catalyze most biological reactions in a living organism. Other proteins perform a structural role for the cell - either in the cell wall, the cell membrane or in the cytoplasm.

Primary Structure of Protein

Protiens are polymers of amino acids. Amino acids are primary amines that contain an alpha carbon that is connected to an amino (NH3) group, a carboxyl group (COOH), and a variable side group (R) - see Figure 6. The side group gives each amino acid its distinctive properties and helps to dictate the folding of the protein.

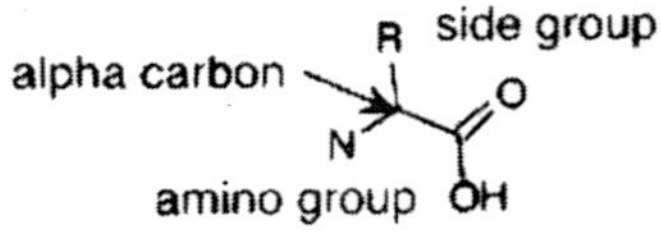

Figure 6: A general amino acid.

Polymers of amino acids are created by linking an amino group to a caroboxyl group on another amino acid. This is termed a peptide bond (Figure 7).

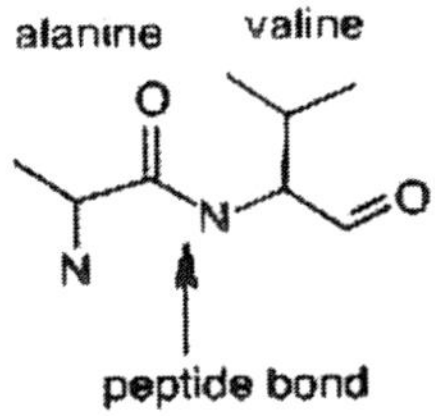

Figure 7: A peptide bond

There are 20 common amino acids found in proteins and these amino acids can be classified into 3 groups; polar, non-polar and charged. Polar and charged amino acids will most often be found on the surface of a protein, interacting with the surrounding water, while the non-polar (or hydrophobic) amino acids will bury themselves in the interior. The number and position of these types of amino acids in protein can greatly influence its function. Peptides and proteins are formed when a ribosome and the rest of the translation machinery link 10 - 10,000 amino acids together in a long polymer. This long chain is termed the primary sequence.

The properties of the protein are determined, for the most part, by this primary sequence. In many cases an alteration of any amino acid in the sequence will result in a loss of function for the protein (a mutation). Genetic diseases in humans are often caused by changes in important proteins that causes illness. Sickle cell anemia is caused by a single amino acid change from glutamic acid to valine at position 6 of the hemoglobin protein. Below is the primary sequence of hemoglobin, the oxygen carrying protein found in humans and other mammals.

NH_2—Val His Leu Thr Pro Glu Glu Lys Ser Ala Val Thr Ala

Leu Trp Gly Lys Val Asn Val Asp Glu Val Gly Gly Glu--

Figure 8: Hemoglobin amino acid sequence. Only the first 26 amino acids are shown.

Secondary Structure

During and after synthesis, the primary sequence will associate in a fashion that leads to the most stable, "comfortable" structure for the protein. How a protein folds is largely dictated by the primary sequence of amino acids. Each amino acid in the sequence will associate with other amino acids to conserve the most energy. This structure is stabilized by hydrogen bonds, hydrophobic interactions, ionic interactions, and sulfhydryl linkages.

Sulfhydryl linkages. These are covalent bonds between cysteine groups. Cysteine is a unique amino acid in that it has a sulfur group available for binding to other groups. Often in proteins, adjacent sulfhydryl groups on cysteines will form a covalent link in a protein - Figure 9 and are often crucial for the mature protein to perfom its function.

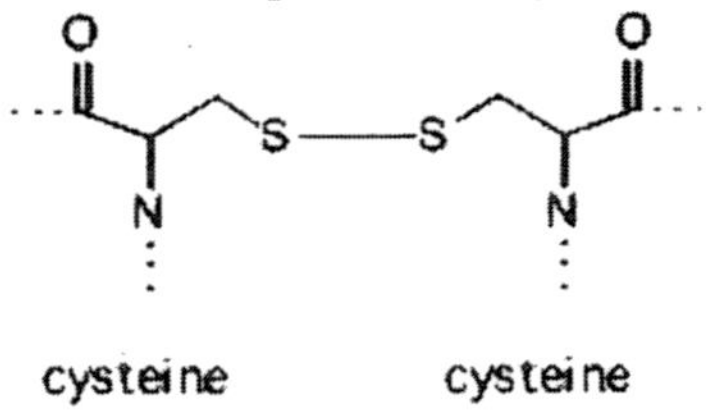

The chemical structure of a sulhydryl bond

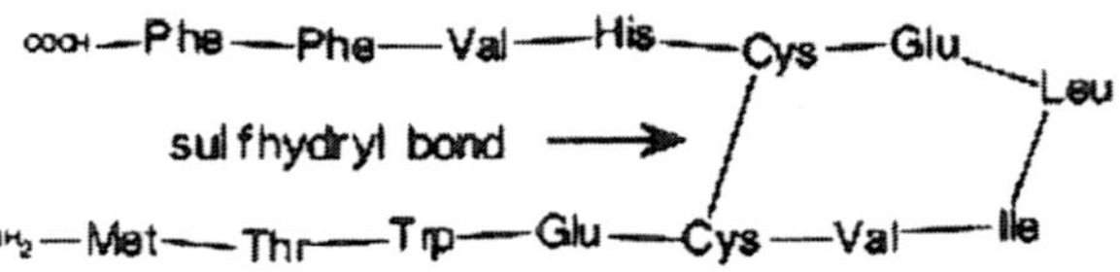

A sulfhydryl bond in a peptide

Figure 9. Two views of sulfhydryl linkages

Proteins will often have stretches of amino acids that will associate into two common structures. These are the alpha helix and the beta (pleated) sheet. Formation of these structures is driven by favorable hydrogen bonding and hydrophobic interactions between nearby amino acids in the protein. The alpha helix resembles a ribbon of amino acids wrapped around a tube to form a stair case like structure. This structure is very stable, yet flexible and is often seen in parts of a protein that may need to bend or move.

2

Microbial World and You

If you ask the average person how microbes (or germs) impact their lives, they would immediately think of disease. This is not a silly view, as pathogenic microorganisms have greatly affected human populations throughout our existence. In 1900 in the United States the infant mortality rate was near 50%, mostly due to childhood infectious disease and until about 1930, microbes were the major cause of death in humans.%. From todays perspective this is a horrendous statistic, over half of all infants did not make it to adulthood! With the advent of antibiotics, vaccines and better water sanitation, humanity has reduced the impact of pathogenic microbes in developed countries, but they will always remain an important social concern.

The discipline of microbiology emerged from the study of these diseases and most advances in treating various ailments had their roots in this relatively young science. While death from infectious disease in the U. S. has been greatly diminished, infection rates in developing nations remain unacceptably high. "Ancient" diseases continue to be a problem where nutrition and sanitation are poor, and emerging diseases such as AIDS are even more dangerous for such populations. The Centers for Disease Control and Prevention estimates that about 9% of adults between the ages of 18-49 in Sub-Saharan Africa are infected with HIV.

Yet AIDS is only one of a number of new diseases that have emerged, many of which have no known cure. Influenza and pneumonia are leading killers of the elderly even in the U. S. and other developed nations. Even the common cold causes illness and misery for almost everyone and drains the productivity of all nations. Many of these new diseases are viral in nature and these are notoriously difficult to treat. Disease due to food-borne pathogens also remains a problem, largely because of consumption of improperly processed or stored foods. Understanding the sources of contamination and developing ways to limit the growth of pathogens in food is job of food microbiologists.

Surprisingly, many diseases that were previously thought to have only behavioral or genetic components have been found to involve microorganisms. The clearest case is that of ulcers, which was long thought to be caused by stress and poor diet. However the causative agent is actually a bacterium, Helicobacter pylori, and many ulcers can be cured with appropriate antibiotics. Work on other non-infectious diseases such as heart disease, stroke and some autoimmune diseases also suggest a microbial component that triggers the illness.

Finally, some pathogenic microbes that had been "controlled" through the use of antibiotics are beginning to develop drug resistance and therefore reemerge as serious threats in the industrialized world as well as developing nations. Tuberculosis, an illness that was on the decline until the middle 80's is become more of a problem, partly due to drug resistance and partly due to a higher population of immunosuppressed individuals from the AIDS epidemic. Staphylococcus aureus strains are emerging that are resistant to many of the antibiotics that were previously effective against them. These staph infections are of great concern in hospital setting around the world. Understanding both familiar killers and new pathogens will require an understanding of their biology and thus an understanding of the field of microbiology.

Microbes and the Environment

Microbes are the major actors in the synthesis and degradation of all sorts of important molecules in environments. Cyanobacteria and algae in the oceans are responsible for the majority of photosynthesis on earth. They are the ultimate source of food for most ocean creatures (including whales) and replenish the worlds oxygen supply. Cyanobacteria also use carbon dioxide to synthesize all of their biological molecules and thus remove it from the atmosphere. Since carbon dioxide is a major greenhouse gas, its removal by cyanobacteria affects the global carbon dioxide balance and may be an important mitigating factor in global warming.

In all habitats, microorganisms make nutrients available for the future growth of other living things by degrading dead organisms. Microbes are also essential in treating the large volume of sewage and wastewater produced by metropolitan areas, recycling it into clean water that can be safely discharged into the environment. Less helpfully (from the view of most humans) termites contain microorganisms in their guts that assist in the digestion of wood, allowing the termites to extract nutrients from what would otherwise be indigestible. Understanding of these systems helps us to manage them responsibly and as we learn more we will become ever more effective stewards.

A sampling of the different types of environments where microbe flourish Microbes are capable of growing in a wide variety of environments. Bacteria will grow in frigid glaciers to boiling volcanic springs, dry sands to the open ocean. Energy is essential for our industrial society and microbes are important players in its production. A significant portion of natural gas comes from the past action of methanogens (methane-producing bacteria). Numerous bacteria are also capable of rapidly degrading oil in the presence of air and special precautions have to be taken during the drilling, transport and storage of oil to minimize their impact.

In the future microbes may find utility in the direct production of energy. For example, many landfills and sewage treatment plants capture the methane produced by methanogens to power turbines that produce electricity. Excess grain, crop waste and animal waste can be used as nutrients for microbes that ferment this biomass into methanol or ethanol. These biofuels are presently added to gasoline and thus decreasing pollution. They may one-day power fuel cells in our cars, causing little pollution and having water as their only emission.

We are increasingly taking advantage of the versatile appetite of bacteria to clean up environments that we have contaminated with crude oil, polycholorinated biphenyls (PCBs) and many other industrial wastes. This process is termed bioremediation and is a cheap and increasingly effective way of cleaning up pollution.

Helpful Microbes

The microbial community in humans not only protects us from disease, but also provides needed vitamins, such as B_{12}. Human health also depends on healthy farm animals, and cows, sheep, horses and other ruminant animals utilize their microbial associates to degrade plant material into useful nutrients. Without these bacteria inside ruminants, growth on plant material would be impossible. Commercial crops are also central to human prosperity and much of agriculture depends upon the activities of microbes. For example, an entire group of plants, the legumes, forms a cooperative relationship with certain bacteria. These bacteria form a symbiotic relationship within the plant: the plant provides carbon and energy, while the bacteria convert atmospheric nitrogen gas into a useful nitrogen source for the plant.

Microbes also serve as small factories, producing valuable products such as cheese, yogurt, beer, wine, organic acids and many other items. In conclusion, while it is less apparent to us, the positive role of microbes in human health is at least as important at the negative impact of disease-causing pathogens.

Role of Microbes as Model Systems

Microorganisms used in research have many useful properties. They will grow on simple, cheap medium and will often rise to large populations in a matter of 24 hours. It is easy to isolate their genomic material, manipulate it in the test tube and then place it back into the microbe. Due to their large populations it is possible to identify rare events and then with the use of powerful selective techniques isolate interesting bacterial cells and study them. These advantages have made it possible to rapidly test hypothesis in laboratory microorganisms that would have taken much longer in other organisms. Using microbes scientists have expanded our knowledge about life; here are a few examples.

In scientific research, microorganisms have been indispensable instruments for unlocking the secrets of life. The molecular basis of heredity and how this is expressed as proteins was described through work on microorganisms. Due to the similarity of life at the molecular level, this understanding has helped us to learn about all organisms, including ourselves. Some prokaryotes are capable of growing under unimaginably harsh conditions and define the extreme limits of where life can exist. Some species have been found growing at near100°C in hot springs and well above that temperature near deep-sea ocean vents. Others make their living at near 0°C in freshwater lakes that are buried under the ice of Antarctica.

The ability of microbes to live under such extreme conditions is forcing scientists to rethink the requirements necessary to support life. Many now believe it is entirely possible that Jupiter's moon Europa may harbor living communities in waters deep below its icy crust. Until recently, while we could study specific types of bacteria, we lacked a cohesive classification system, so that we could not readily predict the properties of one species based on the known properties of others.

Visual appearance, which is the basis for classification of large organisms, simply does not work with many microbes because there are few distinguishing characteristics for comparison between species even under the microscope. However, analysis of their genetic material in the past 20 years has allowed such classification and spawned a revolution in our thinking about the evolution of bacteria and all other species. The emergence of a new system organizing life on Earth into three domains is attributable to this pioneering work with microorganisms.

The fruits of this basic research have been used by scientists to understand microbial activity and therefore to shape our modern world. Human proteins, especially hormones like insulin and human growth factor, are now produced in bacteria using genetic engineering. Our understanding of the immune system was developed using microbes as tools. Microorganisms also play a role in treating disease and keepïng people healthy. Many of the drugs available to treat infectious disease originate from bacteria and fungi.

One last recent role of microbes in informing us about our world has been the tools they provide for molecular biology. Enzymes purified from bacterial strains are useful as tools to perform many types of analyses. Such analyses allow us to determine the complete genome sequence of almost any organism and manipulate that DNA is useful ways. We now know the entire sequence of the human genome, with the exception of regions of repetitive DNA, and this will hopefully lead to medical practices and treatments that improve health.

We also know the entire genome sequence of many important pathogens and analysis of this data will eventually lead to an understanding of the function of critical enzymes in these microbes and the development of tailor-made drugs to stop them. The tools of molecular biology will also affect agriculture. The complete genome sequence of the plant Arabidopsis is now known. This opens a new avenue to a better understanding of all plants and hopefully improvements in important crops.

Microbes have a profound impact on every facet of human life and everything around us. Pathogens harm us, yet other microbes protect us. Some microbes are pivotal in the growth of food crops, but others can kill the plants or spoil the produce. Bacteria and fungi eliminate the wastes produced in the environment, but also degrade things we would rather preserve.

Developmentsof Microbiology

Like all human history, the history of microbiology is not a catalog of linear progress, but is more of an interweaving of the careers of bright individuals and their insights. Microbiology is a relatively young science. It was only 130 years ago that it became possible to seriously study microorganisms in the laboratory with most of our understanding of microbes coming in the last 60 years. Each new discovery relied on previous ones and in turn spawned further inquiry.

The science of microbiology had its most significant early impact on human health, discovering the cause of the major killers of the day, and then methods to treat them. As microbiology matured, scientists began to look at what non-pathogenic microbes were doing in the environment and we will look a bit at the history of general microbiology.

Discovery of Microbes

For years the existence of microorganisms was suspected, but could not be proven, since bacteria were too small to be seen with the naked eye. It took the microscope to expose their tiny world and that instrument has been linked to microbiology ever since. Robert Hooke devised a compound microscope and used it to observe fleas, sponges, bird feathers, plants and molds, among other items. His work was published in Micrographia and became a popular and widely read book at the time.

Several years later Anton van Leeuwenhoek, a fabric merchant and amateur scientist, became very adept at grinding glass lenses to make telescopes and microscopes. While crude by modern standards, his were a technical marvel for the time, able to magnify samples greater than 200-fold. They also produced clearer images than the compound microscopes of the time and by peering through his microscope, Leeuwenhoek observedtiny organisms or wee animacules as he called them.. He spent months looking at every kind of sample he could find and eventually submitted his observations in a letter to the Royal Society of London, causing a sensation.

Hooke was asked to confirm the findings of Leeuwenhoek and his affirmative assessment garnered them wide acceptance. Surprisingly the work of these two scientists was not followed up for almost 200 years. Human societies had neither the technical prowess nor the inclination to develop the science of microorganisms. It was not until the rise of the industrial revolution that governments and people dedicated the financial and physical resources to understand these small inhabitants of our world.

With the development of better microscopes in the 19th century, scientists returned to an examination of microorganisms. After finishing his education, Ferdinand Julius Cohn was able to convince his father to lay down the large sum necessary to purchase a microscope for him, one better than that available at the University in Breslau, then part of Germany. He used it to carefully examine the world of the microbe and made many observations of eukaryotic microorganisms and bacteria. His landmark papers on the cycling of elements in nature was published in Ueber Bakterien in 1872 and a microbial classification scheme including descriptions of Bacillus were published in the first volume of a journal he founded, Beitraege zur Biologie der Planzen.

Cohns work with microscopes popularized their use in microbiology. This and his other work inspired many other scientists to examine microbes and his encouragement of Robert Koch, a German physician by training, began the field of medical microbiology. Koch was convinced that microbes caused some diseases. However, to test this idea, he needed to isolate the causative agent. Almost all samples from diseased animals or any natural surface contained many different microbes and it was impossible to tell which one was the problem. A method was needed to separate these different bacteria.

The most common method of isolation was to continually dilute a sample in liquid broth in hopes that at high enough dilution, only one type of microbe would be found. A problem with this method is that only the most populous microbe would be isolated, but that might not be one causing the disease. There were other technical problems as well with such a liquid-based system, so a solid medium would provide distinct advantages. Koch has tried gelatin for these experiments with unsatisfactory results. Building on the work of Brefeld and Schroeter, Koch used potato slices as a solid medium and observed that a boiled potato left in the open air would develop tiny circular raised spots.

Examination of these spots revealed they were made up of microorganisms and each spot had just one type of microbe in it. He realized that these colonies were pure cultures of bacteria and probably arose from a single species of microbe from the air that landed on the potato. By boiling a potato, slicing it with a hot knife and keeping it in a sterile container with a lid, Koch could keep the potato sterile. But if a sample from a disease animal was smeared across the potato, colonies arose, each being pure isolates from the animal. By then testing these isolates in animals, Koch was able to isolate the cause of anthrax, Bacillus anthracis.

Potatoes failed to support the growth of many microorganisms and Koch and his laboratory were constantly frustrated by the lack of a good solid medium. Walter Hesse joined Kochs laboratory to do studies on air quality, showing a remarkable attention to detail and patience in his work. His wife, Angelina Fannie Hesse along with raising their three sons, also would assist her husband with his research in the laboratory. Walter was attempting to do his air quality experiments using medium containing gelatin as the solidifying agent. In the summertime temperatures would often rise above the melting point of gelatin.

In addition, microbes would often grow in the cultures that were capable of degrading gelatin and in both cases this would cause liquefaction of the medium, ruining the experiments. One day the frustrated scientist asked Lina (as she was called) why her jellies and puddings stayed solid even in the hot summer temperatures. She told him about agar-agar, a heat resistant gelling agent that she had learned about while growing up in New York from a Dutch neighbor who had emigrated from Java.

Development of the new agent by Angelina and Walter led to a resounding success. Few microbes are able to degrade agar and it melts at 100°C yet remains molten at temperatures above 45°C. This allows the mixing of the agar with heat-sensitive nutrients and microbes. After solidification, it will not melt until a temperature of 100°C is again attained, allowing the easy cultivation of pathogens. It can also be stored for long periods of time allowing the cultivation of slow-growing microorganisms.

Any type of broth can be mixed with agar and this gives great flexibility in the kinds of medium that can be made, thus many more types of microbes could be cultivated. Koch laboratory also developed methods of pure culture maintenance and aseptic technique. Aseptic technique involves the manipulation of pure cultures in a manner that prevents their contamination by outside microorganisms and equally important prevents their spread into the environment.

Koch was studying some of the most devastating microbial pathogens of the period and their release could potentially cause disease in the scientists working on them. These procedures were also absolutely critical because they allowed careful study of pure microorganisms, making it possible to identify the role of each microbe in a given situation. Another problem in the cultivation of microbes was solved by Julius Petri while working in Kochs laboratory. Solid medium was poured on glass plates and allowed to spread and harden. Once cooled it allowed a solid surface for streaking. However, creation of these plates required great care since exposure to the air (and the microbes in it) often lead to contamination.

In addition, to prevent contamination of plates during incubation, a cumbersome bell jar was used. If one wanted to view samples, the plate had to be removed from the jar, further exposing it to unwanted microbes in the air. In 1887 Petri developed a shallow glass dishes, with one having a slightly larger diameter than the other. Medium is poured into the smaller dish and the larger one serves as a cover. This simple device solved all of the above problems and has taken on the name of its inventor, the petri plate.

These same techniques are essential in studying all microorganisms. Collectively the above techniques have been used to isolate and identify thousands of different microorganisms. As a testament to the significance of their achievement, these techniques are practiced with remarkably little change in every laboratory that works with microorganisms today.

Spontaneous generation is the hypothesis that some vital force contained in or given to organic matter can create living organisms from inanimate objects. Spontaneous generation was a widely held belief throughout the middle ages and into the latter half of the 19th century. In fact, some people still believe in it today. The idea is attractive because it meshed nicely with the prevailing religious views of how God created the universe. There was a strong bias to legitimize the idea because this vital force was considered a strong proof of Gods presence in the world.

Many recipes and experiments were offered in proof To create mice, a recipe called for dirty underwear and wheat grain be mixed in a bucket and left open outside. In 21 days or less, you would have mice. The real cause may seem obvious from a modern perspective, but to the proponents of this idea, the mice spontaneously arose from the wheat kernels.

Another often-used example was the generation of maggots from meat that was left in the open. The failing here was revealed by Francesco Redi in 1668 with a classic experiment. Redi suspected that flies landing on the meat laid eggs that eventually grew into maggots. To test this idea he used three pieces of meat. One piece of meat was placed under a piece of paper. The flies could not lay eggs onto the meat and no maggots developed. The second piece was left in the open air, resulting in maggots. In the final test a third piece of meat was overlaid with cheesecloth. The flies were able to lay the eggs into the cheesecloth and when this was removed no maggots developed.

However, if the cheesecloth containing the eggs was placed on a fresh piece of meat, maggots developed, showing it was the eggs that "caused" flies and not spontaneous generation. This helped to end the debate about spontaneous generation for large organisms. However, spontaneous generation was so seductive a concept that even Redi believed it was possible in other circumstances. The concept and the debate were revived in 1745 by the experiments of John Needham. It was known at the time that heat was lethal to living organisms. Needham theorized that if he took chicken broth and heated it, all living things in it would die.

After heating some broth, he let a flask cool and sit at a constant temperature. The development of a thick turbid solution of microorganisms in the flask was strong proof to Needham of the existence of spontaneous generation. Lazzaro Spallanzani later repeated the experiments of Needham, but removed air from the flask, suspecting that the air was providing a source of contamination. No growth occurred in Spallanzanis flasks and he took this as evidence that Needham was wrong. Proponents of spontaneous generation discounted the experiment by asserting that air was required for the vital force to work.

It was not until almost 100 years later that the great French chemist Louis Pasteur put the debate to rest. He first showed that the air is full of microorganisms by passing air through gun cotton filters. The filter trapped tiny particles floating in the air. By dissolving the cotton with a mixture of ether and alcohol, the particles were released and then settled to the bottom of the liquid. Inspection of this material revealed numerous microbes that resembled the types of bacteria often found in putrefying media.

Pasteur realized that if these bacteria were present in the air then they would likely land on and contaminate any material exposed to it. He then entered a contest sponsored by The French Academy of Sciences to disprove the theory of spontaneous generation. Similar to Spallanzani's experiments, Pasteur used heat to kill the microbes, but left the end of the flask open to the air. In a simple, but brilliant modification, the neck of the flask was heated to melting and drawn out into a long S-shaped curve, preventing the dust particles and their load of microbes from ever reaching the flask.

After prolonged incubation the flasks remained free of life and ended the debate for most scientists. A final footnote on the topic was added when John Tyndall showed the existence of heat-resistant spores in many materials. Boiling does not kill these spores and their presence in chicken broth, as well as many other materials, explains the results of Needham's experiments.

While this debate may seem silly from a modern perspective, remember that the scientists of the time had little knowledge of microorganisms. Koch would not isolate microbes until 1881. The proponents of spontaneous generation were neither sloppy experimenters nor stupid. They did careful experiments and interpreted them with their own biases. Detractors of the theory of spontaneous generation were just as guilty of bias, but in the opposite direction.

In fact, it is somewhat surprising that Pasteur and Spallanzoni did not get growth in their cultures, since the sterilizations conditions they used would often not kill endospores. Luck certainly played a role. It is important keep in mind that the discipline of science is performed by humans with all the fallibility and bias inherent in the species. It is only the self-correcting nature of the practice that reduces the impact of these biases on generally held theories. Spontaneous generation was a severe test of the scientific experimentation, because it was such a seductive and widely held belief. Yet, even spontaneous generation was overthrown when the weight of careful experimentation was against it.

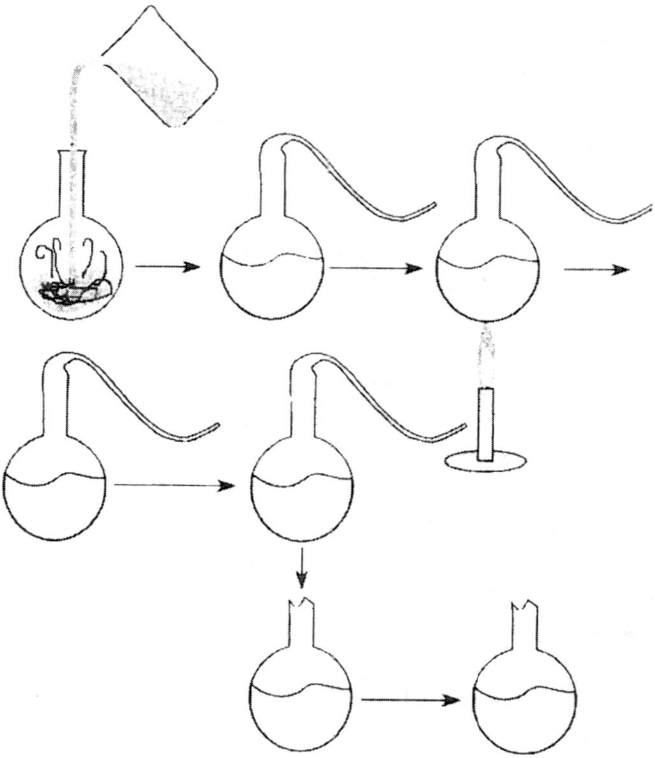

The swan neck flask experiment: Pasteur filled a flask with medium, heated it to kill all life, and then drew out the neck of the flask into a long S. This prevented microorganisms in the air from entering the flask, yet allowed air to flow freely.

Nature of Disease

Ignaz Semmelweis, a Hungarian physician working in Vienna, made the first breakthrough in the true nature of disease. He realized that asepsis in obstetrical wards could prevent the transmission of childbirth fever from patient to patient and instigated a policy for all attending physicians to wash their hands with with chloride of lime (a mixture of calcium chloride hypochlorite, CaCl(OCl); calcium hypochlorite, $Ca(OCl)_2$; and calcium chloride, $CaCl_2$) between patients. This innovation dropped the mortality rate or mortality from 18% to 2.4%. Ignaz became a vigorous proponent of these ideas, but the Hungarian doctor's efforts were opposed by many who could not accept that physicians themselves could be responsible for spreading bacterial infection.

Ridicule of his idea caused him to move from Vienna to Pest, Hungary and ultimately played a role in a nervous breakdown. Ironically Semmelweis died from an infection that he contracted during a surgery he performed, while recovering from his nervous breakdown. Before his death he published his ideas in a paper The Cause, Concept, and Prophylaxis of Childbed Fever in1861. The work was then ignored for 17 years, which raises an interesting point about the culture of science. Radical ideas, even those that are correct and can save lives, are sometimes ignored. It takes time to overcome the dogma of the day.

In a seemingly unrelated event, Louis Pasteur found something interesting while working on wine souring, a problem where wine fermentations produce a sour taste and very little alcohol. Fermentation of alcoholic beverages was thought to be a simple chemical reaction. Heating, common in most beverage preparations, was thought to cause the breakdown of sugar into alcohol.

Pasteur was asked to help out the wine industry in France because wine souring was pushing it close to ruin. His work on wine-making revealed that the process of converting sugar to alcohol is actually performed by various yeast strains. He then showed that the wine was going bad because a contaminating microbe was generating lactic acid instead of alcohol from the sugar. This idea was controversial, but gained credibility when Pasteur solved the problem by heating the wine and killing the contaminant. The heating process was named pasteurization in his honor and is still widely used today.

In a brilliant step of generalization, Pasteur realized that souring of wine and infectious disease shared a common thread in that they both might involve infection by a microorganism. His suggestion that microbes cause disease became known as the germ theory of disease. Joseph Lister became aware of Semmelweis's work and together with Pasteur realized the true nature of disease. He then recognized that he could use this idea to help his surgery patients. At this time, major injuries, broken bones or surgery would often result in infection of the damaged area, sometimes leading to amputation or death.

Lister found he could greatly reduce the number of microorganisms on wounds and incisions by using bandages treated with phenic acid, a compound that killed microorganisms (phenic acid, now known as phenol, is the active ingredient in Listerine). During surgery he began the practice of spraying the wound with a fine mist of phenic acid to kill microbes. These practices greatly reduced the rate of infection and mortality of surgery patients, lending further credence to the germ theory of disease.

In 1876 Robert Koch provided definitive proof of the germ theory by isolating the cause of anthrax and showing it to be a bacterium. From this came the development of Koch's Postulates, a set of rules for the assignment of a microbe as the cause of a disease.

Koch's postulates

1. The specific organism should be shown to be present in all cases of animals suffering from a specific disease, but should not be found in healthy animals.

2. The specific microorganism should be isolated from the diseased animal and grown in pure culture on artificial laboratory media.

3. This freshly isolated microorganism, when inoculated into a healthy nonimmune laboratory animal, should cause the same disease seen in the original animal.

4. The microorganism should be reisolated in pure culture from the experimental infection.

This is his most famous contribution to science and it is a testament to the utility of these postulates that they are stilled used today to discover the cause of new emerging diseases. Koch went on to apply these principles in the study of many other diseases including tuberculosis, cholera and sleeping sickness. It should be pointed out that Kochs postulates cannot be applied to all diseases.

For example if a disease-causing microbe has humans as its sole host and has a significant possibility of causing death, it would be unethical to apply this microbe to test humans as dictated by postulate 3. Also, it is not always possible to obtain a disease-causing microbe in pure culture. Koch developed the tools for obtaining pure cultures to attack the problem of disease.

Advances in science often come from innovations in the available technology. Robert Koch was an important microbiologist because his pioneering work in the isolation and characterization of bacterial diseases helped to identify the causes of many of the maladies plaguing humanity. Further work by other scientists then began the long road to conquering them.

Virology

The ensuing years brought numerous discoveries about the nature of disease. In the latter half of the 19th century the causative agents for anthrax, tuberculosis, gonnorhea, diptheria and many more were discovered. Great strides in understanding maladies caused by bacteria were made at this time, including the solidification of the germ theory of disease. However, some illnesses seemed not to have bacterial origins.

Microscopic examination of sera from ill patients revealed no organisms and the causative agents could not be grown on any known medium. Yet if these sera were injected into a susceptible host, disease resulted. In 1886 John Brown Buist devised a method for staining and fixing liquid from a cowpox vesicle. Observations of this slide showed tiny bodies that he believed were spores. Although he did not realize it, he was the first person to see (and photograph) a virus. It is not until the middle of the twentieth century with the invention of the electron microscope that the true shape and structure of viruses was understood.

In 1884 C. Chamberland in Pasteurs laboratory created an unglazed porcelain filter that had pores much smaller than bacteria (0.1-1 m). It was possible to pass a solution containing bacteria through these filters and completely remove them from the solution. This enabled the creation of sterile medium without the use of heat, and also became a standard test for the removal of all bacteria, especially when testing transmission of disease. By removing the microbes, he clearly demonstrated that an infectious agent, and not the solution, was causing the illness. This concept seemed reasonable until scientists began to investigate a tobacco infection.

Europeans had recognized the effects of a disease, termed tobacco mosaic disease, soon after tobacco was introduced from the New World in the 17th century. This disease was characterized by light and dark green areas on plant leaves in a mosaic pattern and led to stunting of growth and therefore reduced yields. Adolph Mayer first described transmission of the disease by injecting fluid from a diseased plant into a healthy one. Nine out of ten times the healthy plant would become heavily diseased.

In 1892 Dmitrii Ivanowski extended this research by the shocking discovery that the causative agent could pass through Chamberlands porcelain filter. He reported his findings, but the idea that the causative agent could pass through the filter was so troublesome to Ivanowsky he attributed the phenomenon to a cracked filter or to small spores that passed through the pores. It was Martinus Beijerinck in 1898 who realized the true nature of these particles, making the intellectual leap that the causative agent of the disease must be so small as to pass through the filter known to trap all bacteria. He coined the term contagium vivum fluidum a contagious living fluid.

In the same year, Friederich Loeffler and Paul Frosch discovered that a filterable agent also caused foot-and-mouth disease. Some scientists thought these agents were toxins in the fluids of the hosts, but further study revealed that tobacco mosaic disease could cause illness through many transfers from plant to plant (and the same was true for foot-and-mouth disease on animals).

A toxin might cause damage on the first plant, but subsequent transfers should make it so dilute that it would no longer have any effect. These filterable entities were different from bacteria and appeared to depend on their host in order to multiply. The term ultrafiltrable viruses and later just viruses (virus means poison in Latin) was coined to describe these tiny pathogens. Bacterial viruses were described independently by Frederick Twort in 1915 and Felix dHerelle in 1917. Felix d.Herelle was studying a plague of locusts in Mexico when he noticed that they were being killed by a natural agent that turned out to be a microorganism.

During experiments to characterize this microbe, d'Herelle noticed the appearance of clear, circular spots two or three millimeters in diameter on cultures growing on agar. At this point d'Herelle studied the spots enough to determine that they came from an agent small enough to pass through a porcelain filter, but then dropped the investigation. However, this phenomenon had made an impression and in 1915 he recalled these observations whjile studying dysentery. The illness was affecting soldiers fighting in World War I and he soon determined the cause to be the bacterium Shigella dysentery. In the process of investigating Shigella similar areas of clearing were observed and d'Herelle realized that something in these areas of clearing was killing the bacterium. He eventually determined these were viruses of bacteria, coining the term bacteriophage (devourer of bacteria).

Protection from Disease

Role of vaccines

As soon as it was realized that microbes cause disease, the search was on for ways to kill or to prevent them from causing disease. Smallpox was a feared disease throughout human history and justifiably so. It was highly contagious and almost everyone eventually became infected. Mortality rates were as high as 25% in adults and closer to 40% in children. Those who did survive often had scarring due to the blister-like pustules that form on the skin, but they obtained life-long immunity to the disease.

As far back at the 11th century in India and China it was realized that liquid from the pustules of a smallpox victim, when scratched on the skin of a healthy patient, would most often cause mild disease. This intentional infection, termed variolation, would also give life-long protection against the virus. Lady Mary Wortley Montgue, wife of ambassador to the Ottoman Empire, introduced variolation to England in 1721 and it became a popular practice throughout Europe.

Variolation had some deleterious side effects. Serious skin lesions inevitably resulted at the site of inoculation, often accompanied by a generalized rash or even a full case of smallpox. The fatality rate from variolation was 1 to 2 %. Today we would find this level of fatality to be unacceptable, but this risk still represented a significant advance. In the 1796, Edward Jenner, an English country physician, went in search of a more predictable and safer method of protection against the disease. He noticed that milkmaids rarely contracted smallpox. Further investigation revealed they often contracted cowpox from their charges.

In a perceptive leap of faith, Jenner hypothesized that cowpox was related to smallpox and contraction of the former would protect against the latter. In a classic experiment (and one that would land you in jail today), Jenner inoculated a young patient with cowpox and later challenged him with smallpox. The boy did not become ill and Jenner was responsible for the creation of a safer method of protection against small pox. It is important to stress that the nature of these diseases and their viruses would not be known for over 100 years. Jenner was ahead of his time.

Beginning around 1876 Pasteur's studies on chicken cholera led to the development of vaccines to fight the disease. Cholera was a serious problem since it was able to spread through a barnyard and wipe out a flock in as little as 3 days. It was transmitted by contaminated food or animal excrement. Pasteur had identified the cholera bacillus and was growing it in pure culture. When injected with it, a chicken invariably died within 48 hours. Then, as often happens in scientific research, luck intervened. During the heat of the summer, Pasteur returned to Paris and left the cholera cultures used for infection stored on the shelves of his laboratory in Arbois, France.

Upon returning, something had happened to the cultures, they no longer caused disease when tested in chickens. With some impatience for the time they were wasting, his group set to work making new cultures of the bacillus and tested these batches on both new birds and also those previously inoculated with the ineffective strain. To their amazement the previously injected birds were unaffected by the fresh bacillus culture, while the new birds all died. Pasteur immediately realized that this was similar to the studies of Jenner. Pasteur then developed a method for creating cultures that would confer immunity, but not cause disease.

In honor of Jenner's accomplishments Pasteur coined the term vaccination (vacca = cow in Latin) for the process of immunization against disease. In this and several of Pasteur's other discoveries, luck played a part, but it was only helpful because he tenaciously pursued "odd" results and had the insight to arrive at important conclusions. In Pasteur's famous words, " In the field of observation, chance favors only the prepared mind."

Pasteur's technique of weakening a strain by a damaging treatment or passing it through a susceptible host was termed attenuation and resulted in the creation of vaccines against anthrax, plague, yellow fever, rabies and many other diseases. Many vaccines have been developed over the years and children today receive a number of shots, greatly decreasing infant mortality.

Antimicrobial Compounds

We now pick up another thread though the web of change that began with the work of Paul Ehrlich. By 1885 it was becoming clear that the causative agents of many illnesses were microorganisms. As scientists manipulated these microbes in the lab they found that certain dyes and other compounds were able to inhibit their growth. This inspired Ehrlich to propose that chemicals may exist that will kill the microbe, but not the patient. The hope was that by having a patient take these chemicals they could cure the illness.

One of the diseases he hoped to cure was syphilis, which had reached epidemic proportions in Europe. Little did he realize it would be a 17-year odyssey before he would develop salvarsan, the first effective chemotherapeutic agent. Salvarsan was the 606th chemical he tried and is an arsenic compound that effectively kills Treponema pallidum, the causative agent of syphilis. However, the treatment had many problems, causing long lasting health complications for those individuals who used it.

In addition, despite Treponema being quite sensitive to salvarsan, the physician had to administer it intravenously for optimum effectiveness. This type of injection was a recent development and many doctors were leery of trying the procedure. In London a young physician by the name of Alexander Fleming, then in the Army Medical Corps, was one of the few that was willing to treat patients, even getting the nickname private 606 from his burgeoning practice. His work validated the effectiveness of salvarsan against syphilis and convinced others to try the treatment.

Fleming was a physician by training, but spent most of his time studying bacteria, and his success with salvarsan motivated him to search for other antibacterial agents. His first discovery was lysozyme, an enzyme produced by many organisms, including humans, that lysed some bacteria. This enzyme is not useful as a therapeutic agent because it is difficult to administer as a drug, but Fleming did develop titration methods and assays that would become very useful. In September of 1928, before leaving on a summer holiday, Fleming streaked some plates of Staphylococcus aureus and left them to incubate until his return.

In an improbable set of circumstances, the beginning of the holiday was cold, allowing some contaminating mold spores (that had blown in from a nearby window) to grow up on some of the plates. The temperature then increased encouraging the growth of the Staphyloccoccus. Many experimenters when confronted with a contaminated plate will look for the trash bin, but Fleming instead spent some time examining it. The fungus had a zone of clearing around it where the Staphylococcus colonies would not grow, suggesting the fungus was producing an antibacterial compound that had diffused into the medium.

Intrigued, he cultured the fungus, a Penicillium mold, and eventually isolated a soluble extract that could kill bacteria and treat localized infection. He called the new compound penicillin after the mold it came from. Due to the technology available, it was very difficult to prepare a solution that could be used throughout the body without causing problems. World War II added a greater urgency to the search for compounds that could fight infectious disease. Wounded soldiers, if they survived the initial injury, would often develop life-threatening infections and there were no effective drugs to combat them. In 1939 Howard Florey and Ernst Chain began a systematic study of antimicrobial compounds in hopes of developing treatments for these soldiers and ran across Fleming's report written 9 years earlier. They now were able to purify the compound completely and describe its high potency against microbes.

The availability of penicillin during World War II saved countless lives. The rediscovery of penicillin touched off a search for other microbes producing substances that could kill or inhibit microbes, leading to the discovery of many more antimicrobials. With Florey and Chain, Fleming was awarded the Noble prize in Medicine and Physiology in 1945. In the ensuing decades the search and discovery of numerous antimicrobial compounds, combined with the development of vaccines, has eliminated many of the deadly diseases that plagued humankind. While we now realize this is a continuing war and not a one-time battle, our understanding of these microbes and the nature of disease will likely keep infectious disease at bay for the foreseeable future.

Contrary to what you would believe from news and advertising, the vast majority of bacteria are harmless to humans and a large number are actually helpful. Understandably, early work in microbiology focused on pathogenic microbes and treatment of the diseases they caused. Martinus Beijerinck and Sergei Winogradsky began the transition from this early work into the present era where we study the molecular biology of a wide variety of microorganisms. Both were interested in microbes present in the soil and water and their work founded the discipline of general microbiology. Much of what we understand about bacteria in the environment and their impact can be traced back to the efforts of these two scientists.

Martinus Beijerinck was originally trained as a botonist and began his work studying the microorganisms that were present in and around plants. He soon began experiments with microbes in the soil. His greatest contribution was the development of enrichment media. Previously, microbes were cultivated on medium consisting of potatoes or extracts of left-over animal renderings. Such media would support the growth of many different bacteria, with chance and population density dictating what became dominant in the culture. In many cases this was exactly what was desired, but in other cases it was of interest to find bacteria capable of performing certain chemical conversions.

Beijerinck discovered that by adding or removing certain compounds from the medium or incubating under different conditions, it was possible to favor the growth of certain microbes and prevent the growth of others. An example is Beijerinck's work with nitrogen-fixing bacteria, which are important in agriculture and the global cycling of nitrogen. They are capable of taking nitrogen gas (N_2) from the air and reducing it to ammonia (NH_3). This is an important property since reduced nitrogen compounds such as ammonia are the only compounds most organisms, including agriculturally important plants, are able to use as a nitrogen source. Beijerinck wanted to isolate an organism capable of fixing nitrogen in the presence of air, because all previous isolates fixed nitrogen only under anaerobic conditions.

By making medium that did not contain a source of fixed nitrogen and then incubating in the presence of air (containing N_2), he demanded that any microbe growing in the medium had to be able to derive its nitrogen by performing aerobic nitrogen fixation. By this method he succeeded in isolating a new microbe (Azotobacter chroococum) with these capabilities. Similar selective culture techniques (as he liked to call them) enabled his laboratory to isolate sulfur-reducing and sulfur-oxidizing bacteria, Lactobacillus species, green algae and many other microbes.

Sergei Winogradsky, the Russian microbiologist who developed the concept of autotrophy, was also interested in soil bacteria, especially those involved in the cycling of nitrogen and sulfur compounds. He was one of the first to isolate microorganisms responsible for the conversion of these elements in the soil, obtaining pure cultures of bacteria capable of the conversion of ammonia to nitrate by microorganisms in the soil. Winogradsky also studied the consumption of hydrogen sulfide gas by sulfur-oxidizing bacteria directly in their natural habitat.

When working with Beggiatoa he discovered it was obtaining its cell carbon from carbon dioxide. He used the term autotrophy to describe this property, a radical idea at the time. This led Winogradsky to propose the concept of chemolithotrophy - bacteria capable of growth using purely inorganic sources of carbon and energy. He realized the impact these processes have on our environment long before others accepted the idea. As a result of the work of Winogradsky and Beijerinck there was great enthusiasm for identifying and classifying the bacteria inhabiting our natural world.

For the first part of the 20th century many scientists isolated microbes and made proposals for their organization into genera and species. In 1909 Sigurd Orla-Jensen suggested a classification scheme based on the functions and abilities of the bacteria, such as growth on certain compounds or the production of specific by-products. The Society of American Bacteriologists, later to become the American Society of Microbiology, applied this technique to prepare a report on the classification of bacteria. This eventually evolved into Bergey's Manual of Determinative Bacteriology in 1923 and subsequent editions have become authoritative reference works.

There was great optimism that as more bacteria were brought into pure culture a clear organization, based on the evolutionary history of microbes, would emerge from studies of their physiology. However, y the 1940's it became clear that bacteria were unwilling to go along with this idea because classification based on one set of properties was often inconsistent with classification using a different set of properties. Scientists threw up their hands and gave up the idea of finding a system of classification based on growth and morphological characteristics.

Several decades passed during which bacteria became tools for understanding life, but their place in evolution was of little interest. Then in 1961 McCarthy and Bolton developed methods for the comparison of genetic material between species and Pauling and Zuckerkandl formalized the idea of using the makeup of biological molecules, their sequence, as a way to determine phylogenetic relationships.

Carl Woese, The American microbiologist who applied the concept of molecular phylogeny to 16 S rRNA and pioneered modern microbial taxonomy and he began to use this insight. This analysis was a watershed event for the evolutionary classification of bacteria and in 1977 Woese used this technique to assert that known bacteria should be divided into two separate domains that we now call

Bacteria and Archaea, radically changing our view of the microbial world. Lynn Margulis proposed the remarkable notion that some bacteria fused with archaea to crate eukaryotes. This hypothesis, termed endosymbiosis, has been strongly supported by a range of subsequent biochemical data.

In subsequent years, determination of 16S rRNA sequences, and then complete genomes, of microorganisms has enabled the natural classification of microorganisms. A review by Olsen, Woese and Overbeek provided a catalyzing summary of the tree of life for microbes, including eukaryotic microorganisms. This reorganization has reshaped our view of the tree of life for all organisms and helped to reassert the important role of microbes in shaping the past and affecting the future of the earth. A renewed interest in environmental microbiology, using new molecular tools based often on 16S rRNA, is revealing much more about the microbes present in our world and their influence on it.

Life at the Molecular Level

The very nature of genetic material was being hotly debated when in 1928 Fred Griffith discovered transformation in bacteria. Griffith knew that when Streptococcus pneumoniae are injected into mice, they cause rapid deterioration and death. Griffith isolated strains of the bacteria that were no longer capable of producing an outer slime layer and appeared rough when grown on solid medium in contrast to the smooth colonies of the original isolate. When these rough strains were injected into mice, no illness resulted.

Similarly, when a smooth microbe was heat-killed and then injected, the mice showed no signs of infection. A surprise was waiting for Griffith when he mixed the dead cells of a smooth isolate with live cells of a rough isolate and then injected this into mice; they died. When bacteria were isolated from these dead mice, they were all smooth.

Griffith hypothesized that the ability to create the slime layer was passed from the dead smooth cells to the viable rough cells, making them pathogenic again.

The process became known as transformation. He was ridiculed, as most scientists believed his preparation were contaminated with viable smooth cells. It was not until 1944 that his student Oswald Avery and coworkers repeated the experiments of Griffith, reproducing his results and discovering that DNA was the material from the dead smooth cells that transformed the rough mutant. This was strong proof that the hereditary material in cells was DNA, though the actual structure of DNA was not to be discovered for years. Further experiments in the 1940's clearly established this observation with Joshua Lederberg discovering two more ways that DNA could be transferred between bacterial cells, conjugation and transduction.

In 1943 Beadle and Tatum reported experiments with the fungus Neuropsora crassa that eventually established the idea that each gene in the DNA typically codes one protein (the one gene-one enzyme hypothesis). About 10 years later, James Watson and Francis Crick wrote their landmark letter to the journal Nature describing the structure of DNA and making predictions about how it was replicated. It was now clear that DNA stored the information for proteins and that proteins performed the many functions of the cell.

The important question now became, how does one convert the information in DNA into protein. A major contribution in understanding this puzzle was made by Paul Zemecnik and his lab who developed cell-free systems, first with rat liver and later using the bacterium E. coli. This allowed the study of translation in the test tube and He and other scientists used these systems to discover the important molecules involved in the process. An intense effort to describe these molecular events then ensued. The first light came when Crick, Sydney Brenner and colleagues proposed the existence of transfer RNA (tRNA), a molecule that helps to create amino acid polymers based on nucleic acid sequence.

Another critical player in the processing of information was revealed when Brenner, Francois Jacob and Matthew Meselson discovered that translation of genetic material into protein takes place on the ribosome and that the molecule being translated at the ribosome is RNA, not DNA. The next mystery was solved by Marshal Niremberg and J. H. Matthaei when they developed methods to decipher the genetic code that dictates the correspondence of nucleic acids to amino acids. After the stunningly productive decade of the 1960's, the nature of the framework for the conversion of the genetic information into proteins was now understood and the basic mechanism has since been shown to be conserved across all biology.

Genome Control

One final thread we will trace is the rise of molecular microbiology and the technique of genomics. This pathway begins in 1885 with the seemingly unimportant isolation of a common intestinal microorganism by Theodor Escherich. The microbe is eventually renamed Escherichia coli in his honor. It could not have been understood at the time, but this bacterium would play a central role in our understanding of life. E. coli achieved this position because it has several properties that made it invaluable as an experimental system.

1. E. coli is easy to take care of. It can grow on a wide variety of media at temperatures ranging from 20-45°C in the presence or absence of air.

2. E. coli grows quickly. Under normal laboratory conditions it will go through a complete life cycle, doubling its population about every 30 minutes. With this rapid growth rate it is possible to generate large

populations in just a few hours. Most experiments can be set up one day and the results observed the next.

3. It can survive storage for long periods of time without losing viability using relatively simple preservation techniques.

4. It was available. There is an element of arbitrariness that this microbe came to serve such a vital role in biology. Many other bacteria probably could have filled this position, but E. coli was the one chosen.

Several key discoveries laid the foundation for future developments in molecular biology. The first of these was the discovery of autonomously replicated pieces of DNA separate from the bacteria chromosome. Plasmids, as Joshua Lederberg called them, were capable of carrying genes that could be regulated and moved from one microbe to another independently of the bacterial chromosome.

The ability of some plasmids to move between different cells meant that different bacteria could rapidly inherit genes carried on these plasmids. It was found that one class of plasmids encoded resistance genes that would enable the bacteria to grow in the presence of an antibiotic. It later became clear it was possible to select for the presence of these plasmids by demanding growth of the bacterial strain on medium containing the antibiotic to which the plasmid encoded resistance.

A second discovery that greatly impacted modern genetic engineering was that bacteria have their own parasites. As mentioned earlier, there are viruses that infect and kill bacteria, just as viruses infect animals and plants. The analysis of bacterial viruses was a major avenue to understanding the bacteria themselves. For example, investigation of the ability of some viruses to grow well on certain strains of bacteria and not others lead to the discovery of restriction-modification systems in bacteria.

These systems allow bacteria to recognize and destroy foreign DNA and consist of two parts.

A modification enzyme that labels DNA as belonging to the bacterium and a restriction enzyme that recognizes a certain 4-8 base pair sequence in the DNA and cuts it into two if it has not been modified. The landmark paper of Smith and Wilcox, characterizing one of the restriction enzymes of Haemophilus influenzae, showed these enzymes were capable of cleaving double-stranded DNA into discrete pieces and the authors correctly hypothesized that the enzyme was recognizing a sequence of DNA and cutting it.

Joan Mertz and Ronald Davis quickly made restriction enzymes into tools for the manipulation of DNA when they showed that many of the breaks these enzymes made in the DNA produced single-stranded complementary ends. Cohen, Chang, Helling and Boyer then demonstrated that any DNA can be broken into fragments with restriction enzymes and by mixing that with a plasmid digested in a similar manner, it was possible to create recombinant molecules.

Moving the plasmid into a microbe and growing it on selective medium could produce any desired amount of these recombinant molecules. Genetic engineering was born. Another discovery was "brewing" in the western United States. In the mid 1960s, Thomas Brock was on a trip to Yellowstone and became intrigued by the mats of green, brown and pink material that were found in many of the hot springs. Brock was sure that these were living communities of microorganisms, yet the springs were at temperatures near boiling. Subsequent research proved his hypothesis correct and lead to the isolation of a microbe, Thermus aquaticus, capable of growth at 85°C.

Organisms capable of growing at this high a temperature were unheard of at the time and this spawned two major developments. First, work with this isolate and other unusual microbes by Woese and many others lead to the discovery of the Archaea. Second, the enzyme responsible for replicating DNA in T. aquaticus was found to be extremely heat stable, surviving temperatures of 95°C and copying DNA at 72°C.

The polymerase chain reaction (always referred to as PCR) was developed in 1988, an incredibly useful technique for amplifying even small quantities of DNA. Originally the technique required fresh addition of polymerase enzyme after each step, which could become prohibitively expensive. The use of T aquaticus polymerase made the procedure much more economical and sped its adoption. PCR has become a pivotal technique in many areas of science, from detecting bacteria in the environment to the analysis of evidence at crime scenes.

In 1977 Walter Gilbert and Fred Sanger independently developed methods for determining the exact sequence of bases in DNA. Gilbert was interested in finding the sequence of a bacterial operon and Sanger in determining the sequence of a virus that infected E. coli, bacteriophage ?X174. These techniques became immediately useful in determining the sequence of numerous important genes being investigated in countless laboratories. Further refinement has made DNA sequencing more efficient.

In 1985 Robert Sinsheimer convened a meeting of a number of biologists active in genetics and gene mapping. Out of this meeting came a proposal to sequence the entire three billion base pairs of the human genome. This was equivalent at the time of proposing a mission to the moon, technically possible, but with unpredictable value. The initial cost of the project was estimated to be $10 a base pair or a staggering 30 billion dollars. There was resistance from a significant portion of the scientific community, fearing that the project would siphon funds away from other worthy scientific projects.

However, the clarity of the goal ignited the imagination of Congress and the public, creating unstoppable momentum for the project. After about a decade of effort, a preliminary draft of the entire genome was released in the spring of 2001, earlier than projected and dramatically under budget. The project itself drove the development of sequencing technology allowing the determination of millions of base pairs of sequence per day at a cost of less than 3 cents per base at large sequencing facilities.

Along with the human genome, many other model organisms have been or are about to be sequenced. These include the genomes of many pathogenic bacteria, the mouse, the fruit fly and the nematode Caenorhabditis elegans, the last being an experimental model for development in eukaryotes. The analysis and application of this sequence data to investigate biological problems has resulted in the development of the field of genomics (the mapping and analysis of DNA) and bioinformatics (the software tools and techniques for examining the huge amount of data generated from genomics). In their infancy, these fields are already producing astonishing findings that are accelerating the progress of fields such as evolutionary biology, immunology, bacterial pathology, bacterial physiology and cancer treatment.

3

Control of Microbial Growth

Bacterial growth is defined as the increase in number of a microbial population. The growth of a microorganism is dependent upon not only the nutrients available to it for growth, but also the environment in which it is growing. Some of the most important influences of the growth or microorganisms are temperature, oxygen concentration, pH and water availability. Amazingly, microorganisms as a group are capable of growing over wide ranges of these parameters. Their metabolic versatility and ability to adapt to many physical variations has allowed them to thrive in incredibly hostile environments.

Division can occur by binary fission, budding or filamentous growth. In all cases the amount of DNA and the overall total mass of the microorganisms increases over time. There are a number of ways to measure cell growth and they will directly measure the cell number or other properties of the culture that increase as the microbial population increases. In a closed system, microbial growth goes through a characteristic set of phases (lag phase, exponential phase, stationary phase and death phase) called the growth cycle. Analysis of these phases can reveal important data about the physiology of the microorganism and the growth rate equation is useful in characterizing a microbial populations expansion during exponential phase.

The object of microbial control can range from complete eradication of microorganisms to the mere inhibition of their growth, and the goal of the treatment will influence the control method chosen. Sterilization is the complete removal of all life forms from a given area (note that this includes viruses even though they are not really living). Treatments causing sterilization tend to be drastic and can sometimes alter the chemistry of the object being treated. Items that need to be sterile before use include medical instruments, syringes, bandages, fermentation vessels, culture media, and some kinds of food.

Contamination of these items with any type of organism would be deleterious, either causing infection or unreliable research results. The next level down from sterilization is the selective removal of a subset of microbes. In many cases only certain microbes are damaging to an item and more gentle treatments can be used to eliminate only these harmful microbes without killing everything.

A good example of this is heat treatment of milk. Treatment of milk at 72°C for 15 seconds (or 66 C for 30 minutes), termed pasteurization, will kill common pathogens transmitted in milk, including tuberculosis bacilli, E. coli and Salmonella enterica strains. While many harmless bacteria are not killed by this treatment, their elimination it is not necessary. Finally, sometimes it is sufficient to inhibit microbial growth in a sample, without killing any of them. Breads contain preservatives such as sodium benzoate that inhibit the growth of molds and lengthen the shelf life of the product. The mold spores find their way onto the bread after baking, but cannot grow as quickly due to the preservative.

Physical Methods

Temperatures significantly above the optimal temperature are normally lethal to a microorganism, while those well below the optimum merely slow or stop its growth.

Heat Treatment

This interactive figure allows you to change the temperature and observe what happens to the thermal death curves of three species; E. coli, Salmonella enterica, and Listeria monocytogenes. Notice that the death curves change at different rates and L. monocytogenes, while more heat resistant at lower temperatures, dies more quickly at higher temperatures.

When trying to develop an effective heat treatment for a food or culture medium it is often necessary to quantitatively determine the rate of death. One of the best methods for achieving this goal is through the determination of decimal reduction times (or D value). The decimal reduction time is a measure of the heat sensitivity of a microbe and is defined as the length of time it takes for the viable population to decrease 10 fold at a given temperature. D can be determined by incubating a culture at a lethal temperature and periodically determining the number of surviving microbes in the sample by viable plate count.

The log of the viable plate count is plotted against time and a straight line is drawn through the points. The negative reciprocal of the slope (-1/slope) of the line is the decimal reduction time. This value is only valid for the microbe under study, at that temperature and in the medium used. In a typical experiment, the D value at a series of temperatures is determined (Figure 1). Any change in sample conditions will require an additional D value analysis. Once a D value is determined it is possible to estimate how long a sample must be heated at a certain temperature to destroy a known population of cells.

Determining the D value at a large number of temperatures for any sample is tedious and the concept of thermal death time (TDT) and the Z value was developed to allow prediction of D values at any lethal temperature. The

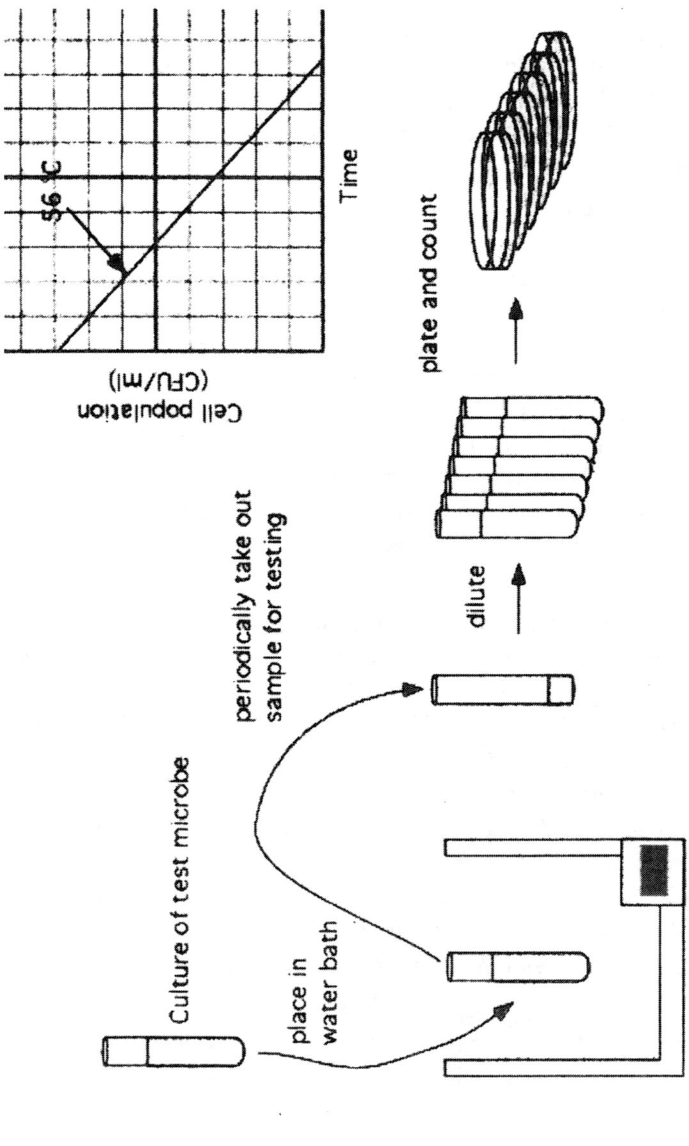

Figure 1: Determining the D value of a culture A culture is incubated at a specific temperature and portions removed at various time points. The population in each sample is determined.

TDT is the time it takes for a population of cells to reach 100 (effectively zero) at a given temperature. This can be determined by multiplying the log10 of an initial cell population by the D value or by determining the X intercept from a D-value experiment. Once several TDTs have been determined for at least three temperatures, the Z value can be obtained.

The Z value measures the sensitivity of a microbe to a change in temperature and is defined as the amount of temperature increase necessary to decrease the TDT ten-fold. To determine the Z value for a microbe, the TDT is plotted (on a log scale) against its temperature and a line is drawn through the points. The Z value is the negative reciprocal of the slope of the line. With a Z value in hand, it is possible to predict the microbes death rate in the specific medium at any lethal temperature. D values, TDT and Z values are very useful in the food industry, where one wants the treatment to appropriately reduce the microbial population with minimum negative effect on the food itself.

Types of heat treatments

One of the most ancient methods of killing microorganisms is incineration. This typically destroys all living things as well as the sample that contains them. Incineration was used in the past to prevent the spread of infectious disease. During the black plague of the 14th century, it was a common practice to burn the corpses of those who succumbed to the illness, sometimes with all their possessions. The burning of houses and possessions is no longer common due to its destructive nature, but during some outbreaks of highly infectious disease, it is still very effective.

Also, incineration is still legally required for the disposal of body parts as well as animals suspected of being infected with anthrax. Another historical method of sterilization was repeated boiling also known as Tyndallization. Boiling a solution for 30 minutes at room temperature will kill most vegetative cells, but not bacterial endospores. In Tyndallization the boiled medium is cooled, incubated for a period of hours and then boiled again and this cycle is repeated three times.

During the cooling periods, the endospores usually germinate and turn into heat-sensitive vegetative cells. Subsequent rounds of heating then kill these cells. More than two rounds of heating are necessary to insure that all spores have germinated. Tyndallization was often used to sterilize media before the invention of the autoclave. It has the drawback that it is time consuming and the growth of germinated spores can alter the medium, possibly making it unsuitable for its intended purpose.

The most common method of sterilization currently used in laboratories and hospitals is autoclaving, which is basically a sophisticated pressure cooker. This employs stream under pressure to raise the temperature to 121°C at 15-17 psi for at least 15 minutes. (Autoclaves are simply steel chambers with pipes for entrance and exit of gas. During sterilization, the autoclave is filled with steam to a pressure of 15-17 psi, resulting in a temperature of 121°C). At this elevated temperature all living cells, including endospores and viruses, are killed. Large liquid volumes and some types of medium need longer autoclaving times to insure complete elimination of microbes. One of the most hardy endospore-forming microorganisms is Bacillus stearothermophilus, which contains spores that can maintain viability for about 13 minutes at 121°C. It can therefore be used as a standard bioassay to verify that an autoclave is working properly.

Dry heat in an oven can also be used to kill microbes. Obviously this treatment will not work for liquid items since they will reach a maximum of 100°C, but for non-liquid items that do not melt at the oven temperature (160-

170°C or above), it can be effective. Items such as metal and glass can be sterilized in this manner, however these treatments can ruin some items. For example surgical instruments loose sharpness when treated in this manner. One problem with all of these high-temperature methods is that they can drastically alter the composition of the sample due to the breakdown of heat-labile components.

In some cases alternatives to high temperature must be found to preserve the integrity of the item. For foods this often means treatment at lower temperatures since most food does not need to be sterile. The first and still most common method is pasteurization, named after the great microbiologist Louis Pasteur. Originally developed to prevent the spoilage of wine, it is commonly used for milk, and eliminates the transmission of Coxiella burnetti, Mycobacterium tuberculosis, Brucella, Staphylococcus, Salmonella and E. coli strain O157:H7.

In the original batch pasteurization method, the food was heated at 66°C for 30 minutes, but most modern applications use flash pasteurization, which is a treatment at 71°C for 15 seconds. The shorter incubation time allows for easier automation and less damage to food during processing. Also, the higher temperature is more effective at killing Coxiella burnetti.. Pasteurization not only eliminates pathogens, but also greatly decreases the number of spoilage organisms. Pasteurization is used extensively in treating many other food products including beer, wine, yogurt, juices and cheese.

In microbiology laboratories, heat sensitive compounds are often necessary additions to culture media preparations. Unlike the case with foods, it is possible to easily separate heat sensitive compounds from the rest of the medium by simply not adding them initially. Heat sensitive compounds are treated separately, using some low-temperature sterilization method, and added back to the medium aseptically after it is autoclaved and cooled. In this way the heat-labile components are undamaged, yet medium containing them can still be made sterile.

Table 1: Common uses of heat to control bacteria

Treatment	Temperature	Effectiveness
Incineration	>500°C	Vaporizes organic material on nonflammable surfaces but may destroy many substances in the process.
Boiling	100°C	Thirty minutes of boiling kills vegetative forms of bacteria but may not kill bacterial endospores. There are also toxins that are not inactivated at 100°C.
Intermittent boiling	100°C	Three 30-minute intervals of boiling, followed by periods of cooling kills bacterial endospores.
Autoclave and pressure cooker (steamunder pressure)	121°C for 15 at 15 minutes p.s.i.	Kills all formsof life including bacterial endospores. The substance being sterilized must be maintained at the effective temperature for the entire time.
Dry heat (hot air oven)	160°C for 2 hours	Used for materials that must remain dry. Good for glassware, metal, but not most plastic or rubber items.
Dry heat (hot air oven)	170°C for 1 hour	Same as above. Note that increasing the temperature by 10° C shortens the sterilizing time by 50 %.
Pasteurization (batchmethod)	63-66°C for 30 minutes	Kills most vegetative bacterial cells, including pathogens such as streptococci, staphylococci and Mycobacterium tuberculosis.

Pasteurization (flash method)	72°C for 15 seconds	Effect on bacterial cells is similar to batch method. For milk, this method has fewer undesirable effects on quality or taste.

High temperature

High temperature kills by causing lysis of the membrane or denaturation of critical enzymes. Two methods of providing heat are generally used. Dry heat involves incubation in an oven-like environment, while moist heat utilizes steam under pressure, and the latter is more effective. Water has a very high heat capacity (ability to carry heat) and moist air is capable of holding more heat than dry air.

Moist heat is therefore more effective because it increases the rate of heat penetration into a substance. With dry heat a higher temperature or longer time of exposure is necessary to obtain the same amount of killing as that seen with moist heat. If you have ever used a wet oven mitt to grab a hot pan you know how much more readily heat travels in a moist environment.

In either case, at temperatures above the lethal limit for a bacterial strain, cell population decrease from heating follows a first-order exponential pattern. Because of this experimental pattern, the initial number of bacteria in a sample will affect the time necessary to eliminate that population from the sample. The goal of a heat treatment is to bring the target population down to some acceptable level. In addition, each species of microbe also has its own characteristic resistance to heat, with some bacteria being much more heat tolerant than others.

A final factor influencing the effectiveness of a heat treatment is the composition of the environment surrounding the microbe. High salt and acidic environments increase the rate of killing at a given temperature due to the damaging effects salt and acid have on the cell. Conversely, fats and proteins in a solution have a protective effect. Because of all these mitigating factors on the effectiveness of heat treatment, determining the success of a given treatment on a given type of sample must be done empirically, that is by experimentation.

Low temperature

Low temperature slows the rate of all chemical reactions, including those catalyzed by enzymes and it also decreases the fluidity of the cell membrane. Freezing the membrane thus prevents much of cellular metabolism by preventing enzymes in the membrane from functioning properly. Refrigerator temperatures (4°C) prevent the growth of many bacteria, extending the shelf life of many products. However, there are a large number of microorganisms still capable of slow growth at 4°C and these will eventually spoil foods. Refrigeration merely slows down the process of spoilage. Freezing a sample at or below 20°C stops all microbial growth. Low temperature, even freezing, is not damaging to most microorganisms and, when brought up to suitable temperatures, the microbes will begin growing again. In fact, microorganisms are well preserved in liquid nitrogen (-196°C) and this is a common method of preserving bacterial strains in research laboratories.

Irradiation

Irradiation destroys microorganisms with high-energy electromagnetic waves such as gamma rays, X-rays, UV light or electron beams. While the electromagnetic spectrum covers wavelengths of energy ranging from gamma rays to radio waves, only high-energy electromagnetic radiation is damaging to microorganisms. Radiation can be split into two types, ionizing radiation and nonionizing radiation. Ionizing radiation has enough energy that it can remove electrons from a target molecule causing it to form ions.

Nonionizing radiation cannot. Other variables being equal, ionizing radiation is more damaging than nonionizing radiation to the cell. X rays, gamma rays and electron beams are all forms of ionizing radiation, while UV light is nonionizing. At very high levels gamma rays and X-rays can denature proteins. At lower doses, gamma rays and X-rays collide with various molecules (often water), producing highly reactive species, such as hydroxyl and hydride radicals. Note that electron beams are a direct source of damaging electrons. All of these are capable of reacting with membranes lipids, DNA and proteins.

Gamma and X-rays can also directly damage DNA, causing double-stranded breaks and other mutations. At high enough intensities of radiation an item can be completely sterilized. Gamma rays, X-rays and electrons penetrate relatively deep into substrates and can be used to process many types of items. UV light damages DNA. It creates covalent linkages between bases that prevent replication and transcription, causing death when not repaired by the cell.

Because UV light is absorbed by a wide range of molecules, it fails to penetrate into samples, and it is therefore most often employed in the disinfection of critical surfaces such as in clean rooms in packaging plants. Short wavelength UV light (185 nm) does penetrate further than higher wavelength UV light and has been used to sterilize water in sewage treatment plants among other uses. The amount of radiation necessary to kill a microbe is species-specific and depends on a variety of factors. Gram-negative bacteria, including spoilage organisms, pseudomonads, and eneterics (i.e. E. coli, Shigella and Salmonella) are more sensitive to radiation than are most gram-positive bacteria.

Spores of Bacillus and Clostridium are more resistant still, due to special proteins in the spore that are thought to protect the DNA. Molds tend to have similar resistance ranges to those of most bacteria, and yeasts are a bit more resistant than bacteria to radiation. There are however some species of microbes that are incredibly resistant to radiation as vegetative cells. Deinococcus radiodurans, for example, can withstand 10 times the radiation that kills E. coli and this ability stems from its unusual efficiently in repairing double-stranded breaks in the DNA.

Table 2: Resistant to radiation of selected species

Microorganism	Type of microorganism	D_{10} (Gy)[a] in fresh food
Pseudomonas putida	Gram-negative rod-shaped bacteria	85
Campylobacter jejuni	Gram-negative slender-rod shaped bacteria	140
E. coli (O157:H7)	Short gram-negative rod-shaped bacteria	260
Lactobacillus species	Gram-positive, rod-shaped bacteria	600
Clostridium perfringens (vegetative cells)	Gram-positive, rod-shaped bacteria.	710
Clostridium botulinum (spores)	Gram-positive, rod-shaped bacteria.	2300
Deinococcus radiodurans	Gram-negative, coccus shaped bacteria	2800
Aspergillus niger	Mold	500
Saccharomyces cerevisiae	Yeast	500
Coxsackievirus	Virus	4500

[a] D_{10} is the decimal reduction dose and is similar to the D value for thermal processes. It is the amount of radiation in Grays necessary to decrease the population 10-fold. One Gray (Gy) is defined as the absorption of 1 joule of radiation per kilogram.

In some parts of Europe, irradiation of fruits and vegetables has gained wide acceptance and increased the shelf life of those products 500 percent. Irradiation is also used to treat vaccines, drugs and most imported spices. Until recently, there was resistance to irradiating food in the United States, even though the FDA has approved it for treatment of meat products. Recent food-borne outbreaks, the anthrax letters of 2001 and positive articles about irradiation from reputable sources are starting to sway public attitude toward this technology.

Filtration

Filtration is used for the removal of microbes from solutions that cannot easily be treated in other fashions. Typically heat-sensitive compounds such as antibiotics and vitamins are filtered before addition to sterile cool media. In the food industry, filtration finds utility in beer making to remove yeast before final bottling. Filtration physically removes microbes because it employs membranes whose precisely defined pores are too small to allow their passage. It is obviously only useful for liquids and gases.

Filtration does not effectively remove viruses from solution because they are typically too small. A filter system with sufficiently small pores to remove viruses would have an extremely slow flow rate due to the viscosity of water. Because viruses are not removed, filtration cannot technically be considered a form of sterilization, although it is common to refer to the process as filter sterilization. There are three major types of filters.

Depth filters, are the oldest type and consist of overlapping layers of fibrous sheets of paper, asbestos or glass fibers. The random nature of the fibers laying on one top of another creates torturous paths through the filter that trap many particles. Due to their nature they do not trap all particles of a given size, but they find utility as pre-filters before final filtration. That is, their ability to remove the vast majority of things means that this removed material does not plug up the more efficient filters noted below. They are also useful for the filter sterilization of gases. Glass and asbestos depth filters can tolerate high heat and can be conveniently sterilized with steam.

The membrane filter is the most common type of filtration system used in modern microbiology laboratories. These are made from high tensile strength polymers of cellulose acetate, cellulose nitrate, polycarbonate, polyester, polypropylene or polysulfone. At high magnification the polymers appear as a thick mesh of interconnected strands with rather precisely defined spaces between the polymer. By adjusting polymerization conditions, the size of the spaces or pores can be controlled to create membranes with various maximal sizes.

Nucleopore membranes are created by exposing a very thin polycarbonate film (10 m) to nuclear radiation, which creates areas of weakness in the polymer. The membrane is then treated with an etching solution that degrades the weak areas creating pores in the membrane. Changing the strength of the etching solution or the time of exposure of the membrane controls the size of the pores created and results in remarkably precise pore sizes.

Nucleopore membranes are particularly useful for trapping bacteria on the surface of a membrane for subsequent microscopic examination. Filters come in many shapes and sizes from small (13 mm) filters that are used for the filtration of a few milliliters of liquid to industrial filters with surface areas of several square meters that can process hundreds of liters a minute.

Reducing water activity: All living things require water so the removal of water from a sample inhibits the growth of microorganisms. Water can be removed from foods by heating, evaporation, freeze-drying or by addition of salt or sugar. The first three methods directly remove water from the sample and the last two rely on the hydrophilicity of salt and sugar to bind up the water, limiting its availability to microbes.

Before refrigeration, the salting of food was a common method of preserving it for prolonged periods and beef jerky is an obvious example of that. Dried fruits and honey are other examples of low water-activity foods. There are microorganisms that have adapted to low water activity conditions and can grow under very dry conditions. Many of these are molds and yeasts and they are the most common spoilage organisms found on jams, jellies and other low water-activity foods. Pathogens, which have evolved to live on our bodies, cannot tolerate these conditions so they are rarely a hazard in such foods.

Chemical Treatments

Chemical treatments have the advantage of providing continuous protection in contrast to the physical treatments described that often only affect the microbial population at the time of treatment, but not thereafter. Most chemicals when used at low levels are also less likely to change the physical characteristics of the environment being treated. However, adding a chemical to a sample does alter the finished product and this may have unwanted consequences.

It is also possible for microbes to develop a resistance to certain chemical treatments so that they cease to be effective. This is of particular concern in medical situations where significant amounts of antimicrobial chemicals are used. An antimicrobial agent is any chemical that kills or inhibits microorganisms. Many types of synthetic and natural compounds have antimicrobial activity. Chemicals that stop microorganisms from growing have the suffix -static, those that kill cells have the suffix -cidal, and compounds that not only kill microbes, but also cause them to lyse have -lytic appended to them. For example, an agent that kills bacteria is bacteriocidal: one that kills fungi is fungicidal and so on.

The effect of an agent on a microorganism depends on the type of compound and its concentration. Those that cause damage to proteins and membranes tend to require higher concentrations to be effective. Those that cause damage to DNA or can oxidize many types of macromolecules are usually lethal at lower concentrations. Increasing the concentration of an antimicrobial agent often increases its effectiveness and a compound that is bacteriostatic at one concentration might be bacteriocidal at a higher one. This can only be taken so far however. For example, increasing alcohol concentrations above 70% actually decreases its effectiveness.

Antiseptics and Disinfectants

A number of compounds are used to prevent infection or sepsis and are thus called antiseptics. These compounds inhibit or kill microorganisms and are safe to use on the skin and mucous membranes, but are normally not taken internally. Examples include mercurials (they contain mercury), silver nitrate, iodine solution, alcohol, and detergents. These find utility in hand-washing soaps and in the treatment of surface wounds.

Antiseptics are often employed to prevent infection with microbes or sepsis. Disinfectants are compounds that kill microorganisms and may or may not kill spores, but are not safe to apply to living tissues. Common disinfectants include chlorine compounds such as hypochlorites, as well as lye, copper sulfate and quaternary ammonium compounds. Some disinfectants are powerful enough to eliminate all life forms from an area and are given the name sterilants. Disinfectants find wide use in places where the use of heat or radiation is impractical.

For example, hospitals, food-processing plants and laboratories that need to control the microbial count on floors, walls and bench tops. The application of disinfectants to these surfaces can greatly decrease the microbial load and therefore reduce contamination.

The distinction between antiseptics and disinfectants can depend upon concentration. For example, treatment of water with sodium hypochlorite at a level of 0.02 % insures the removal of pathogenic microorganisms, yet has no effect on people, but one would never ingest liquid bleach (a 6% solution of sodium hypochlorite). Table 3 lists some common antiseptics and disinfectants along with their mode of action. Most of these compounds have their effect by inactivating proteins in the cell while a few damage DNA.

Table 3: Antiseptics and their actions.

Chemical	Action	Uses
Ethanol (50-70%)	Denatures proteins and solubilizes lipids	Antiseptic used on skin
Isopropanol (50-70%)	Denatures proteins and solubilizes lipids	Antiseptic used on skin
Tincture of iodine (2% I in 70% alcohol)	Inactivates proteins	Antiseptic used on skin
Silver nitrate ($AgNO_3$)	Precipitates proteins	General antiseptic and formally used in the eyes of newborns Erythromycin drops (an antibiotic) are now used
Detergents (e.g. quaternary ammoni--um compounds)	Disrupts cell membranes	Skin antiseptics
Phenolic compounds (e.g. carboloic acid, lysol, hexylresorcinol, hexachlorophene)	Denature proteins and disrupt cell membranes	Antiseptics at low concentrations;

Table 4: Disinfectants and their action.

Chemical	Action	Uses
Formaldehyde (8%)	Reacts with NH_2, SH and COOH groups	Disinfectant, kills endospores
Chlorine (Cl2) gas	Forms hypochlorous acid (HClO), a strong oxidizing agent	Disinfect drinking water; general disinfectant
Mercuric chloride	Inactivates proteins by reacting with sulfide groups	Disinfectant, although occasion- -ally used as an antiseptic on skin
Detergents (e.g. quaternary ammon- -ium compounds)	Disrupts cell membranes	At higher concentr- -ations and with some compounds is a disinfectant
Phenolic compounds (e.g. carboloic acid, lysol, hexylresorcinol, hexachlorophene)	Denature proteins and disrupt cell membranes	Disinfectants at high concentrations
Ethylene oxide gas	Alkylating agent	Disinfectant used to sterilize heat-sensitive objects such as rubber and plastics

A number of factors affect the potency of disinfectants. One important example is the role of biofilms, which are populations of microorganisms that grow on surfaces and encase themselves in excreted layers of polysaccharide. Dental plaque and slimy, slippery rocks in rivers are two very common examples of these types of communities. Biofilms can form on catheters, tubes, pipes and many other surfaces that microbes can attach to, and they cause significant problems in medicine and industry.

Biofilms can greatly retard or even prevent the diffusion of disinfectants to the microbes, eliminating the effectiveness of the compound. Understanding these films and how to combat them is an important research topic. The composition of the item being disinfected can also alter the activity of a disinfectant. High concentrations of organic compounds decrease the potency of disinfectants and it is usually prudent to clean a surface before adding disinfectant. Finally, endospores are characteristically more resistant to disinfectants than are vegetative cells. However, certain agents such as bleach can still kill spores. It is important to be aware of these factors when treating an area in order to insure the maximum potency of disinfectants.

Preservatives

Preservatives are static agents that are added to food and medical supplies to inhibit microbial growth, thus increasing their safety and shelf life. These compounds must be non-toxic and safe for human ingestion, and preservatives added to vaccines must be safe to enter the blood stream. Salts of organic acids (propionate, sorbate, benzoate and lactate) are preservatives that act by increasing the proton concentration of the cytoplasm of many microbes. They are weak acids, so at mildly acidic conditions they are protonated and therefore non-polar, allowing them to penetrate the cellular membrane.

Once inside the cell, these acids dissociate (releasing protons) due to the lower proton concentration of the cytoplasm. Because microorganisms strictly maintain their proton concentration, they must compensate for these acids by pumping out protons using ATP synthase, which also disrupts ATP synthesis in respiring microorganisms. Both of these effects cost the cell energy and slow growth. For organic acids to be effective, they must be prononated, so that any solution containing them must be at a pH of 5.5 or lower for the preservative to be effective.

Parabens are derivatives of phenol and have similar disruptive effects. They inhibit bacterial growth by disrupting the cellular membrane, thereby inhibiting uptake of nutrients and dissipating the proton motive force. Sulfites, in addition to being preservatives, are effective antioxidants, preventing the browning of fruit. The sulfites are extremely reactive, attacking proteins, prosthetic groups, sugars and nucleic acids. Their targets for inhibition include the cytoplasmic membrane, DNA replication, protein synthesis and various enzymes in the cytoplasm. Low concentration sulfites can inhibit bacteria, yeast and molds.

Nitrites are specifically added to cured meats to prevent growth and toxin production by Clostridium botulinum. It has its effect by inhibiting two enzymes, pyruvate-ferrodoxin oxidoreductase and ferrodoxin. Inhibition of these enzymes disrupts the central catabolic processes of C. botulinum, preventing energy generation and thus spore germination and outgrowth. Many food products contain some sort of preservative, including bread, juices, carbonated beverages and snack foods. Common preservatives and their action are listed in Table 5.

Table 5: Common preservatives and their action

Preservative	Effective Concentration	Uses
Propionic acid and propionates	0. 3%	Antifungal agent in breads, cake, Swiss cheeses.
Sorbic acid and sorbates	0. 2%	Antifungal agent in cheeses, jellies, syrups, cakes.
Benzoic acid and benzoates	0. 1%	Antifungal agent in margarine, cider, relishes, soft drinks.
Sodium diacetate	0. 3%	Antifungal agent in breads.
Lactic acid	Variable	Antimicrobial agent in

		cheeses, buttermilk, yogurt and pickled foods.
Methyl, propyl and heptyl paraben	0.04 0.2 %	Antimicrobial agent in beer, fruit based beverages, jams, jellies, syrups, and wine.
Sulfur dioxide, sulfites	0.02-0.03 %	Antimicrobial agent in dried fruits, grapes, molasses.
Sodium nitrite	0.02 %	Antibacterial agent in cured meats, fish.
Sodium chloride	Variable	Prevents microbial spoilage of meats, fish, etc.
Sugar	Variable	Prevents microbial spoilage of preserves, jams, syrups, jellies, etc.
Wood smoke	NA	Prevents microbial spoilage of meats, fish, etc.

Antibiotics and chemotherapeutic agents: Antibiotics are another class of compounds that inhibit or kill microorganisms. They are low molecular weight compounds that inhibit or kill other microorganisms and are effective at very low concentrations. They were first discovered as excreted metabolites of some microorganisms, but many are now synthetic or semi-synthetic compounds (that is, natural metabolites are isolated and then chemically modified) produced by the pharmaceutical industry.

Measuring antimicrobial activity: Determining the antimicrobial activity of a compound is often essential for its effective use. For example, to fight a bacterial infection a series of antibiotics and antimicrobials will be tested to determine which should be prescribed as a treatment. In a food processing plant the concentration of disinfectant to use for cleaning equipment can be determined experimentally to maximize killing power, yet minimize the amount of antimicrobial used. A good antimicrobial assay will achieve two purposes, it first verifies that the compound actually has the desired antimicrobial activity and second it indicates the concentration of the antimicrobial that will be needed to inhibit the target organism.

To determine the activity of an antimicrobial compound against microorganisms, it is tested under carefully controlled conditions. The effectiveness of a compound is dependent upon a number of conditions such as the nature of the target microbes, concentration of the microbes, composition of the environment, time in contact with the compound, temperature, pH and amount of aeration. A standard assay often used to gauge the effectiveness of an antimicrobial is the minimum inhibitory concentration (MIC) test (figure 2).

The MIC is the lowest concentration of a compound that still inhibits its growth. The MIC of a given compound for a certain bacterial species is determined using a series of test tubes containing medium in which the microbe will normally grow, but where each tube contains progressively lower concentrations of the test compound. Each tube is inoculated with the microbe and after incubation the tubes in which growth does not occur are noted. The lowest concentration of the antimicrobial compound that prevents growth defines the MIC. Since many parameters affect MIC, it is only valid for the specific conditions tested.

If it is desired to compare the effectiveness of different antimicrobials on a certain strain or to examine the resistance of a number of microbes to a single agent, test conditions need to be rigorously standardized. In some situations it is important to determine the minimum concentration at which a compound is lethal to a microorganism and this is defined as the minimal lethal concentration (MLC). Antimicrobials that are cidal will normally kill a microorganism at two to four times their inhibitory concentration, while a static agent will require a much higher concentration and may not ever be lethal.

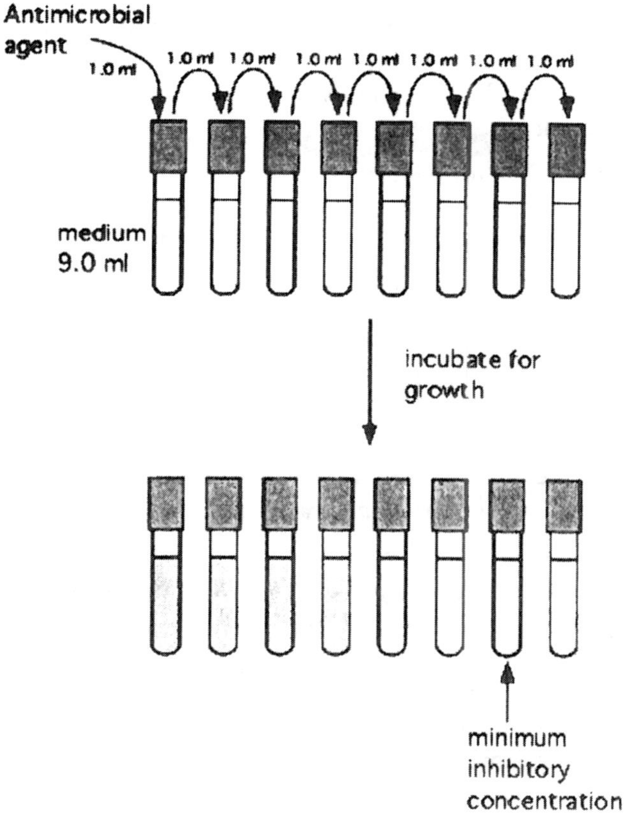

Figure 2: Assessing the antimicrobial activity of a compound using the minimum inhibitory concentration method

A compound to be tested is serially diluted into growth medium, inoculated with culture and then incubated. The minimum inhibitory concentration is indicated in the lowest dilution of compound that prevents growth as shown by the arrow.

Another commonly used assay to assess the potency of an agent is the agar diffusion method. A microbial culture is spread evenly on the top of an agar plate containing medium that will support its growth. Disks impregnated with antimicrobial compounds are then placed onto the agar and the plate incubated at an appropriate temperature for that microbe.

During incubation the antimicrobial compound diffuses away from the disk and into the agar creating a concentration gradient that is highest near the disk and decreases as one moves away from the disk. If a microbe is inhibited by the agent, it will be unable to grow near the disk, which we see as a zone of clearing in the lawn of growth. Farther away from the disk, where the concentration of the antimicrobial compound is much lower, growth will be evident. The size of the zone of clearing around the disk is an indication of the potency of the antimicrobial for the tested microbe.

Using the agar diffusion method it is possible to test a number of different compounds simultaneously on the same agar plate. Unlike the previous method, this one does not readily provide the MIC, since we cannot easily know the concentration at different places in the agar. The agar diffusion method is most useful in determining the approximate antibiotic sensitivity of a microbe.

4

Functional Anatomy of Prokaryotic and Eukaryotic Cells

Living cells are divided into two types:

1) prokaryotic and

2) eukaryotic.

This division is based on internal complexity.

Eukaryotic: The cells of protozoa, higher plants and animals are highly structured. These cells tend to be larger than the cells of bacteria, and have developed specialized packaging and transport mechanisms that may be necessary to support their larger size. Here are representive drawings of plant and animal cells showing their respective organelles.

Prokaryotic: These cells are simple in structure, with no recognizable organelles. They have an outer cell wall that gives them shape. Just under the rigid cell wall is the more fluid cell membrane. The cytoplasm enclosed within the cell membrane does not exhibit much structure when viewed by electron microscopy.

Prokaryotic Cell

Prokaryotes (from Old Greek *pro-* before + *karyon* nut, referring to the cell nucleus, + suffix *-otos*, pl. *-otes*; also spelled "procaryotes") are organisms without a cell nucleus (= karyon), or indeed any other membrane-bound organelles, in most cases unicellular (in rare cases, multicellular). This is in contrast to eukaryotes (also spelled "eucaryotes"), organisms that have cell nuclei and may be variously unicellular or multicellular.

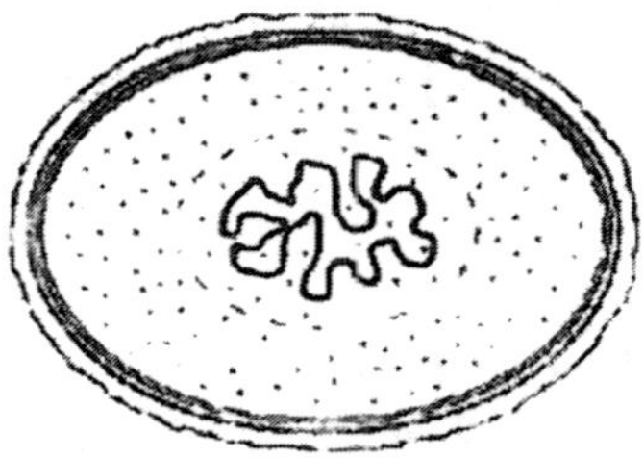

Prokaryotic Cell

The difference between the structure of prokaryotes and eukaryotes is so great that it is considered to be the most important distinction among groups of organisms. Most prokaryotes are bacteria, and the two terms are often treated as synonyms. However, Woese has proposed dividing prokaryotes into the Bacteria and Archaea (originally Eubacteria and Archaebacteria) because of the significant genetic differences between the two. This controversial arrangement of Eukaryote, Bacteria, and Archaea is called the three-domain system.

Structure

The cell structure of prokaryotes differs greatly from eukaryotes in many ways. The defining characteristic is, of course, the absence of a nucleus or nuclear envelope. Prokaryotes also were previously considered to lack cytoskeletons and do lack membrane-bound cell compartments such as vacuoles, endoplasmic reticulum, mitochondria and chloroplasts.

In eukaryotes, the latter two perform various metabolic processes and are believed to have been derived from endosymbiotic bacteria. In prokaryotes similar processes occur across the cell membrane; endosymbionts are extremely rare. Prokaryotes also have cell walls, while some eukaryotes, particularly animals, do not. Both eukaryotes and prokaryotes have structures called ribosomes, which produce protein. Prokaryotes are usually much smaller than eukaryotic cells.

Prokaryotes have a single circular (only exceptionally linear, as in *Borrelia burgdorferi*) chromosome, contained within a region called *nucleoid*, rather than in a membrane-bound nucleus, but may also have various small circular pieces of DNA called plasmids spread throughout the cell. Reproduction is exclusively asexual, through binary fission, where the chromosome is duplicated and attaches to the cell membrane, and then the cell divides in two. However, they show a variety of parasexual processes where DNA is transferred between cells, such as transformation and transduction.

While prokaryotes are nearly always unicellular, some are capable of forming groups of cells called colonies. Unlike many eukaryotic multicellular organisms, each member of the colony is undifferentiated and capable of free-living. Colonies are formed by organisms that remain attached following cell division, sometimes through the help of a secreted slime layer. Some prokaryotes contain protein-enclosed *microcompartments* which can be seen as primitive organelles.

Prokaryotes are found in nearly all environments on earth. Archaea in particular seem to thrive in harsh conditions, such as high temperatures or salinity. Organisms such as these are referred to as extremophiles. Many prokaryotes live in or on the bodies of other organisms, including humans. Sometimes this leads to a life-threatening bacterial infection, but in many cases the organisms are harmless or even beneficial to the host.

Evolution of Prokaryotes

It is generally accepted that the first living cells were some form of prokaryote. Fossilized prokaryotes 3.5 billion years old have been discovered, and prokaryotes are perhaps the most successful and abundant organism even today. While earth is the only known place where prokaryotes exist, some have suggested structures within a Martian meteorite should be interpreted as fossil prokaryotes, but this is extremely doubtful.

Prokaryotes diversified greatly throughout their long existence. The metabolism of prokaryotes is far more varied than that of eukaryotes, leading to many highly distinct types of prokaryotes. For example, in addition to using photosynthesis or an organic form of carbon for energy like eukaryotes do, prokaryotes may obtain energy from inorganic chemicals such as hydrogen sulfide.

Eukaryotic Cells

Eukaryotes (also spelled "eucaryotes") are organisms with complex cells, in which the genetic material is organized into membrane-bound nuclei. They include the animals, plants, and fungi, which are mostly multicellular, as well as various other groups collectively referred to as protists, many of which are unicellular. In contrast, other organisms such as bacteria lack nuclei and other complex cell structures, and are called prokaryotes. The eukaryotes share a common origin, and are often treated formally as a superkingdom, empire, or domain. The name comes from the Greek *eus* or true and *karyon* or nut, referring to the nucleus.

Structure

Eukaryotic cells are generally much larger than prokaryotes, typically a thousand times by volume. They have a variety of internal membranes and structures, called organelles, and a cytoskeleton composed of microtubules and microfilaments, which play an important role in defining the cell's organization. Eukaryotic DNA is divided into several bundles called chromosomes, which are separated by a microtubular spindle during nuclear division. In addition to asexual cell division, most eukaryotes have some process of sexual reproduction via cell fusion, which is not found among prokaryotes.

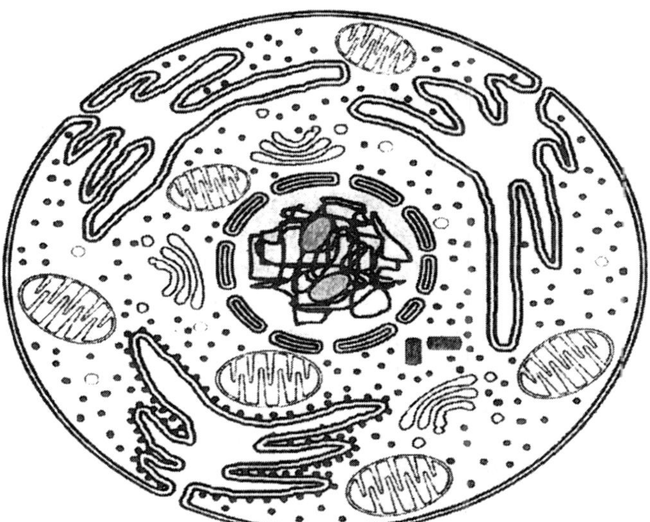

Eukaryotic (Animal) cell

Internal Membranes

Eukaryotic cells include a variety of membrane-bound structures, collectively referred to as the endomembrane system. Simple compartments, called vesicles or vacuoles, can form by budding off other membranes. Many cells ingest food and other materials through a process of endocytosis, where the outer membrane invaginates and then pinches off to form a vesicle. It is probable that most other membrane-bound organelles are ultimately derived from such vesicles.

The nucleus is surrounded by a double membrane, with pores that allow material to move in and out. Various tube- and sheet-like extensions of the nuclear membrane form what is called the endoplasmic reticulum or ER, which is involved in protein transport. It includes rough sections where ribosomes are attached, and the proteins they synthesize enter the interior space or lumen. Subsequently, they generally enter vesicles, which bud off from the smooth section. In most eukaryotes, the proteins may be further modified in stacks of flattened vesicles, called Golgi bodies or dictyosomes.

Vesicles may be specialized for various purposes. For instance, lysosomes contain enzymes that break down the contents of food vacuoles, and peroxisomes are used to break down peroxide which is toxic otherwise. Many protozoa have contractile vacuoles, which collect and expel excess water, and extrusomes, which expel material used to deflect predators or capture prey. In multicellular organisms, hormones are often produced in vesicles. In higher plants, most of a cell's volume is taken up by a central vacuole or tonoplast, which maintains its osmotic pressure.

Mitochondria and Plastids

Mitochondria are organelles found in nearly all eukaryotes. They are surrounded by double membranes, the inner of which is folded into invaginations called cristae, where aerobic respiration takes place. They contain their own DNA and are only formed by the fission of other mitochondria. They are now generally held to have developed from endosymbiotic prokaryotes, probably proteobacteria. The few protozoa that lack mitochondria have been found to contain mitochondrion-derived organelles, such as hydrogenosomes and mitosomes.

Plants and various groups of algae also have plastids. Again, these have their own DNA and developed from endosymbiotes, in this case cyanobacteria. They usually take the form of chloroplasts, which like cyanobacteria contain chlorophyll and produce energy through photosynthesis. Others are involved in storing food. Although plastids likely had a single origin, not all plastid-containing groups are closely related. Instead, some eukaryotes have obtained them from others through secondary endosymbiosis or ingestion.

Endosymbiotic origins have also been proposed for the nucleus and eukaryotic flagella, but this is not generally accepted, both from a lack of cytological evidence and difficulty in reconciling this with cellular reproduction.

Cytoskeletal Structures

Many eukaryotes have slender motile projections, usually called flagella when long and cilia when short, that are variously involved in movement, feeding, and sensation. These are entirely distinct from prokaryotic flagella. They are supported by a bundle of microtubules arising from a basal body, also called a kinetosome or centriole, characteristically arranged as nine doublets surrounding two singlets. Flagella also may have hairs or mastigonemes, scales, connecting membranes and internal rods. Their interior is continuous with the cell's cytoplasm.

Centrioles are often present even in cells and groups that do not have flagella. They generally occur in groups of one or two, called kinetids, that give rise to various microtubular roots. These form a primary component of the cytoskeletal structure, and are often assembled over the course of several cell divisions, with one flagellum retained from the parent and the other derived from it. Centrioles may also be associated in the formation of a spindle during nuclear division.

Some protists have various other microtubule-supported organelles. These include the radiolaria and heliozoa, which produce axopodia used in flotation or to capture prey, and the haptophytes, which have a peculiar flagellum-like organelle called the haptonema.

Reproduction

Nuclear division is often coordinated with cell division. This generally takes place by mitosis, a process which allows each daughter nucleus to receive one copy of each chromosome. In most eukaryotes there is also a process of sexual reproduction, typically involving an alternation between haploid generations, where only one copy of each chromosome is present, and diploid generations, where two are present, occurring through nuclear fusion (syngamy) and meiosis. There is considerable variation in this pattern, however.

Origin and Evolution

The origin of the eukaryotic cell was a milestone in the evolution of life. Although eukaryotes use the same genetic code and metabolic processes as prokaryotes, their higher level of organizational complexity has permitted the development of truly multicellular organisms. Without eukaryotes, the world would lack mammals, birds, fish, invertebrates, mushrooms, plants, and complex single-celled organisms.

Eukaryotes are generally held to have originated around 2 billion years ago, but this has been disputed. Early fossils such as acritarchs are difficult to interpret. Forms that can be related to modern groups start appearing around 800 million years ago, and most fossil lines are known by the end of the Cambrian, around 500 million years ago.

Genetic studies during the 1980s and 1990s left most eukaryotes in an unresolved "crown" group, usually divided by the form of the cristae in their mitochondria. The few amitochondriate groups branched first on rRNA trees and so were considered basal, but this is now considered to be an error caused by long branch attraction. A new picture has been slow to develop. Most eukaryotes are now included in several supergroups:

Opisthokonts	Animals, fungi, choanoflagellates, etc.
Amoebozoa	Most lobose amoebae and slime moulds
Rhizaria	Various amoeboid protozoa
Excavates	Various flagellate protozoa
Plantae *sensu lato*	Land plants, green and red algae
Chromista	Brown algae, diatoms, water moulds, etc.
Alveolates	Ciliates, Apicomplexa, dinoflagellates, etc.

However, some protists are not closely related to any of these lines, and the relationships between the different supergroups remain almost entirely uncertain. In particular, there is dispute about where the root of the evolutionary tree belongs, and as a result what the earliest eukaryotes were like.

Eukaryotic vs. Prokaryotic Cells

All cellular life has the following characteristics in common.

— all cells have a cell membrane that separates the chaos outside a cell from the high degree of organization within the cell. A cell without a cell membrane is not a cell.

— all cellular life contains DNA as its genetic material. All cells contain several varieties of rna molecules and proteins, most of the latter are enzymes.

- all cells are composed of the same basic chemicals: carbohydrates, proteins, nucleic acids, minerals, fats and vitamins.
- all cells regulate the flow of nutrients and wastes that enter and leave the cell.
- all cells reproduce and are the result of reproduction.
- all cells require a supply of energy.
- all cells are highly regulated by elaborate sensing systems (chemical "noses") that allow them to be aware of every reaction that is occurring within them and many of the environmental conditions around them; this information is continually processed to make metabolic decisions.
- for example: many flowers close up at night and open during the day. How do they know when the sun is up?
- when you were developing in your mother's uterus how did the cell that eventually became your eyes know to turn into an eye and in the right place at the correct moment in fetal development and relative to the other cells around it that will be turning into something else?

The above criteria are the minimal requirements of life. Two general cell types have evolved. These are called prokaryotic and eukaryotic cells. Current data supports the theory that prokaryotic cells represent the initial or primitive cell type on earth and that eukaryotic cell types evolved from them.

Prokaryotic cells are less complex than eukaryotic cells at several levels. Eukaryotic cells are structurally & biochemically more complex and are considered to represent a later stage of evolution. There is strong data to support the idea that eukaryotic cells evolved from aggregates of prokaryotic cells that became interdependent upon one another and eventually merged or fused into a single larger cell. Eukaryotic cells have a higher degree of organization than do prokaryotic cells, in that they contain many organelles or structures separated from the other cytoplasm components by a membrane, whereas prokaryotic cells contain no organelles. The major eukaryotic organelles are:

— the nucleus, which contains the DNA and

— the enzymes for DNA synthesis and the process of transcription.

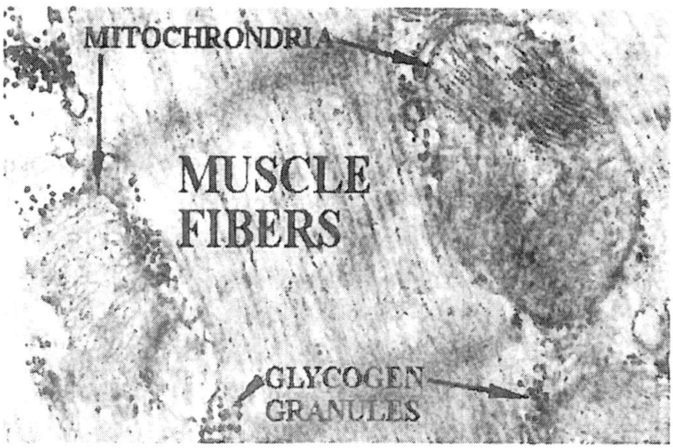

Figure 1: Eukaryotic muscle cell.

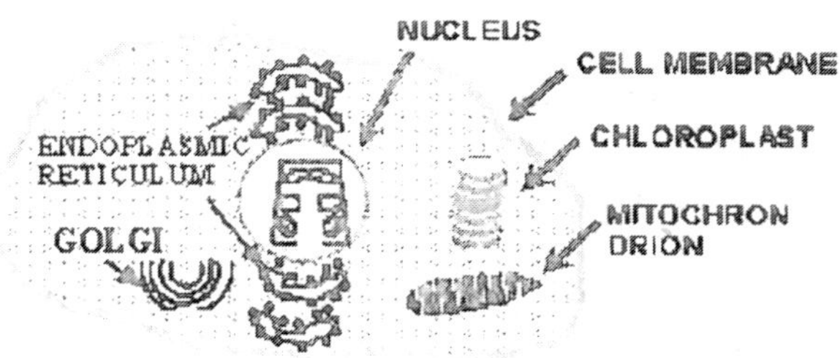

Figure 2: Composite eukaryotic cell structure

— mitochondria are the energy producing structures of eukaryotic cells and supply the cells with ATP. The mitochondria contain some DNA and some protein synthesizing machinery that resembles similar prokaryotic machinery (fig. 1). The human mitochondria are inherited entirely from the mother (the egg) and thus changes (mutations) in mitochondrial DNA are traced through the mother only.

— chloroplasts which allow plants to trap sunlight as energy and to carry out photosynthesis. It is photosynthesis, the process of using the trapped sunlight to fix carbon dioxide in the form of sugar, that makes human life possible on this planet since plants ultimately provided the food for most eukaryotes.

— golgi apparatus is a structure in eukaryotic cells that secretes substances.

— ribosomes which are the structures upon which proteins are made. All cells contain these, but they are different in prokaryotes and eukaryotes.

— photosynthetic cells contain forms of the light-trapping pigment, chlorophyll. Almost all life on earth is dependent upon chlorophyll. There are many photosynthetic bacteria (prokaryotes), but many of them have a mechanism of photosynthesis that is different from that in eukaryotic photosynthetic cells.

— motility structures. Not all cells are motile, but both groups have cells that are. Some cells have flagella that are long thin structures that rotate so as to propel the cell; others crawl across solid surfaces and others have stiff fiber-like structures that move like oars. The bacterial flagella is composed of repeating protein subunits that form a stiff organ. The base of the bacterial flagella acts like a motor and contains a flexible "joint". The motor can change direction when necessary, but it only moves forward when the flagella turns in a counterclockwise direction for most bacteria. The eukaryotic flagella is very complex and is composed of several filaments.

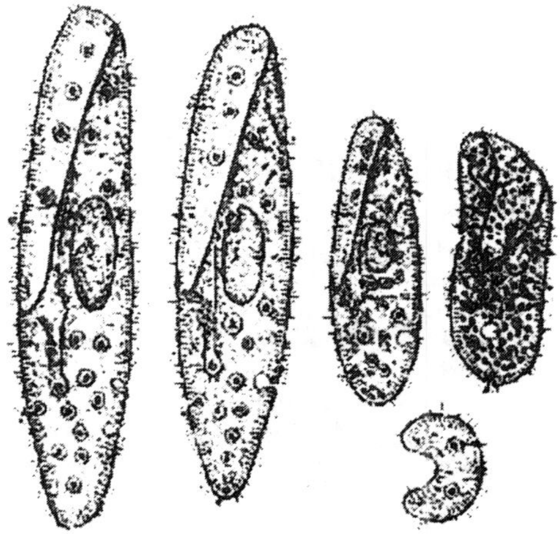

Figure 3: Protozoan cells.

The fine stiff hairs on the outside of these protozoa beat in rhythm to move these cells through liquid. In the first two laboratory exercises you will see a number of such protozoa.

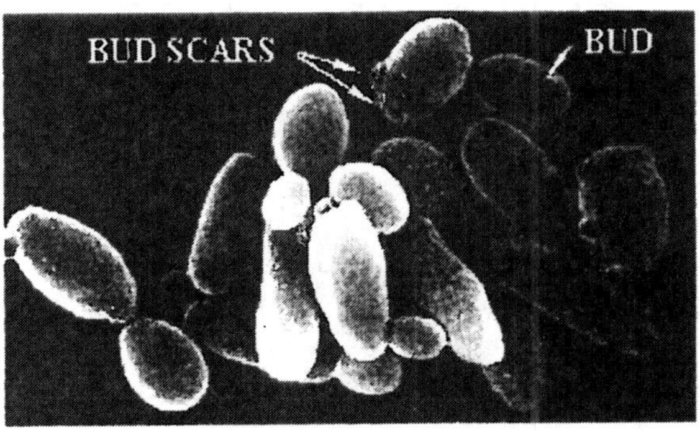

Figure 4: Actively reproducing yeast cells showing buds and bud-scars

These are actively growing yeast with lots of daughter yeast budding off from the parental cell. Note that every daughter cell leaves a "Bud Scar" behind on the parent yeast cell. What do you think happens when these scars build up to a high number?

Most cells divide by a process called binary fission where a cell divides in half forming two daughter cells which are smaller duplicates of each other. A few cells reproduce by budding, where the daughter cell grows out of the parent and gradually increases in size.

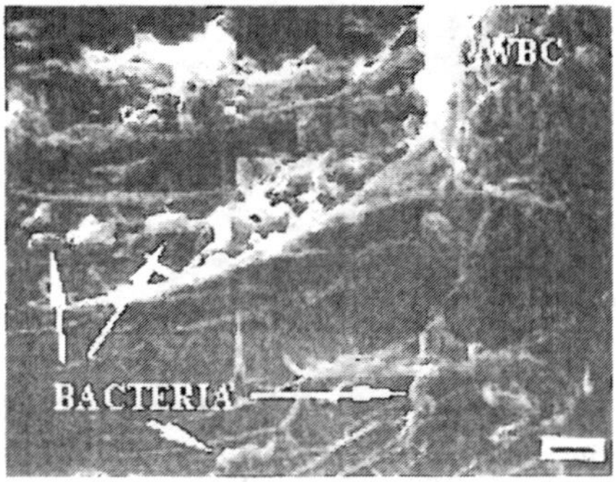

Figure 5: White blood cell attacking bacterial cells

All cells have their genes arranged in linear chains called chromosomes. Eukaryotic cells contain 2 (or more) copies of each gene (with some exceptions) carried in duplicate chromosomes. During cell division the chromosomes of eukaryotic cells undergo an organized process of chromosome replication that is visible under the light microscope. This process, called mitosis, insures that each daughter cell receives a complete copy of the parental genome. Prokaryotic cells usually contain only a single chromosome and, while its process of replication etc. Is also highly organized, it is not visible under the light microscopes.

Eukaryotic cells range in size between 2 and 100 micro meters ($=10^{-6}$ meters) and are usually much larger than prokaryotic cells which run between 0.5 and 2 micrometers. However, a large prokaryotic cell that is 600 micro meters long has recently been discovered. This bacterium is much larger than the paramecia you observed in lab and can be seen by the naked eye. So far it can't be grown in culture.

Until recently, only eukaryotic cells were thought to exist in multicellular coordinated groups such as organs and tissues, but recent evidence indicates that some prokaryotic cells contain differentiated cells in their colonial mass that do different activities important to the survival of the colony. This is not too unexpected when you consider that whatever a bacterium does is regulated by its immediate environment and that the environment in a colony is very different (pH, nutrients, wastes) in different parts of the colony (e.g. The colony center vs the outer edge of the colony).

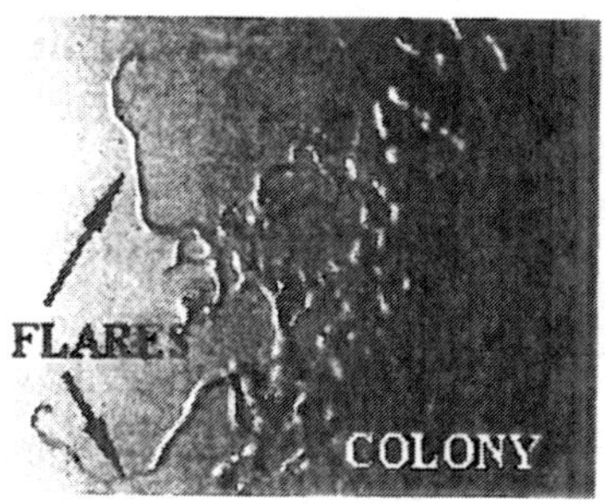

Figure 6. Mobile cells forming flares at the edge of a colony.

Some highly motile cells produce aggressively spreading colonies. At the edges of these colonies special large motile cells are formed. These cells move in a coordinated fashion, forming long chains of unconnected giant cells which produce "flares" or streams of giant cells that rapidly move out from the colony edge in this characteristic fashion.

Recent data indicate that these flare-cells are differentiated from the cells further back in the colony.

Figure 7: Electron micrographs of fungi

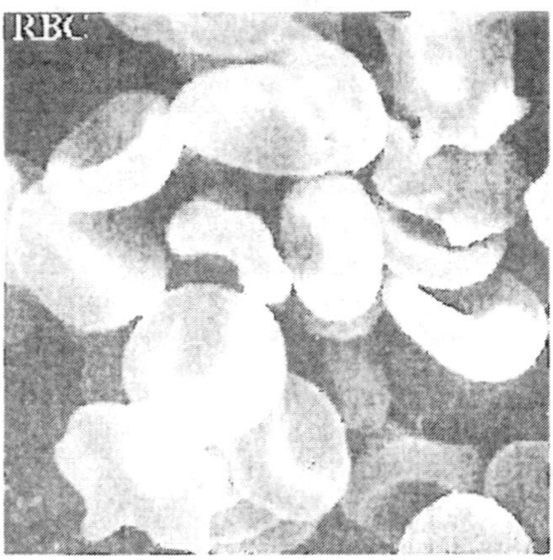

Figure 8. Electron micrographs of blood cells

Most of the cells (hole in center) in the picture are red blood cells (RBC) that carry oxygen to the tissue cells. Rbc cells are unusual in that they lack a nucleus, which is discarded after they are formed.

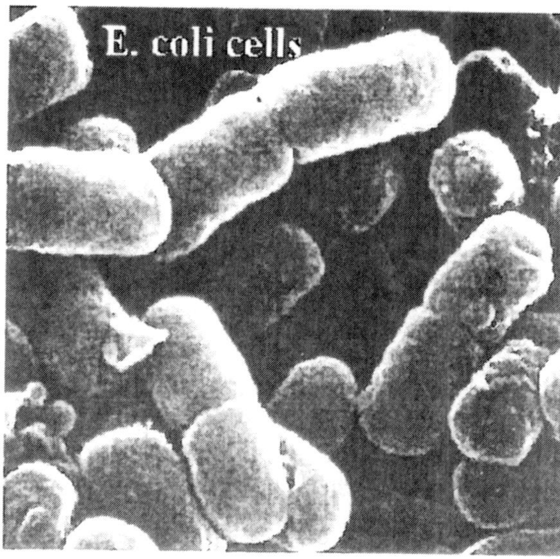

Figure 9: Electron micrograph of E. coli *cells.*

These cells are approximately 2 micrometers long and 0.5 to 1.0 micrometers wide. The number of cells in the process of binary fission indicates that this was a rapidly growing culture.

5

Genomics and Genetics

Genomics is the analysis and utilization of DNA sequence information. Even within the field of biology, where the amount of information doubles every few years, the change in genomics is stunning. First, genetics and genetic engineering are essential for understanding fundamental issues of all of biology at the molecular level. As argued elsewhere in the text, it is only by examining the effect of a mutation on the behavior of the organism that we can make firm conclusions about the role of the gene product in the cell. Second, an understanding of genetics will also provide a sense of how people can (and cannot) interpret the genomics information that is flooding into scientific publications and even the popular press. Third, it provides a bit of a sense of "how we know what we know," since microbial genetics was instrumental in the understanding of virology, the central dogma, and metabolism.

Fourth, it provides a background for understanding how scientists are manipulating microbes to generate valuable products and to understand virulence and disease. Understanding genetics therefore provides a sense of how microbes have evolved and how they continue to adapt to changes in their environment, to the advantages and perils of humans.

Genomics generates testable hypotheses about the function of genes, but the tests typically require the application of the methods of biochemistry and genetics. The discipline of biochemistry allows the precise analysis of biological phenomena, but it is typically limited to analyses in vitro. In other words, biochemistry typically examines the processes of cells using cell extracts in test tubes, which can be very different from the situation inside a cell.

Genomics suggests the number and identity of many of the genes whose products are involved in a specific biochemical process. However, the generation and characterization of mutants altered in that process - that is, genetics - tests those hypotheses. Genomics can suggest that a given protein might have a certain biochemical activity because it is evolutionarily related to a protein in which that activity has already been demonstrated. Biochemical characterization of mutants created through genetics lacking that protein can confirm if the metabolic defect is consistent with that hypothesis.

In vitro biochemical assays of the protein itself, perhaps after it has been overexpressed with the tools of genetic engineering, can verify the ability of the protein to run that reaction. There are obvious biotechnological values in the generation of mutants created by genetic means with desirable properties like overproduction of the desired gene products or metabolites, production of novel gene products or metabolites, or the easily regulated production of gene products or metabolites.

The specific power of microbial genetics (which includes the genetics of small eukaryotes like yeast) reflects several features. Perhaps most importantly, because microbes are very small, we can easily work with vast populations of them. These huge populations mean that very rare, but important and useful strains exist in a single test tube and the power of genetic screen and selections allows us to find these. One can examine as many bacteria in a single test tube as there are humans on earth.

Secondly, it is relatively easy to create specific mutations in regions of cloned DNA from microbes in vitro, and then move those mutations into the genome of the organism. This allows us to precisely create desired strains and test their behavior. This is not in the toolbox of scientists working on most higher eukaryotes, so there are questions that can be asked with microbes that simply cannot be addressed with other organisms. Because genomics has made it clear that all organisms are evolutionarily related, studying microbes has allowed us to ask about important biological properties that they share with higher organism.

For example, applying microbial genetics to te analysis of a bacterial protein that is similar to a human protein not only elucidates the protein's role in the microbe, but will generate a hypothesis about its role in humans, where actual experiments are either impossible or unethical.

To make sense of any field of science, you must speak the language. That is, you must develop an understanding of both the denotations and connotations of the terms used. Therefore we will start off with a number of definitions that are used in genetics. You will often see the term wild type. This refers to the specific strain that has been arbitrarily chosen as the benchmark for each species. It is not necessarily the best or most robust strain of the species and it was probably just the first isolate that was described in the scientific literature. Nevertheless, such a strain serves as a standard to which all other strains of the species are compared. A term with roughly the same meaning is the type strain of a species.

The terms phenotype refers to the behavior or appearance of a strain. A strain that behaves like the wild type is said to have a wild-type phenotype. A strain that behaves differently under some condition, whether it grows better or worse that does the wild type, has a mutant phenotype. Genotype refers to the precise genetic makeup of the organism and increasingly refers to the genome sequence. As above, the genotype of the wild type is arbitrarily defined as the wild-type genotype and any variation from the sequence is termed a mutant genotype.

A change in the nucleotide sequence of DNA (or RNA, in the case of viruses with RNA genomes) from what is found in the wild type is called a mutation, irrespective of its effect on the phenotype. A strain carrying such a genetic change is termed a mutant. These definitions imply that just because a strain has a wild-type phenotype does not mean that it has a wild-type genotype, it might simply be that the mutation does not cause a mutant phenotype.

Mutations can either be tight or leaky. A tight mutant displays its mutant phenotype distinctly and clearly. In other words, it looks much different from the wild type. In contrast, a leaky mutant displays a phenotype that is only a bit different from that of wild type. Mutants can also be stable or unstable and this is an indication of the frequency with which they revert to an apparently wild-type phenotype; reversion is the return of a mutant to a wild-type phenotype.

A conditional mutation is one that it is known to display its mutant phenotype only under certain conditions and under other conditions, it looks like wild type. A particular condition where the mutant phenotype is evident is termed non-permissive, while the wild-type phenotype is observed when conditions are permissive. The typical example is a temperature-sensitive mutant, which is one that displays a mutant phenotype only at low or high temperatures.

A strain that can derive all carbon requirements from the principal carbon source is termed a prototroph. If one or more other organic growth factors (like amino acids, nucleotides, or vitamins) are required by the strain, it is termed an auxotroph. A conditionally lethal mutation is one that causes cell death under the non-permissive conditions regardless of the medium. Such mutations are typically found in genes whose products perform DNA replication, RNA transcription, protein synthesis or other functions essential on any medium.

The wild type of a given species will not necessarily be a prototroph for two reasons. The dumb reason is that the arbitrarily chosen wild type that was plucked out of the environment years ago might not have been representative of the species. That wild type might simply have had a spontaneous mutation that happened to create an auxotrophic requirement. The more biologically important reason that a wild type might be an auxotroph is that some species simply do not possess some biosynthetic pathways.

Similarly, some bacteria that grow only in milk have lost the ability to make some of the amino acids that are abundant in milk. Optimally, wild type refers to a strain that has all of the metabolic and catabolic properties typically found in other strains of that species, but wild type does not mean that the strain can grow under all sorts of conditions.

Nomenclature of Genes, Phenotypes and Proteins

There is a final bit of nomenclature that is used for phenotypes. It looks a bit like the short-hand for proteins in that it is not italicized and does start with a capital letter, but it always has a superscript "+" or "-." The context in which term is used should also avoid confusion. When a strain has a wild-type phenotype for the property in question, it has a "+" superscript, while a mutant phenotype is indicated by a "-" superscript.

Remember though that phenotypes are somewhat arbitrary: when a strain is referred to as His-, you may assume it requires the addition of histidine to the media for optimal (wild-type) growth. You should not assume that it fails to make any of its own histidine, but rather that it does not make enough for optimal growth under the conditions tested. Similarly, a strain might make rather less histidine than does the wild type, but if it is capable of making sufficient histidine so that it grows normally without supplementation, it is designated His+. Again, the assignment of either a His+ or His- phenotype depends on the actual conditions of growth used in the experiment.

To understand the relationship between phenotypes and genotypes, it helps to develop mental pictures of the biochemical processes that you are analyzing genetically. For example, it happens to be true that mutations that destroy a protein product are more common than mutations that make the protein temperature-sensitive. After all, the protein must work pretty well at one temperature, but then fail to work just a few degrees higher. On the other hand, there are lots of mutations that can destroy a protein's function. These would include deletions of some or all of the gene, frameshift mutations, premature stop signals and alterations of the residues that are critical for catalytic activity.

Therefore mutations with a temperature-sensitive phenotype should be rather rare compared to mutations that destroy activity (at all temperatures) since there will be many more alterations that will have the latter result. Without such mental pictures of the biochemistry underlying the phenotypes, genetic analysis will seem to be an arbitrary and formal game. With such images, the genetic result will make sense because it reflects the biochemistry underlying cell behavior.

Genetics and Genetic Engineering

Genetics and genetic engineering are fundamentally similar in that both involve creating mutations and examining the effects of these on the phenotype of the organism. The primary difference is that in traditional genetics, one seeks mutants with interesting phenotypes, and then figures out what mutations make these strains interesting. In genetic engineering, one creates specific mutations and then asks whether or not they cause an interesting phenotype.

You can probably see why the term inverse genetics has been applied to genetic engineering. In traditional genetics, therefore, only mutants with interesting phenotypes are even analyzed; you learn nothing about those strains that you did not even detect as being different. When you deliberately create a specific mutation by genetic engineering, the subsequent analysis will say something about the effect of that mutation, whether or not it causes an interesting phenotype.

By the genetic engineering approach, it takes rather a lot of effort to construct each mutant, so it is very disappointing if the mutants turn out to be uninteresting. This implies that genetic engineering works best if you already have certain information so that the mutations you make have a good likelihood of being useful. Genetic engineering also requires that you know the sequence of the relevant region of DNA and have the ability to isolate small but useful amounts of DNA from the region of interest for in vitro manipulations. Neither of these is necessary for doing genetics.

There are also mutation types that affect multiple base pairs of sequence. Deletions eliminate some number of bases, though of course large deletions of thousands of base pairs are typically not detected because they typically delete essential functions. Duplications are similarly profound changes in the genome but because they rarely alter the phenotype, we tend to ignore their presence. Amplifications are the result of further recombination among a duplicated region and an have important phenotypic effects.

Finally, there are the mobile genetic elements, which are pieces of selfish DNA that move within the genome and dramatically alter whatever gene that they insert into.

Selections and Screens

Successful genetic analysis, whether traditional or inverse, demands that you be able to find and recognize mutants that you want. That means that if the desired mutants are very rare (1 in 100,000,000 or 10-8), then you need a terrific method to find that rare mutant among the huge set of undesired strains. However, if the desired mutant is common (10-2) then you don't need to be very clever. You can simply look at strains one at a time and be fairly sure of finding the desired strain fairly quickly.

The methods that allow us to sort through populations for rare or common mutants are called selections, screens, and enrichments. These tools are relevant to both classical and inverse genetic approaches since you must identify the desired mutants regardless of their mode of generation. Even in inverse genetics, not all the organisms from genetic manipulation in vitro will be the ones you want.

Selections are often more useful than screens, because they allow you to ignore the vast majority of cells (since they will not grow) and focus on the rare desired ones. As an example, let's say that you want to isolate mutants that are resistant to rifampicin, a drug that inhibits RNA polymerase. You plate 108 cells on an agar plate with an appropriate level of rifampicin and after two days incubation you see five colonies. By definition, they have the desired phenotype because these grew in the presence of rifampicin. This was a selection because only cells of that phenotype were able to grow, and the other ~108 cells died on the plate.

Recognize that every growth condition is selective: each selects against mutants that grow less well than the rest and for mutants that grow better than the rest under those conditions. Even growth in rich medium selects for mutants that grow even faster than the rest of the population. However, some selections are more demanding than others. The demand that an auxotroph mutate so that it can grow on minimal medium (termed reversion) is a strong selection, since only prototrophs will grow. Growth of wild type in nutrient medium is a weak selection, since the best strains will only grow slightly better than the rest.

Selections are of course relevant to organisms outside the lab as well. "Survival of the fittest" is just another way of saying that you have a weak selection going on. Under fairly constant conditions, the selection for improved mutants in natural populations of bacteria and other organisms will typically not be so strong because the majority of organisms have already been selected for good growth under that condition. However, when the environment of that population is changing, selections will usually be much stronger because it is more likely that the rare mutants will grow better than the majority under these new conditions.

A screen is the analysis of some number of different bacterial isolates for a given phenotype or property. These are properties like unusual growth, the level of a given enzyme, the presence of an interesting metabolite, the level of a particular antigen, or the presence of a region of DNA capable of hybridizing to a given probe. Screens are not the same as selections, where only cells of the desired phenotype grow. There is no condition under which the desired His- cells will grow better than the His+ majority. However, certain of the screens described below would allow you to easily find His- cells even if they constitute no more than 0.01% of the population.

In the following examples, the frequencies themselves with which mutation types are detected are important, but only as order-of-magnitude estimates. The most difficult screens are those that involve a separate analysis, typically biochemical, of each member of the population to be analyzed. Easier screens are those where a large number of different cells can be analyzed in a single assay.

Hard Screens

If one were searching for a mutant defective in a given enzymatic activity, this could be done by picking a number of single colonies, growing each up in liquid in a test tube, breaking open the cells in each tube and then assaying for the enzyme in question. Industrial screens for bacterial isolates that produce altered levels or types of antibiotics are sometimes performed like this. These screens are so hard that you can really only consider doing a few hundred separate assays or else somehow automate the screen by a machine. This is therefore not a very good way of finding the desired mutants unless they are so common in the population that you are likely to find one in a small sample size.

Easier screens

One of the easiest screens involves replica-printing, which was invented by Joshua and Esther Lederberg in the '40s but variations are still used in modern molecular biology labs. In this system one grows up between 100 and 1000 single bacterial colonies on an agar plate and presses a piece of sterile velveteen onto the surface of the plate. Small numbers of cells from each colony adhere to the velveteen, which is then used to imprint this pattern onto various other media. What one gets is an image of the original master plate superimposed on these other media so that a bacterial colony unable to grow on a certain media can be found. With this screen one can analyze approximately 500 colonies per plate and it is not too tough to do a 200-plate experiment. This means that you can screen up to 105 colonies in a couple of days.

Color indicator plates can also be extremely useful. Chemical compounds have been created that become colored when attacked by specific enzymes. When they are added to agar medium and single cells are plated, colonies that produce the enzyme turn the appropriate color. Mutants defective in the production of that enzyme function will remain uncolored and can be detected. Similarly, pH indicator plates have been used for screening for scoring sugar utilization. The plates turn color when the pH drops, so colonies that metabolize sugars to acidic end products change the plate color immediately around them. As above, you can easily screen hundreds of colonies per plate and hundreds of plates, so finding 1 in a million is possible.

Finally, there are very powerful methods that involve either radiolabeled nucleic acid probes or antibodies to a given protein that are tagged in some way. By this method the colony is printed to a membrane and the cells are broken in such a way that their proteins and nucleic acids stick right there. The membrane with these immobilized cells components is then tested for the ability to hybridize to a particular nucleic acid probe or be recognized by a specific antibody. The colony spots where these sorts of probes stick shows which colony had the desired property. This is clearly a variation of the replica-printing of colonies described above, but with a different assay. Some screens of this sort can be extremely powerful, allowing the screening of more than 106 candidates on a single plate.

Enrichments (counter-selections)

What if the phenotype you want is one where the growth of the mutant is never better than the majority class, but under some conditions is actually much worse? You can hardly use a selection in such a case, because the desired mutant grows less well. You place the culture in a medium where your rare mutant fails to grow, but the majority do. You then add a chemical to the medium that kills only growing bacteria. The desired cells just sit there and a great many of the growing cells are killed. You then remove the chemical from the culture. The desired cells have been enriched for because, even though they did not change in number, the total number of cells in the culture dropped, so that a greater fraction of the survivors are the desired cells. The chemicals that kill only growing cells include those that inhibit cell wall synthesis, such as penicillin.

Mutants

For the isolation of interesting mutants for eventual biochemical characterization, you need to be able to find them. This means that you must generate such mutants at a frequency in the population that allows their detection. The following sections treat the frequency of mutant generation and factors involved in their delectability.

First, however, we should have a brief discussion of why one might want random mutations. Another section will describe how to create specific mutations, but the researcher needs to know quite a bit before undertaking this task: you need to know not only the DNA sequence, but you need to have some reason to believe that a given mutation is worth creating and analyzing. If you lack that sort of information, then it makes sense to make random mutations in your population and then use screens and selections to find the interesting ones. The other reason that you should care a bit about this is because some of the tools we use are mutagens. Even if you have no interest in ever mutating microbes, you should have a general sense about such chemicals because many of the same mutagens that affect bacteria also affect humans.

Chemical Mutagens

Chemical mutagens are defined as those compounds that increase the frequency of some types of mutations. They vary in their potency since that reflects their ability to enter the cell, their reactivity, their general toxicity, and the likelihood that the type of chemical change they introduce into the DNA will be corrected by a repair system. Not surprisingly, the majority of mutagens react directly with DNA, though they can also indirectly affect the fidelity of replication and repair by binding to proteins that serve those processes.

Base analog mutagens are chemicals that look like normal bases and as such fool the DNA replication system. Their essential property is that they base-pair with two different bases thus making mutations because of their lack of consistency in base-pairing. To be mutagens they must be incorporated into the DNA and therefore they need be present during active DNA synthesis.

When chemical mutagens alter DNA, they do not immediately create a mutation, which is a permanent change in DNA, because they initially only alter one strand. Another type of chemical mutagen are alkylating agents that react directly with certain bases and thus do not require active DNA synthesis in order to act, but still do require DNA synthesis in order to be fixed. They are very commonly used because they are powerful mutagens in nearly every biological system. Examples of alkylating agents include ethyl methane sulfonate and nitrosoguanidine. These mutagens tend to prefer G-rich regions, reacting to form a variety of modified G residues. Some of these modified G residues might help mutagenize by inducing error-prone repair although mispairing of the altered base might also be possible. This stimulation of error-prone repair allows all sorts of mutation types to occur as a result of these mutagens, though base substitutions are by far the most frequent.

While not a chemical, UV light is a strong mutagen (in the wavelength that DNA absorbs, roughly 225-300 nm) and primarily generates dimers between adjacent pyrimidine bases on the same DNA strand. Some of the dimers can be repaired by a very specific repair system called photoreactivation repair. As its name indicates, photoreactivation requires light to repair damage and so when trying to make mutations by UV light, it is important to keep the cells in the dark after exposure to UV. However, there are other types of dimers generated by UV light that cannot be corrected by phtoreactivation repair.

Bacterial Mutagenesis

Bacteria and humans do differ in the way they take chemicals up from the environment and process them, so some chemicals are mutagens for bacteria but not for us and vice versa. It is also true, however, that some chemicals are mutagens in almost all studied organisms. This raises the question of how we even know if a chemical is a mutagen in people.

You shouldnt be surprised to hear that this is a difficult question to answer, even using model systems such as mice and rats. It is expensive to perform big enough studies in animal models to provide good statistics.

Transposons as Mutagens

The type of spontaneous mutation caused by mobile genetic elements such as transposons (Tns). Rather soon after these were discovered, scientists realized that they were potentially useful tools for studying microbes. We use Tns as mutagens, since they carry genes that confer drug-resistance and we can therefore select for strains that carry the Tn. Tns also provide a tag that helps you find where the insertion event has occurred.

If you can genetically map the drug-resistance, then you know where the mutation is, or you can physically map the position of the Tn itself with a similar result. As mutagens, Tns destroy the function of the product of the mutated gene and they also tend to disrupt the expression of any other genes that lie downstream in the same operon. Tns, and other mobile genetic elements, typically do not move to all sites in DNA with the same frequency, but have at least some sequences that they favor.

Since it is clear that transposons transpose to new sites at certain frequencies, one might expect that you "mutagenize" a strain by taking a strain carrying the transposon (in an uninteresting location) and look for cases where the Tn has moved and generated an "interesting" mutation. While this will work, it is not smart: (a) you will not know when a transposition has occurred—both the starting and desired strains have the transposon (i.e. you will not have a selection for the acquisition of the transposon, since it was present to start with); (b) because you will be looking for the loss of gene function (the typical result of transpositions), you will often not have a selection for the mutant itself.

These problems are solved if the transposon is introduced into the cell from elsewhere in such a way that every transposon-containing cell (and therefore, drug-resistant, selectable cell type) is generated by an independent transposition event. If this is achieved, then you have a positive selection for mutants (cells not mutagenized by the transposon are drug-sensitive) and every survivor of the selection will contain a Tn-induced mutation. For an organism with about 3,000 genes there will be an insertion in a specific gene in roughly 1/3000 cells. This is a rough estimate and ignores the fact that there is a bit of DNA in microbes that does not code for genes.

Such a mutagenized population is achieved if the Tn is introduced into a recipient cell on a piece of DNA that cannot replicate. This might be a plasmid or a bacterial virus, both of which will be addressed in later sections. Because the Tn and its gene for drug-resistance cannot be maintained on the non-replicating piece of DNA, the only way for a "stably" drug-resistant cell to exist is for the Tn to become associated with a replicating piece of DNA by transposition.

Microbiologists often use Tns as mutagens for the following technical reason. Most mutations leading to the loss of gene function do not have a selectable phenotype. For example, if you want to destroy the hisC gene, you have no way of selecting for such a His- mutant. This also means that such loss-of-function mutations cannot easily (i.e. selectably) be moved from one strain to another using the gene transfer systems described later. However, a mutation caused by a transposon solves these problems, since it has two phenotypes: the loss of function of the affected gene and the drug-resistance of the transposon. The latter phenotype is selectable, but brings the former along, because they are due to the same mutation.

Different mutagens have different effects on genes and their protein products. No mutagen causes all possible types of mutation. Some have a preference for certain types of sequences or cause only certain types of mutations. A base analog mutagen just causes base substitutions, which have variable effects on the function of the gene product. In contrast, a Tn (or insertion sequence) inserts a huge amount of genetic information into a gene and almost certainly destroy the protein that is normally encoded there. So let's say that you want to look for a mutant that degrades a certain compound faster. This would probably happen if you could increase the amount of the critical protein or increase its activity.

These are the sorts of things that might happen with base-substitution mutations resulting from a base analog or an alkylating agent. This is because base substitutions change single amino acid residues and therefore often alter a gene product. However, a mutagen like a Tn, which certainly would destroy the gene product, would almost never give you an increase in protein levels or activity.

When scientists first realized the importance of antibiotic-producing organisms, they wanted to find mutants that made more of these valuable products. They mutagenized the organisms with a variety of mutagens and then screened for those that made more, but you might wonder why this ever worked. If the vast majority of random mutations are deleterious, how would you ever find a mutation that was beneficial? People who do not understand evolution have raised a similar question, If random mutations are generally deleterious, how does anything new and useful evolve? The answer to both concerns is the same: while random mutations are typically damaging, if the rare beneficial mutation provides an advantage for the mutant organism, then the progeny of that mutant will predominate.

In the case of antibiotic production, the vast majority of mutants generated by the random mutagenesis made either the same amount of antibiotics or less than did the starting strain, but with scientists putting huge amounts of work into a screen, the rare valuable mutants were found. In evolution, the beneficial mutations are found by the process of natural selection.

Effects of Mutations

The majority of mutations that occur are base substitutions and an inspection of the genetic code shows that the majority of these cause the substitution of one amino acid for another. The mutations that cause such amino acid changes are termed missense mutations. What determines if such small changes in the encoded protein will actually alter its function enough to change the phenotype of the strain? There are several general factors in answering this question.

The first consideration might be called the toughness of the gene product. If a protein serves a strictly structural role in the cell, there may be no one region critical for function. Thus missense mutations will rarely have a sufficiently detrimental effect on function to change the phenotype. The only mutations that would be detected would be those with drastic consequences for the function of the protein and these will be relatively rare.

The second consideration depends on the gene product's role in metabolism. Cells produce most proteins at levels just sufficient for good growth. Therefore, any significant loss of that activity in a mutant would probably be detectable because it would become rate-limiting for the cell's growth. On the other hand, a protein produced in excess of growth requirements would need to be damaged (in a mutant) much more severely for it to become growth-limiting. However, there is an important complication here that results from the regulatory processes in cells.

Cells are constantly testing their own internal pools and conditions, trying to determine if they need more or less of certain compounds. If a protein suddenly becomes less efficient due to mutation, the cell will probably sense the reduction in the metabolic product, though it will not know why the problem has occurred. The cell will almost certainly try to compensate for the lower protein activity by making more of the protein through changes in gene expression. Obviously if a cell can compensate enough, then the mutant will still have a wild-type phenotype and we will not detect that the cell is a mutant at all.

For example, if a cell senses that it needs more histidine, we know that it will respond by increasing the rate of synthesis of the proteins that make histidine. Imagine what happens then when you have just created a mutation in a gene whose protein product is part of the histidine biosynthetic pathway and let's assume that the mutation causes the protein to only work 10% as well as the normal version. Will we see that this strain requires histidine? Maybe not and one reason why not might be that the cell senses the low level of histidine and simply increases the level of the defective protein so that there is now enough total activity in the cell that the cell makes enough histidine for normal growth. In that case, we would not detect a His- phenotype for the mutation, even though it certainly did significantly damage the protein. Note that the cell is not planning on getting mutations here, but rather that the flexibility of normal regulation can sometimes mask the phenotypes of mutations.

Applications of Genomics

There are a number of possible applications besides those of simply understanding how proteins and their properties have evolved. Here are a few of the many possible examples of how this information is applied to real problems.

Virulence

If we want to protect ourselves from pathogenic bacteria, then it would help to know what properties make them pathogenic - these properties are often termed virulence factors. If one knew, for example, that a certain pathogen used a specific protein to evade host antibody defenses, than that protein might be a terrific target for a drug. The logic would be that if you could give the patient a drug that inhibited that activity of the protein, then the pathogen would no longer elude host defenses. It would be especially nice to target proteins specific for virulence for the following reason, these tend to be proteins that are not carried by non-pathogenic cells. Thus only pathogenic cells would be affected by the drug. In contrast, a drug that affects a protein that is found in both pathogens and non-pathogens (and maybe humans as well) would mean that non-pathogens would also be affected by the drug.

So how would one use genomics to figure out which genes in the complete genome of a newly sequenced pathogen were involved in virulence? One approach is to look for genes whose sequences are related to those of known virulence genes in other pathogens. For example, a pathogen of human cells has to have a way of recognizing those cells. Typically the pathogen will make one or more proteins on its own surface that recognize structures that are found only on the surface of human cells. These genes will continue to evolve in the new pathogen, but there will still be recognizable similarity for a long time. This similarity therefore allows us to screen the genomes of pathogens for sequences similar to those known to be important for pathogenicity in other organisms.

Gene arrays

Technology has given us the ability to make very small glass slides with micro-dots of DNA attached in a regular array. In accordance with the genome sequence each micro-dot contains some DNA for a different specific gene and all genes are represented by dots on the slide. One then isolates mRNA from the organism grown under different conditions and uses that to make a nucleic acid sequence that has been labeled in some way so that we can detect it. This labeled sequence is then allowed to hybridize to the micro-dots on the slide. Through detection of the label, the mRNA can be detected in proportion to its abundance in the cell. Optical scanners and a computer do the rest, revealing a pattern of mRNA accumulation, which primarily reflects gene expression.

Therefore small differences in the apparent expression levels of a gene under different conditions are probably not meaningful. There is also a problem with genes that are expressed at very low levels, as again the noise in the data makes their expression impossible to accurately interpret. Nevertheless, there will always be a huge amount of interpretable data from such experiments. Some of the regulated mRNAs you detect are those that you expected to see, based on more traditional analyses.

Proteomics

There is another relatively new methodology, called proteomics because it looks at the accumulation of proteins instead of mRNA. While mRNA accumulation shows what the cell wants to make at the moment, protein accumulation shows what the cells current metabolic capabilities are. As a consequence, the two methods provide different but related information. Essentially it allows you to see the accumulation of individual proteins as spots on a two-dimensional gel. You can then isolate any given spot from the gel and determine the sequence of the protein. When you also have a genome sequence, you can readily identify which gene encoded the protein. This information in turn helps to suggest the function of the protein in the cell.

Metabolic Pathways

Another application of genomic information is in developing new metabolic pathways, for example, pathways for creating new antibiotics. For some of the evolutionary reasons argued above, many proteins involved in making one antibiotic are often related to proteins that make a somewhat different antibiotic. This allows the possibility of isolating the DNA for the biosynthetic pathways of different antibiotics (because we recognized them based on their sequence similarities) and then reassorting those genes in an organism to see if a new antibiotic can be created with this synthetic pathway. Variations on this theme have allowed the synthesis of antibiotics that had not previously been found in any single microbe.

In a similar fashion, the proteins that degrade certain classes of chemicals are often found to be related. If we want to use microbes to remove problem chemicals from the environment, genomics provides a way of both identifying the relevant genes and also of mixing pathways to create microbes with better abilities to degrade a range of toxins.

Analyzing genome sequences not only tells us about what the genomes encode, but it tells us a great deal about the evolution of the genomes themselves. With higher organisms, for example, one can compare the organization of specific genes and see that vertebrates have evolved in part by rearranging the genes that existed in an ancient vertebrate, long since gone. For example, some human chromosomes have very much the same genes and the same arrangement of genes as certain cat chromosomes. Now there are a lot of other genetic differences in these genes that make us different from cats, but the pattern of genes still reveals the ancient root.

Most bacterial species are wildly older than vertebrates, so any similarities in gene arrangement have disappeared from all but the most similar microbes. However, members of the genera Escherichia, Salmonella and Klebsiella, which probably became genetically distinct 120 million years ago, still show many similarities in genome organization. In these organisms, most homologous genes are present in their respective genomes in about the same relative positions.

In some cases though a piece of one genome, containing a few or many genes, has been placed in the reverse orientation relative to the other genomes, presumably by an odd recombination event. There are also a number of genes present in only one or two of the organisms. Typically such genes allow the organism to use a certain small molecule as a food source or perhaps to interact with a specific host. It is largely these exceptional genes that make each organism appear different to us in the first place.

Genomics has already had a profound influence on the techniques used in genetics and genetic engineering and sped up the pace of scientific discovery. However, the thought processes for approaching genetic problems and analyzing data have remained largely unchanged. The microbiologist is tacking similar questions as before, but with more powerful and straightforward tools. Also, while it is possible to create testable hypotheses by analyzing gene sequence, it is certainly still necessary to make mutants and test these hypotheses in living organisms before drawing conclusions. The most enlightening and powerful insights come from the combination of genomics and genetics.

The advent of genomics is making inverse genetics much less of a shot in the dark and it is often desirable to make a specific change in a specific gene. It might be that we have already studied a gene and its product for a while and want to examine the effect of a specific amino acid change. Alternatively we might have seen a gene in the data banks and guessed that it was important for pathogencity, for example. If the microbe shows diminished pathogencity, then we have found something important to the disease process.

Certainly the first and easiest sort of mutation to create is one that you are certain will destroy the protein product (a loss-of-function mutation). This might be created by the insertion of a drug-resistance gene into your gene of interest. One would then test the mutant's behavior and if a certain phenotype was altered, you could conclude that the missing protein had a role in that behavior. A more subtle and specific question that you could ask would concern the specific properties of the protein product.

For example, you might want to know why a protein could hydrolyze one compound but not a closely related one. By making amino acids substitutions in the active site of the enzyme, one might be able to perturb the activity of the enzyme toward the two compounds and therefore better understand the basis for its normal selectivity. You might also be able to create a different activity of the enzyme - the ability to hydrolyze another compound.

Vitro Manipulation

Performing any of the targeted mutagenesis described above involves manipulation of DNA in vitro, which means that you need a way of getting a reasonable amount (a few micrograms actually! - one millionth of a gram) of reasonably pure DNA for the specific genes of interest. This was essentially impossible in the '60s, excruciatingly difficult in the '70s, laborious in the '80s and, though the use of polymerase chain reaction (always abbreviated PCR), trivial now. Through PCR, one is able to obtain useful amounts of DNA even from relatively uncharacterized organisms. Other uses include:

— Amplification of a region from mutants for direct sequence analysis.

— Use in both site-directed and localized mutagenesis.

— The generation of specific gene (and therefore protein) fusions.

Making Mutations

Now that you have a bit of pure DNA of the region of interest, there are a large variety of ways to create mutations in vitro and we will show only one representative way for creating point mutations, though small modifications allow all sorts of other constructions. An example of the use of PCR to create a mutation. One identifies the base change that is desired and buys two synthetic oligonucleotides that are complementary to each other. Each of these contain the desired change and extend about 10 bases on either side of the change. These are then used as primers in the presence of a thermostable DNA polymerase and the single-stranded (melted with temperature) plasmid and the polymerase extends each primer to make a longer-than-plasmid-length copy.

The polymerization is halted by another cycle of heating, which again denatures the plasmids and then cooled, which allows the excess pool of primers to rebind and the thermostable polymerase to again extend all primers bound to template. After a number of cycles, a large pool of double-stranded DNA molecules is created that has overlapping single-stranded ends. This pool is then transformed into recipient cells, selecting a drug-resistance gene on the plasmid, and the cell re-circularizes these plasmids and ligates the gaps together. Only cells with the desired plasmid can grow, though plasmids should be isolated from candidate colonies and sequenced to make certain that there have not been errors in amplification.

The methods above actually create mutations in a piece of DNA, not mutants (i.e. organisms with changes in their DNA). The fragments of DNA carrying these mutations then must be introduced into an organism in some way, so we can create the desired mutant to test the effect of the mutation.

Gene Transfer Systems

Whether the genetics is being done by scientists or by nature there must be a way of moving genes around, which we term gene transfer systems. These systems really do have a role in gene transfer in natural populations of cells and they certainly have had a huge role in the evolutionary process. With any gene transfer system, the transferred DNA is useful only if it is replicated in the recipient. If it does not replicate, then none of the progeny cells will have it. The first way this replication can be accomplished is if the introduced DNA is itself a plasmid, which means it is able to replicate in the cytoplasm of the new cell.

The general term for such pieces of DNA that can replicate is replicons. However, if the introduced DNA is not itself a replicon, then the only way any of it will be stably inherited is if it becomes part of a replicon. This requires that some sort of recombinational event occurs, such as the addition of the introduced DNA to an existing replicon in the recipient. Alternatively, homologous recombination can replace a similar sequence already associated with a replicon with a portion of the introduced DNA.

Transformation

Transformation is defined as the transfer of genetic material from a donor cell to a recipient using naked DNA. The recipient takes DNA up from the medium, and there is no requirement for cell-to-cell contact. It is relevant to us for two different reasons. Some organisms are naturally transformable, which means that take up DNA in their normal environments and this process therefore has biological and evolutionary implications.

It certainly affects the way genes such as antibiotic-resistance might move into pathogens, for example. The other reason for our interest is that most prokaryotes can be forced to be transformable, and this has become a very valuable tool in genetics and genetic engineering. Indeed, E. coli, the bacterium most central to the history of genetics and to genetic engineering, falls into this group.

Naturally transformable bacterial species include Bacillus, Streptococcus pneumoniae, Haemophilus, and Neisseria. This has historical importance because it was the natural transformation of pneumococci that allowed Griffith to change their antigenic surfaces in 1928. With many of the naturally transformable bacteria, the competence to accept DNA is normal, but often is dependent on the cells being in a particular growth stage.

In some organisms the DNA in the environment is bound by particular receptors on the surface. Normally these strains will only take in one strand of the DNA and degrade the other. One assumes that any microorganism that naturally takes up DNA does it for the express purpose of altering its own genetic information, but that has not been proven.

Certainly it is a bit dangerous taking up random DNA from the environment. One might acquire potentially dangerous DNA such as mobile genetic elements as often as one would obtain something potentially useful as drug resistance. Indeed, many of these naturally transformable strains only take up DNA that has certain sequences that are relatively common in their own DNA but relatively rare in DNA from other organisms. Quite possibly the reluctance to take up double-stranded DNA is also an effort to avoid acquiring potentially dangerous plasmids.

Natural and induced transformation

Induced transformation is the act of tricking a normally non-transformable bacterium into taking up DNA from the medium. Induced transformation is critical for genetic engineering because there needs to be a way of taking the DNA that we have manipulated in vitro and putting it into cells.

Conjugation

One of the most common solutions is to transform a different bacterium, perhaps E. coli, and then conjugate the DNA into the desired strain, since most strains can serve as recipients in conjugation. Conjugation involves the transfer of DNA from one cell to another through cell-to-cell contact. Conjugation is probably the major route by which DNA has been exchanged between bacteria through evolution and it continues to be of broad utility in the genetic manipulation of prokaryotes (there is no apparent conjugation system in yeast or other eukaryotes).

The description of the conjugation process makes it clear that it does not depend on plasmids, but it also happens that almost all conjugation seen in natural systems involves plasmids. One view of why plasmids should have developed these abilities holds that plasmids are just selfish pieces of DNA like viruses and mobile genetic elements. As such, they try amplify themselves in the environment and conjugation is an excellent mechanism for doing so.

There are two different functions involved in conjugative ability: the first is a site on the DNA where transfer of DNA is initiated and this is called either *oriT* or mob. The former term is a mnemonic for origin of transfer and the second is short for mobility. In each case they refer to a site on the DNA and not to a diffusible protein product. The second group of functions are those proteins that act at these sites and cause the range of functions necessary for mobilization to occur. These are encoded by the tra (for transfer of DNA) genes and have a variety of functions described in the example below.

Conjugation, with F^+ as the model

F factor (termed "F^+") is a conjugative plasmid that has been studied for many years and its use was at the core of most of the gene transfer systems that were used by bacterial geneticists in the '50s through the '70s. The plasmid is about 100 kb in size (roughly 1% the size of the E. coli chromosome) and encodes about 26 tra genes. If one takes a culture with this plasmid in each cell and mixes it with a culture that lacks this plasmid, a little while later all the cells in the culture will have the same plasmid.

The protein products of the tra genes are critical for the entire process and certain of them regulate the expression of other tra genes in the entire process. The cell with the F^+, termed the donor cell, places some tra proteins on the outside of the cell to catch appropriate cells for mating, termed recipient cells. These appendages are pili, which are long polymers with a special protein at the tip to attach to potential recipients. When a contact is made, the pilin is de-polymerized at the surface of the donor cell, which draws the two cells together. Other tra proteins then form a tiny pore between the two cells.

Finally, other tra proteins recognize the *oriT*/mob site on the F+ and make a nick. A DNA polymerase then starts copying one strand starting at that nick, re-making double-stranded DNA in the donor, but the single strand that is displaced in this process is transferred through the pore into the recipient cell, where a complementary strand is synthesized and the double-stranded molecule is re-circularized in the recipient. This re-circularization involves a protein, TraI, that is actually covalently attached to the 5' end of the transferred DNA strand. For a circular replicon, reforming a circular molecule is critical if the plasmid is to continue to replicate in the new cell. The net effect of all this is that the donor strain still has a copy of the plasmid and now the recipient strain does also.

While conjugation of the chromosome looks a lot like conjugation of a plasmid up to this point, there is something fundamentally different. With chromosomal transfer, the amount of DNA to be transferred is vast, which happens to make it very difficult for it to re-circularize in the recipient cell. Indeed, it happens that transfer takes so long, about 100 min in the case of the E. coli chromosome, that only about 1/1000 transfers is actually completed. The partial chromosome that is transferred is still converted to a double-stranded form, but it has no way of circularizing.

Even if it did, there is only one origin of replication in a chromosome (this is not the same as the origin of transfer) so that the chances of bringing it along are small. Any DNA in a cell that cannot replicate will be lost, but the transferred DNA might become associated with a replicon if it undergoes recombination with the chromosome.

Applications of Conjugation

But now we have a bit of a problem. Small plasmids were the ones that were easy to work with in vitro, but also that conjugative plasmids were large, since they contain all the tra genes. As long as a plasmid carries an *oriT* site, which is only a few dozen base pairs, then it can be conjugated. For this to be successful, the tra genes must be present in the cell, but they do not need to be on the plasmid itself. For example, assume that you have two plasmids in the cell: an F^+ with its tra genes and your little plasmid with your genes of interest and a copy of *oriT*. As before, the tra proteins would form mating pairs and perform transfer of the DNA with the *oriT*, but now they would transfer one or both of the plasmids in the cell, since they both have an *oriT*. You could identify which recipient cells had the desired plasmid by genetic markers, such as drug-resistance. Such an *oriT*-containing plasmid will therefore be small enough to be manipulated in vitro and will be mobilizable, but will not be self-conjugative.

Certainly it might be an effort by cells to promote exchange of chromosomal genes, but this seems unlikely, in part because of where the genes for conjugation are found. These genes are rarely found associated with normal chromosomes, but rather with plasmids or other genetic elements that are not part of the normal chromosome. It therefore seems like that conjugation is the primary result of selfish DNA trying to move itself through the population and only occasionally does it do some good for the cells themselves.

Certainly the case of conjugative plasmids are best understood, but there are other conjugative elements. Perhaps the most surprising is that of conjugative transposons. These elements are typically in the chromosome (as transposons, they rely on being within a replicon in order to be inherited) and they move between cells by starting a conjugation process like the Hfrs above, but where their own DNA is transferred first. Once in the recipient, they are made double-stranded, but, unlike transferred chromosomal genes, they do not need to rely on homologous recombination to become associated with a replicon. Rather, they can merely transpose themselves into a replicon like the chromosome or some plasmid. In this way they can move themselves between rather different prokaryotes.

When one examines the genome sequences of many prokaryotes, it becomes clear that portions of their genomes have been acquired from other species. This is evident either because some regions have unusual codon usage or because some genes are clearly more related to those of other organisms than is the rest of the genome. While it is difficult to prove, it is the prevailing view among scientists that these gene transfer events almost certainly came about through some form of conjugation. Natural transformation is too rare to explain most organisms that have apparently received genes from elsewhere and, as described below, phage transduction does not seem a realistic way of moving DNA between very different microorganisms.

Transduction

Transduction is defined as the transfer of genetic information between cells through the mediation of a virus particle. It therefore does not require cell-to-cell contact, nor is the DNA ever exposed to the environment. In order to understand transduction it is necessary to understand a bit of the biology of bacteriophage. Much of the relevance of transduction is historical, as it was one of the best ways to move DNA between cells in the case of both E. coli and Salmonella typhimurium.

Transduction has also been used for some aspects of genetic engineering, as noted below. However, as microbiologists work on an ever broader range of prokaryotes, there has not been time to develop transduction systems for each organism and other more general tools have become readily available. Therefore, unless you happen to work with the handful of organisms for which transducing phage have been developed, you will probably never even read about a transduction experiment.

Generalized Transduction

Imagine what would happen if a phage incorporates host DNA instead of phage DNA inside a fraction of the produced phage heads. The cell would still lyse, and these novel particles, termed transducing particles, could still recognize an appropriate bacterium because the protein portion of the particle would be completely normal. They could also attach and inject their DNA into the recipient cell, but in this case, it would be host DNA that was injected. The result would be the transfer of host DNA from one cell to another. This type of movement of DNA is called generalized transduction since any part of the chromosome can enter a transducing particle.

Then when a phage with host DNA goes on to infect another cell, it actually injects that host DNA (and no phage DNA). With some frequency that injected DNA can recombine with the chromosomal DNA in the infected cell, which represents an exchange of DNA from the cell that was originally infected to the new host by means of the phage itself. This recipient cell therefore just sees a section of DNA that looks a lot like its own and it recombines it into its own chromosome. As always, for the transferred DNA to become stably inherited, it must become associated with a replicon in the recipient cell.

Since the transferred DNA is a linear molecule, this stable inheritance requires two homologous recombination events with the net result that a portion of the chromosome in the recipient is replaced by a portion of the incoming DNA. Thus, in contrast with specialized transduction (see below), generalized transduction requires that the recipient possess both a functional recombination system and DNA homologous to the transferred fragment. The net effect is that a piece of one bacterial genome has been transferred to another bacterial cell through the action of a phage.

Specialized Transduction

The phenomenon of lysogeny whereby some phage integrate their DNA into that of the host chromosome. Sometimes these phage genomes excise from the bacterial chromosome improperly, and a portion of the bacterial chromosome replaces a portion of the phage genome. Then this piece of DNA, which consists of both host and phage DNA in the same molecule, replicates to produce many identical copies. Then these are packaged into virions, all of the phage particles carry the same portion of the bacterial chromosome (hence the term specialized), in contrast to the case with generalized transduction.

Such phage are typically mutant in some way since they lack a portion of their normal phage genome and they might need the presence of a normal phage to make all the proteins necessary for normal phage growth. This normal phage is typically supplied as a lysogen in the strain being infected by the specialized phage. Now what happens if one of these phage injects its DNA, both phage and bacterial in a single piece, into a recipient cell? As always, if the transferred DNA is to become inherited, it must become associated with a replicon.

The primary way that the DNA of a specialized phage does this involves the normal phage integration system. By this means, the entire specialized phage DNA is integrated at the phage attachment site This generates a merodiploid (a strain partially diploid for a portion of its genome) for the region carried by the phage. Remember the normal bacterial copy of the region has not been altered. Certain aspects of specialized phage now serve as the basis for many of the commonly used commercial cloning systems, but specialized phage by themselves are no longer an important genetic tool.

Phage as gene transfer agents in the lab and the real world. Phage are parasites that steal a great deal of the machinery of the host. As a consequence it is important that they only infect hosts in which they can replicate, so they tend to be able to attach to only a narrow range of prokaryotes. If phage only infect hosts that are of a single type, then they will never move DNA between very different hosts. Phage are therefore unlikely to have been major factors in moving genes around between unrelated bacteria.

There are, however, some interesting wrinkles on the role of phage in evolution. Some phage have clearly been implicated in helping recipient cells become virulent toward animal hosts, since pathogenic clostridia very often have critical toxin genes that are actually residing in the host genomes in the middle of an integrated temperate phage. Presumably the phage in this case are helping their hosts prosper in the environment by making them better pathogens. Phage can apparently be smart as well as selfish. Phage have also certainly played some role in evolution. Even if they do not move a lot of DNA around for horizontal transfer, they are constantly providing a selection for hosts that are phage resistant, which will almost certainly have other implications for the physiology of those hosts.

Genetic Mapping

There is probably no aspect of microbial genetics that has been more greatly changed by recent technology than the issue of mapping. Mapping is the process of figuring out where mutations are on the chromosome. The results also tell you where the genes are that contain those mutations. There have been two general reasons why one would care about this. In fine-structure mapping, where one actually ordered the mutations within a gene, you could begin to learn something about the organization of the protein product. For example, you might get a sense of what part of the gene encoded the active site or an allosteric site.

The other type of mapping, what might be called gross mapping, was far more common and essentially asked if mutations fell in the same region of the chromosome or not. This information helped us to start to think about the nature of chromosomes, but the primary use was to sort mutations into different groups. For example, let's say you were studying genes involved in virulence and isolated a number of mutations causing avirulence and mapped them to five different regions of the chromosome, you could assume that there were at least five different genes involved. Fine-structure mapping was previously performed by generalized transduction or transformation, while gross mapping involved conjugation by Hfrs.

The new technology that has completely transcended genetic mapping is sequencing. Where genetic mapping identifies the position of a mutation relative to that of other analyzed mutations, sequencing identifies the position of a base (or mutation or gene) in absolute terms: "gene X lies exactly here on the chromosome." Fine structure mapping is completely obsolete, since entire genes are rapidly sequenced, so one finds out not only "where" a mutation is in the gene, but precisely what the mutation is. This text will say nothing more about fine structure genetic mapping, as its interest is only historical.

Sequencing

Sequencing provides better information than does genetic mapping for both gross and fine-structure mapping. It relates the gene product to other evolutionarily similar products, so we can form hypotheses about the gene product we are studying based on the work of other scientists on other genes from other organisms. Obviously too, the sequence of a given mutation can be thought about in the context of that same data bank, to form hypotheses about why this specific genetic change might have affected the gene product to cause the phenotype that we observe.

Complementation Analyses

In complementation, one takes a region of DNA that makes proteins that supply a product necessary for growth of the cell and mutate that region so that the required product is no longer made. Then you supply another copy of that region that similarly has been mutated and is also unable to produce the necessary product. If a cell with both of those two different versions of the region can grow, then the two copies must together supply all the functions necessary for making the product, even though neither copy could by itself. In such a case, the mutations in the two copies are said to complement each other and this implies that one or the other copy must provide a protein product lacking from the other copy. In other words, when two mutations complement, they cannot be damaging the same gene product. In contrast, if the cell with both copies fails to grow, then the mutations do not complement. This implies that there is at least one critical; protein product that cannot be made by either copy of the region.

As with genetic mapping, complementation analysis was at one time absolutely central to the way microbiologists employed genetic methods to address biological questions. Mapping told us the relative position and order of mutations, while complementation indicated the number of genes and the number of gene product functions encoded by a genetic region. While sequencing does not provide quite the same information, there is sufficient overlap that complementation analyses is performed less and less. However, the underlying idea of asking about the number of critical proteins encoded by a region is still useful and variants on complementation are still performed. Understanding the old approach also raises some very important points about genetics and biochemistry, even if the actual application of the method has become relatively less important in current microbiology.

Let's say that you have a mutation that causes a deleterious phenotype and you know where that mutation lies on the chromosome. As an example, let's assume that you have a mutation in one of the genes whose product is involved in histidine biosynthesis. The mutant therefore requires histidine for optimal growth and is termed His- You manage to clone the his genes of the chromosome from a wild-type strain of the same species, place it on a replicating plasmid and introduce that plasmid into your mutant. You then ask if the strain with the plasmid is His+ or His-. This is, more or less, a complementation assay.

Fusions

A plasmid designed to express whatever gene is cloned into it is termed an expression vector. The other type of fusion is where you take the promoter and other regulatory regions for your gene of interest and place them upstream of some other gene whose product is easily assayed. In this way, you can study the regulatory system that usually controls your gene by simply monitoring the activity of the easily assayed gene product. This is typically called a transcriptional fusion or a reporter.

Expression Vectors

Very often we want to make a lot of a certain protein - much more than the cell usually makes. We might do this because we want to see the impact on the cell when we over-express the protein (to gain an insight into its normal function). Alternatively, we might already know a lot about the normal protein, but wish to get greater insights by making mutants that encode variants of the protein and seeing how they are biochemically different. Or, we might have a protein that is clinically useful, so we need to synthesize a lot of it, so that it can be purified away from other proteins and provided to patients.

For all these situations, we want a promoter that provides maximum expression when the promoter is "on", and we want to be able to regulate the expression of that promoter in some way. As described in the regulation of metabolism section, we have already figured out how cells control gene expression in a number of cases, so scientists have taken those regulatory systems and rebuilt them for gene expression purposes. A classic example would be to start with a very strong promoter, but have the expression regulated by the LacI protein, which will prevent RNA polymerase from binding. One then regulates expression with the chemical IPTG (an artificial effector of the LacI repressor). IPTG binds to LacI and prevents it from binding DNA. When LacI falls off the DNA it then allows RNA polymerase to bind to the strong promoter and transcribe the gene of interest. The result is a high level of gene expression of whatever is placed downstream of the strong promoter whenever we provide IPTG. The level of IPTG can actually be varied, so that we can tune the level of expression as well.

In the course of analyzing a regulated gene or genes, it is often useful to monitor the regulatory system by putting a foreign gene under the control of that system. The foreign gene typically encodes an easily assayed reporter - galactosidase, encoded by?molecule like the enzyme lacZ.

Suppression

Suppressors are the class of second-site mutations that, in the presence of the original mutation, modify the original phenotype of the mutant strain so that it behaves like wild type under the condition tested. For example, if you start with a His- cell and demand it grown on minimal medium with no histidine, you will isolate a number mutants that are called revertants because their phenotype has reverted to one like that of wild type. Many of these will correct the original mutation, but some will be in other parts of the

DNA that compensate for the original His- mutation. This second class of mutations are suppressors because they suppress the phenotype of the original mutation.

The reason scientists create and study suppressors, especially non-informational ones, is that they tell us an enormous amount about how a cell thinks. That is, when we start with a cell with a certain defect in metabolism and demand that we obtain mutants that have "solved the metabolic problem", we find all sorts of extraordinary changes in metabolism, which reveals connections and capabilities that we would never have guessed at.

All suppressor mutations have the possibility of causing one or both of two general problems for the cell: (1) they often entail the loss of a normal gene product function (the suppressor mutation does, after all, alter a gene and therefore its product), and (2) they often involve the acquisition of new, possibly deleterious, functions. Suppressors come in two rather different forms: those that change the way the information encoded by the original mutation is processed (termed informational suppressors) and those that solve the problem caused by the original mutation in a completely different way.

Informational suppressors

An informational suppressor is one that does not change the mutated gene's sequence, but rather affects the way the information (of the original mutant gene) is expressed as a product. One example of this class of suppressors are altered tRNAs that now misread the mutant codon. The suppressor formed could suppress missense, nonsense, or frameshift mutations, depending on the nature of the tRNA alteration. Similarly, there are enzymes that modify and process tRNAs to active forms. An alteration in these modification enzymes can occasionally give rise to an altered tRNA that misreads and thus suppresses certain mutations. A third class of suppressors involves alterations that affect the fidelity of ribosomes and these suppress some forms of base substitution mutations. Much of what we know about the process of translation has come about through the generation and analysis of informational suppressors. The other types of suppressors come in a huge variety of possibilities, depending on the exact nature of the original mutation and the biology that it affects.

6

Recombinant DNA and Biotechnology

Biotechnology is the use of microorganisms, cells, or cell components to make a product. Closely related organisms can exchange genes in natural recombination. Genes can be transferred between unrelated species via laboratory manipulations called genetic engineering. Recombinant DNA refers to DNA that has been artificially manipulated to combine genes from two different sources.

Recombinant DNA Procedures

1. A desired gene is inserted into a DNA vector such as a plasmid or viral genome.
2. The vector inserts the DNA into a new cell, which is grown to form a clone.
3. Large quantities of the gene or the gene product can be harvested from the clone.

Tools of Biotechnology

Selection

Microbes with desirable traits are selected for culturing by artificial selection.

Mutation

1. Mutagens are used to cause mutations that might result in a microbe with desirable traits.
2. Site-directed mutagenesis is used to change a specific codon in a gene.

Restriction enzymes

1. Prepackaged kits are available for many genetic-engineering techniques.
2. A restriction enzyme recognizes and cuts only one particular nucleotide sequence in DNA.
3. Some restriction enzymes produce sticky ends-short stretches of single-stranded DNA at the ends of the DNA fragments.
4. Fragments of DNA produced by the same restriction enzyme will spontaneously join by hydrogen bonding. DNA ligase can covalently link the DNA backbones.

Vectors

1. Prepackaged kits are available for many genetic-engineering techniques.
2. A restriction enzyme recognizes and cuts only one particular nucleotide sequence in DNA.
3. Some restriction enzymes produce sticky ends

Polymerase chain Reaction

1. The polymerase chain reaction (PCR) is used to make multiple copies (amplification) of a desired piece of DNA enzymatically.
2. The PCR can be used to increase the amounts of DNA in samples to detectable levels, a process known as

amplification. This may be used to allow for sequencing of genes, diagnosis of genetic disease, or detection of viruses.

Inserting Foreign DNA into Cells

1. Cells can take up naked DNA by transformation. Chemical treatments are used to make cells that do not naturally transform competent to take up DNA.
2. Pores made in protoplasts and animal cells by electric current in the process of electroporation can provide entrance for new pieces of DNA.
3. Protoplast fusion is the joining of cells whose cell walls have been removed.
4. Foreign DNA can be introduced into plant cells by shooting DNA-coated particles into the cells with a "gene gun."
5. Foreign DNA can be injected into animal cells by using a fine glass micropipette (microinjection).

Obtaining DNA

1. Gene libraries can be made by cutting up an entire genome with restriction enzymes and inserting the fragments into bacterial plasmids or phages.
2. cDNA (complementary DNA) made from eukaryotic mRNA by reverse transcription can be cloned in gene libraries. This avoids the problem of eukaryotic intron DNA that does not code for a gene product.
3. Synthetic DNA can be made in vitro by a DNA-synthesis machine.

Methods for Selecting a Clone

1. Antibiotic resistance markers on plasmid vectors are used

to identify cells containing the engineered vector by direct selection.

2. In blue/white screening, the vector contains the genes for ampR (ampicillin resistance) and ß-galactosidase. The growth medium contains ampicillin and X-gal, a substrate of ß-galactosidase that turns blue when catalyzed.

   The desired gene is inserted into the ß-galactosidase gene site, destroying the gene. Clones containing the recombinant vector will be resistant to ampicillin and unable to hydrolyze X-gal and thus the cloned colonies will be white. Clones containing the vector without the new gene will be blue. Clones lacking the vector will not grow because they are sensitive to the ampicillin in the medium.

3. Clones containing foreign DNA can be tested by detecting the desired gene product.

4. A short piece of labeled DNA called a DNA probe can be used to identify clones carrying the desired gene.

Making a Gene Product

1. E. coli is used to produce proteins by genetic engineering because it is easily grown and its genetics are well understood.

2. Efforts must be made to ensure that E. coli's endotoxin (a component of the lipopolysaccharide (LPS)) does not contaminate a product intended for human use.

3. To recover the product, E. coli must be lysed or the gene must be linked to a gene that produces a naturally secreted protein.

4. Yeasts can be genetically engineered and are likely to secrete the gene product continuously.

5. Mammalian cells can be engineered to produce proteins such as hormones for medical use.

6. Plant cells can be engineered and used to produce plants with new properties.

Recombinant DNA Techniques

Researchers are now able to manipulate DNA sequences in order to remove isolated pieces that correspond to a specific gene or protein. One technique for isolated specific genes from whole DNA is by a process called Polymerase Chain Reaction (PCR). With this technique, DNA can be cut at specific sites in order to remove the DNA segment of interest for futher genetic research. A second technique for cloning specific genes within DNA is by removing the sequence and placing it into bacteria. When the bacteria replicate, they also replicate the gene. Although this sounds like a rather easy process, the techniques involved in bacteria transformation and DNA cloning have only recently been accepted as a standard for genetic manipulation.

Before the process of DNA cloning can begin, the nucleotide base arrangement must be known. The base order is important, first of all, because the special molecular scissors called restriction endonucleases only cut at specific areas within DNA. Restriction endonucleases are proteins that cleave DNA at specific regions called restriction sites. These restriction sites usually consist of four to six nucleotides. Cleavage by these specialized scissors creates a variety of unique surfaces which can be designed to connect pieces of DNA from different sources. Some of the common restriction endonucleases are listed below along with their specific areas of DNA cleavage.

Enzyme	Recognition and Cleavage Site
BamHI	5' - G GATCC - 3'

	3' - CCTAG G - 5'
EcoRI	5' - G AATTC - 3' 3' - CTTAA G - 5'
HaeIII	5' - GG CC - 3' 3' - CC GG - 5'
HindIII	5' - A AGCTT - 3' 3' - TTCGA A - 5'

When restriction enzymes cleave DNA, they produce what is called a "sticky end." As seen in the table above, stickky ends are produced when an area of overhang is produced in the cleavage process. These sticky ends allow for pieces of DNA with complementary ends to be rejoined, forming a recombinant piece of DNA. Bacteria DNA is circular, and when a section of genetic material is inserted from another source, a recombinant plasmid is produced. Bacterial transformation is a process by which genetic information is transfered to a new cell. This recombinant plasmid is reproduced several times each time a bacteria replicates itself.

Over time, millions of copies of the inserted DNA sequence can be produced. In order to distinguish between bacteria that have the plasmid insert and those who do not, scientists can place some type of antibiotic resistance gene into the plasmid along with the recombinant DAN. As a result, bacteria that have the gene being studied will be able to survive in a colony plate that has been treated with that antibiotic. Normal bacteria do not have a resistance to this bacteria and will die.

Removal and Separation of Cloned DNA

Once the bacteria has cloned several million copies of the specific gene sequence of interest, the DNA containing the gene must be isolated and removed from the bacteria. The first step is to break the cell walls of the bacteria so that the recombinant plasmid is in solution and not contained within the bacteria. This process of lysing open cell walls can be done either chemically or by mechanical means. Most often, the bacteria are subjected to sonication which is simply a power wave of sound that acts to disrupt and break open a bacteia's cell wall. This releases its contents into the free solution.

After this the solution can be concentrated by centrifugation and then resuspended in a buffered solution containing the same restriction endonuclease that was used to cleave it earlier. Addition of the restriction enzyme separates the two segments of DNA so that they can be separated by gel-electrophoresis. Because an electrical current will have different attractions to various sizes and shapes of DNA, the segment of DNA being studied can be removed from all other contaminants. All gene manipulation is based on microbial genetics—ways of doing in the test tube what bacteria and viruses do naturally.

Gene Manipulation

All gene manipulation is based on microbial genetics--ways of doing in the test tube what bacteria and viruses do naturally.

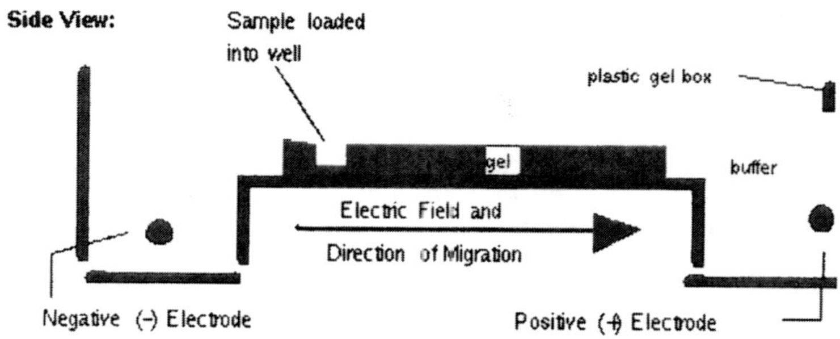

Gel Electrophoresis

This technique separates molecules on the basis of their size. Cast slab of gel material, usually agarose or polyacrylamide. The gel is a matrix of polymers forming sub-microscopic pores.

The size of the pores can be controlled by varying the chemical composition of the gel. The gel is set up for electrophoresis in a tank holding pH buffer. Electrodes apply an electric field:

The molecules to separate (DNA RNA) carry a net negative charge (why?) so they move along the electric field toward the positive cathode. (To separate proteins, a detergent would be included which coats the protein with negative charge.)

The larger molecules are held up as they try to pass through the pores of the gel, while the smaller molecules are impeded less and move faster. This results in separation by size, with the larger molecules nearer the well and the smaller molecules farther away.

Note that this separates on the basis of size (volume in solution), which is not necessarily molecular weight. For example:

— Two DNA molecules of the same molecular weight will run differently if one is supercoiled, because the supercoils constrain the shape to be smaller.

— Two RNA molecules of the same molecular weight will run differently if one has much intramolecular base pairing, making it "smaller."

Aside from the above exceptions, the distance migrated is roughly proportional to the log of the inverse of the molecular weight (the log of 1/MW). Gels are normally depicted as running vertically, with the wells at the top and the direction of migration downwards. This leaves the large molecules at the top and the smaller molecules at the bottom. Molecular weights are measured with different units for DNA, RNA, and protein:

— *DNA*: Molecular weight is measured in base-pairs, or bp, and commonly in kilobase-pairs (1000bp), or kbp.

— *RNA*: Molecular weight is measured in nucleotides, or nt, and commonly in kilonucleotides (1000nt), or knt.

— *Protein*: Molecular weight is measured in Daltons (grams per mole), or Da, and commonly in kiloDaltons (1000Da), or kDa.

Molecular weight standards run in one well of the gel are used to calibrate the molecular weights of sample molecules. Below is a gel stained with a dye: a colored molecule which binds to a specific class of macromolecules in a sequence-independent manner (probes bind in a sequence-dependent manner).

Sample 1 contains only one size class of macromolecule - it could be a plasmid, a pure mRNA transcript, or a purified protein. In this case, you would not have to use a probe to detect the molecule of interest since there is only one type of molecule present. Blotting is usually necessary for samples that are not complex mixtures. By interpolation, its molecular weight is roughly 3.

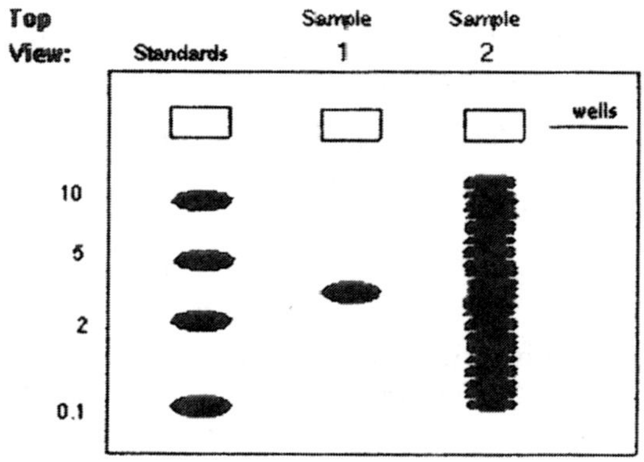

Sample 2 is what a sample of total DNA cut with a restriction enzyme, total cellular RNA, or total cellular protein would look like in a gel stained with a sequence-independent stain. There are so many bands that it is impossible to find the one we are interested in. Without a probe (which acts like a sequence-dependent stain) we cannot get very much information from a sample like this.

Different stains are used for different classes of macromolecules. DNA and RNA are generally stained with ethidium bromide (EtBr), an intercalating agent. The DNA-EtBr complex fluoresces under UV light. Protein is stained with Coomassie Blue or Silver Stain.

Cloning genes

In nature, DNA molecules recombine for various functions—even DNA between different species. DNA was still thought to be the "master molecule," not to be violated by "unnatural" manipulation. When scientists began to manipulate DNA in the test tube, many scientists feared that disastrous monsters would result, with unspecified dangers to people. In 1977 scientists proposed sweeping regulation on so-called "recombinant DNA," technologies which recombine DNA from different species in the test tube.

Since then, the dangers have appeared to be little more than those of "natural" genetic mixing. But we remain concerned about issues such as:

— Engineering food crops to resist pesticides. The pesticide resistance genes can escape into natural populations of weeds.

— Engineering a human symbiont microbe, such as E. coli, to produce a deadly toxin such as botulin. In theory this could be done, although it's not clear where such an organism would live, or how well it could "compete" with natural flora.

— Societal dilemmas of human cloning. How far shall we use reproductive technology to shape future humans?

How do we manipulate these natural processes for biotechnology; for instance, to make a bacterium that produces large quantities of insulin? One approach would be to cut the appropriate gene from human DNA and paste, or splice, it into a vector such as a plasmid or phage DNA.

Restriction Endonucleases

An "endonuclease" is an enzyme that cuts duplex DNA in the middle, not at an end (for exonuclease). Different species of bacteria have evolved different restriction endonucleases, each to cut foreign DNA that gets into their cells by mistake. To be cut, the DNA has to lack their own pattern of protective methylation. There are well over a hundred restriction enzymes, each cutting in a very precise way a specific base sequence of the DNA molecule.

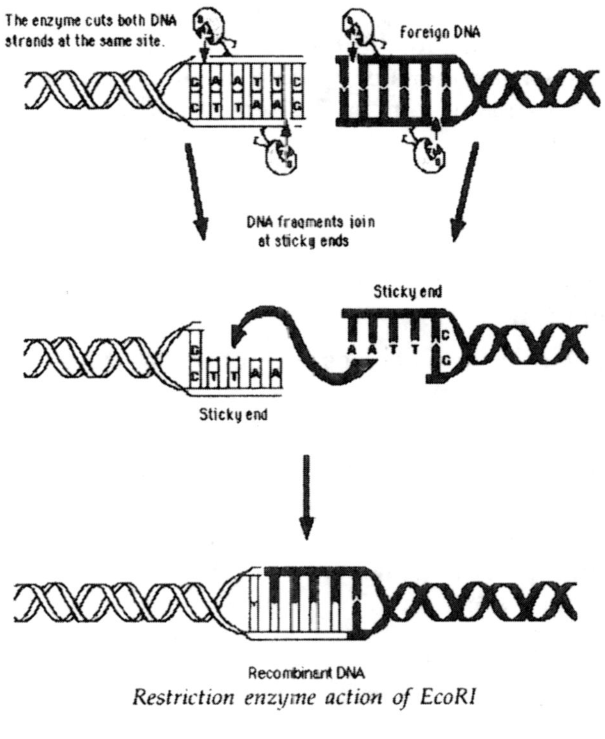

Restriction enzyme action of EcoRI

A restriction endonuclease cuts DNA only at a specific site, usually containing 4-6 base pairs. The enzyme has to cut the DNA backbone twice, recognizing the same type of site; therefore, the site "reads" the same way backwards as forwards—a palindrome.

This "sticky ends" from two different DNA molecules can hybridize together; then the nicks are sealed using ligase. The result is recombinant DNA. When this recombinant vector is inserted into E. coli, the cell will be able to process the instructions to assemble the amino acids for insulin production. More importantly, the new instructions are passed along to the next generation of E. coli cells in the process known as gene cloning.

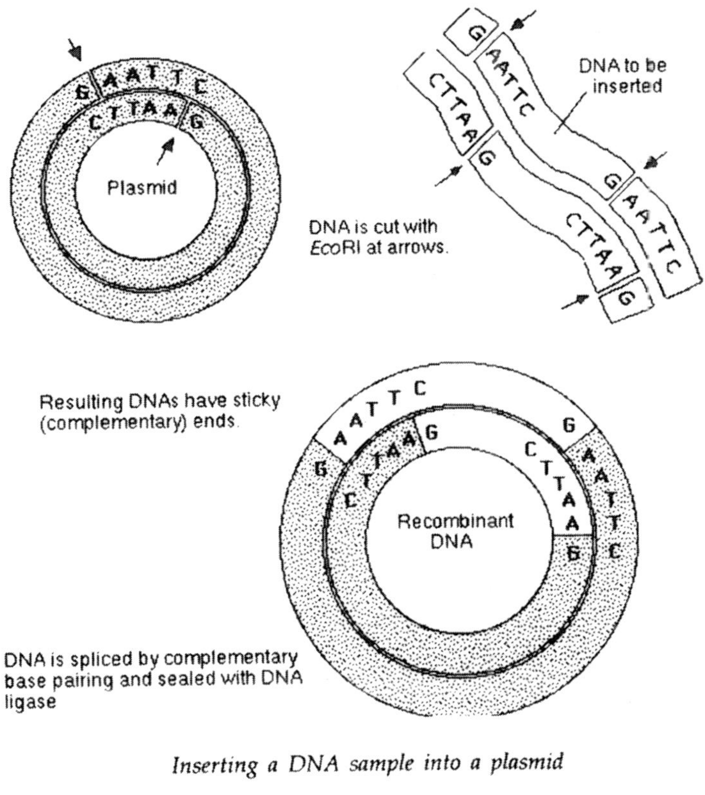

Inserting a DNA sample into a plasmid

How do we get the recombinant molecule into a bacterial cell? Usually by transformation (for a plasmid) or by in vitro packaging into a phage head coat (for a phage vector such as lambda phage).

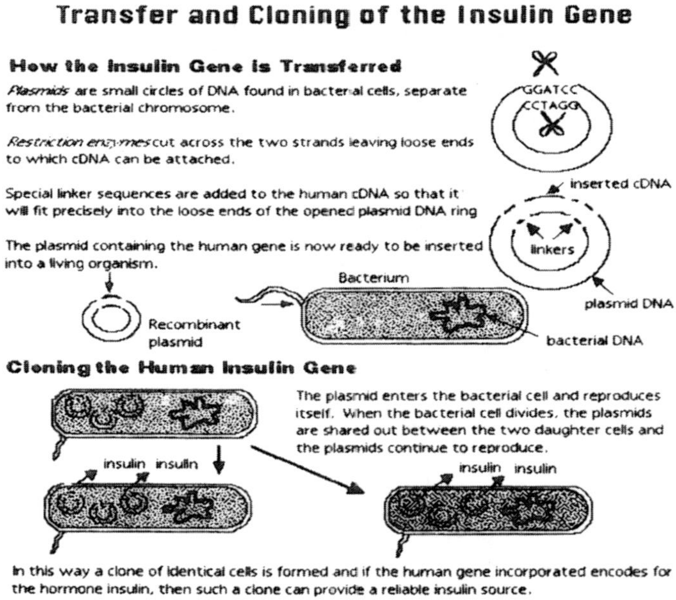

The above is a highly simplified description of recombinant DNA technology. How would we actually locate the appropriately cloned gene? There are many different ways, depending on the specific case. Here is one example, in which a partial sequence of the protein enables us to reverse the code and determine an approximate DNA sequence to use for a radiolabeled probe. The DNA probe will hybridize to clones containing the correct DNA, even if it is just one piece cut out of an entire genome.

The radioactive probe is made by determining a short segment of the protein sequence, then "back translating" to the possible DNA sequences. Short DNA sequences are

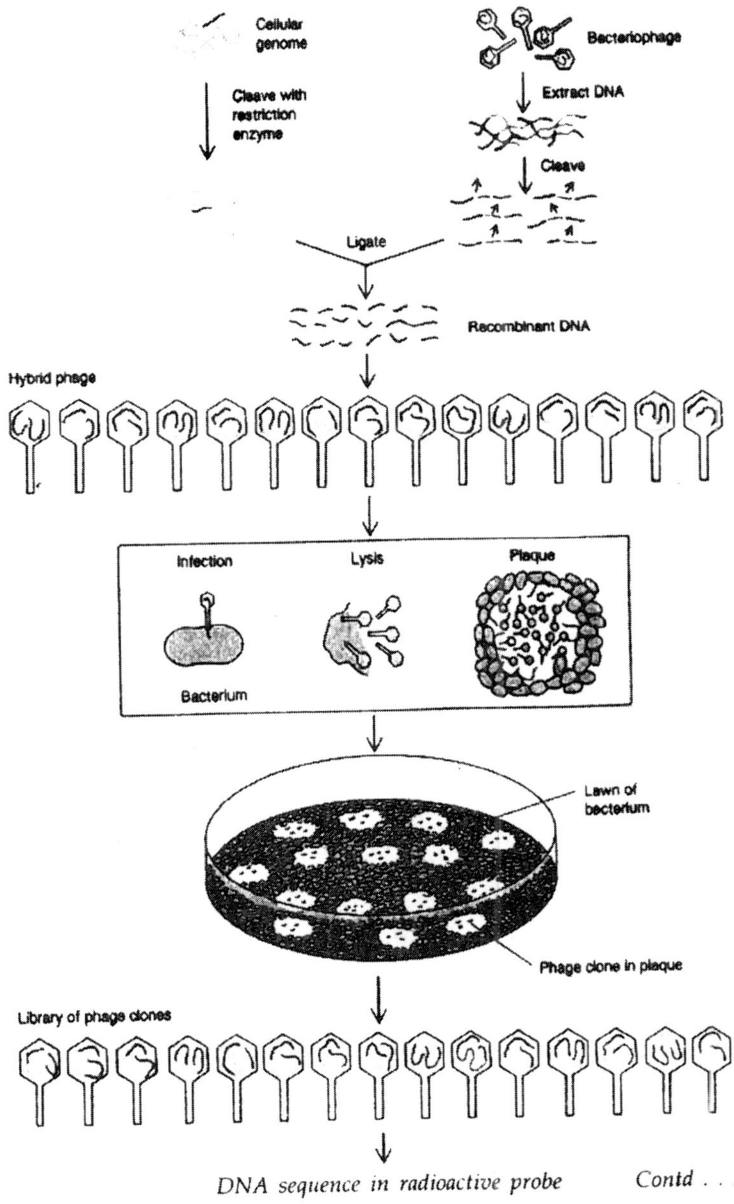

DNA sequence in radioactive probe *Contd . . .*

Contd . . .

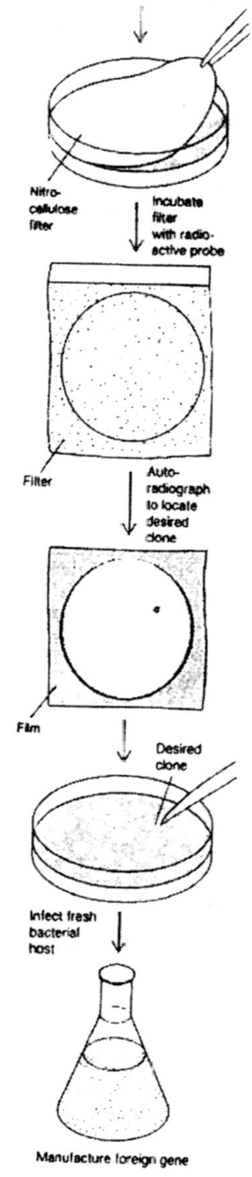

Nitro-
cellulose
filter
Incubate
filter
with radio-
active probe
Filter
Auto-
radiograph
to locate
desired
clone
Film
Desired
clone
Infect fresh
bacterial
host
Manufacture foreign gene

synthesized to match the protein sequence. Then these DNA oligomers (known as "oligos") are radiolabeled, and applied to the blotted clones. They should hybridize only to clones containing sequence encoding the desired protein.

Reverse Transcription: cDNA Cloning

To overcome this problem, we can start with mRNA isolated from tissues that produce the desired protein. We then use reverse transcriptase enzyme (produced by a retrovirus related to HIV) to reverse transcribe the mRNA into a DNA molecule that now is free of introns. Now we can ligate "sticky ends" onto the cDNA and recombine it into a phage or plasmid vector.

In PCR, a heat-stable DNA polymerase is used, most commonly Taq Polymerase from the thermophilic microbe Thermus aquaticus. More recently, an even more heat-resistant polymerase has been developed from a hyperthermophilic microbe growing at 110 degrees C in hydrothermal vent ecosystems in the deep ocean; it's called "Vent Polymerase."

The Taq Polymerase is put with the DNA to be amplified, plus all four NTPs, plus two primers facing each other, about 200 - 6000 kb apart. The primers are selected based on the DNA region you want to amplify. The tube is placed in a thermal cycler.

DNA gets synthesized from each primer, for about 2 minutes. Then the temperature is raised to 95 degrees C — enough to denature (split apart) the DNA base pairs. But the Taq Polymerase remains intact, because it comes from an organism that evolved to grow at this temperature. Now the temperature is decreased again, and primers again can hybridize to the DNA--both the old AND the newly synthesized strands. Again, Taq Polymerase extends new DNA strands. Again, the temperature is raised.

After repeated cycles, the amount of DNA sequence between the two primers increases exponentially. First 2 strands, then 4, 8, 16, up to about a million. Thus, in a couple of hours, you can get million-fold amplification of a DNA sequence.

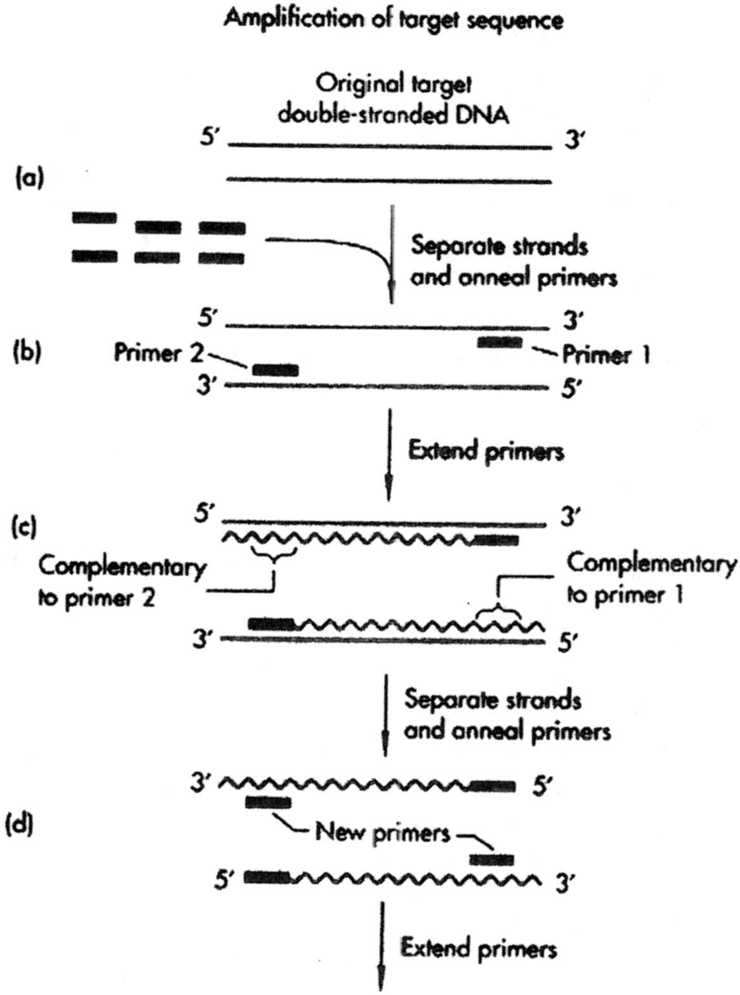

Application of target sequence

Applications of PCR

PCR has replaced cloning for many purposes, particularly the sequencing of DNA. It is faster and requires no vectors, which can mutate as they reproduce. It can be used forensically, to amplify tiny amounts of DNA from criminal evidence; or clinically, to detect DNA sequences linked to inherited disorders.

The main limitations of PCR are:

— Only relatively short sequences can be amplified reliably. Anything more than 10,000 base pairs is unlikely to be amplified.

— You need to know the right primer sequences to use, at both ends of the sequence you want to amplify. If two related genes have the same end sequences, you might amplify the wrong gene.

— You only obtain a DNA fragment. To see this DNA at work inside a living organism, some type of cloning has to be done.

The sequence of DNA base pairs can be analyzed by Restriction mapping. Construct a "road map" of restriction sites.

DNA Sequence Analysis

Cut and clone various restriction fragments, and determine the exact sequence of base pairs. All sequence information is deposited in GenBank. If you just want the sequence of the peptide translated from the RNA, you have to look for insulin mRNA or cDNA.

Once we have a piece of DNA cloned, it is amplified (available in many copies) and we now have a living clone which provides, in theory, an indefinite source of the DNA sequence. How do we analyze the sequence?

DNA Sequence Determination

Once you have identified a particular region of DNA of interest, you need to find out the precise sequence of DNA nucleotides. This is done by di-deoxy sequencing, in which a DNA polymerase is put together with dNTPs in four different reactions, each containing a small amount of one di-deoxy NTP (ATP, TTP, CTP, or GTP). The di-deoxy nucleotide lacks a 3'OH to continue chain extension, so the chain terminates. Each reaction produces a population of fragments terminated at A, T, C, or G.

The fragments are either radiolabeled or enzymatically labeled. They can be separated on a gel, or on a fluorescence analyzer. All published DNA sequences in the world are deposited in GenBank.

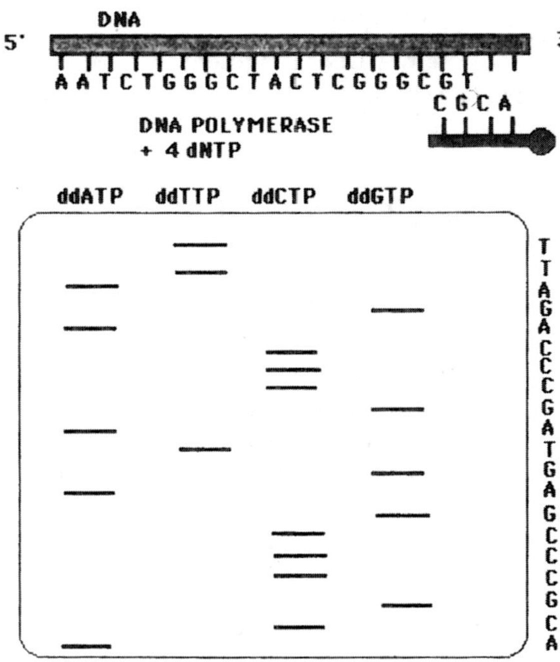

Contd. . .

Contd. . .

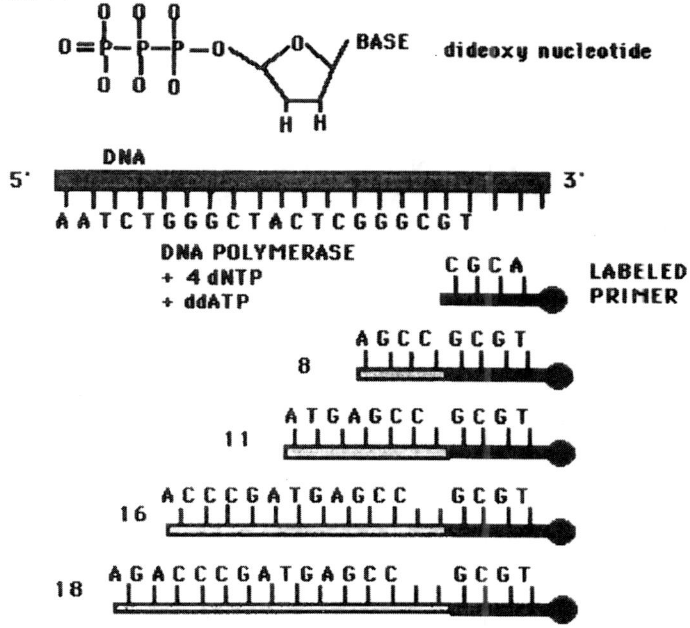

DNA Sequence Determination

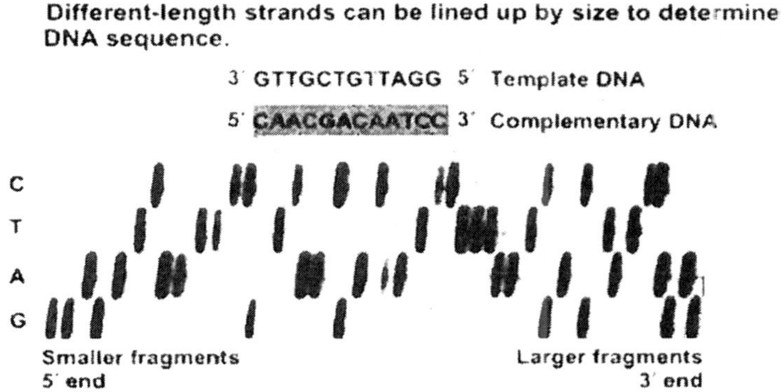

Historically, the products of dideoxy sequencing reactions were subjected to electrophoresis in four different lanes of a gel. Each lane contained a reaction using a different dideoxy terminator nucleotide. The data looked like in the previous page.

Today, products of all four sequencing reactions are loaded in a single gel lane or capillary tube and subjected to electrophoresis. Molecular labels consist of fluorescent dyes instead of radioactive nucleotides.

7

Bacterial Diversity

The large number of microorganisms present in the bacteria display a wide diversity of overlapping abilities and these traits do not match up neatly into any form of classification. For example, the metabolic capabilities of the proteobacteria seem almost randomly dispersed throughout the group and do not fall into any discernable arrangement. Therefore, any scheme to organize bacteria will have its problems, and unavoidably, certain abilities appear several times in different places. Sulfate reduction and photosynthesis are two examples of abilities dispersed throughout this domain.

alpha-Proteobacteria

Proteobacteria are evolutionarily related to each other, but have so evolved that one of the few things they have in common is their gram-negative cell wall. They are one of the largest collections of cultured microorganisms and many microbes important to humans fall into this group. There is tremendous diversity within the group. Strict aerobes, facultative anaerobes and strict anaerobes are found in this family and a number of different cellular morphologies are also present, although they tend to be rod-shaped.

There are five subgroups of Proteobacteria α, ß, γ, δ, and ε and it will examine a few species from each subgroup to give you a sense of the wide variety of microorganisms and metabolisms.

α subgroup

Rhizobia a plant symbiont

Rhizobia were originally identified as bacteria that form nodules on leguminous plants and were all lumped into one genus, Rhizobium. However, you wont be surprised to learn that phylogeny based on such a quality happens to be incorrect and phylogenetic evidence has since made it clear this group of microbes is quite diverse. The rhizobia have been split into six different genera based upon 16S rRNA analysis, Rhizobium, Sinorhizobium, Mesorhizobium, Bradyrhizobium, Azorhizobium and Allorhizobium. These plant-nodulating bacteria do not form a self-contained group, but are intermingled with a number of species that do not form symbiotic relationships. In other words, members of the Rhizobium and Bradyrhizobium are less related to each other than to genera that fail to nodulate plants.

Rhizobia are gram-negative chemoheterotrophic organotrophs and are capable of growth on a large array of carbohydrates. They are normally rod-shaped and do not form endospores. They are motile by one polar or subpolar flagellum or by 26 peritrichous flagella, and grow by aerobic respiration of various carbon compounds. They are easily cultivated on medium containing carbohydrates and a considerable portion of this carbohydrate is converted to extracellular slime, which presumably serves a role in the environment.

The behavior of rhizobia toward carbohydrates no doubt reflects the fact that this material is available in the vicinity of plants where rhizobia are often found. Because of photosynthesis, plants produce an excess of carbohydrates that can be available to bacteria that are either in the vicinity of plant roots or have formed a symbiotic relationship in nodules.

Rhizobia can be divided into fast-growing strains, with generation times of less than 6 hours, and slow-growing strains. Fast growing strains utilize the Entner-Meyerhoff-Parnas pathway, while most of the slow-growing rhizobia utilize the Enter-Douderoff pathway. Fast-growing strains are capable of catabolizing glucose, galactose, fructose, xylose, mannitol, sucrose, trehalose, and dulcitol. Slow-growing strains can utilize these sugars, except for surcrose, trehalose and dulcitol. Slow-growing strains also tend to have growth factor requirements in addition to the carbon and energy source.

The fast-growing rhizobia have the genes for nodulation and nitrogen fixation on very large plasmids. These plasmids are actually larger than the entire chromosomes of other bacteria and are so large (~1 Mbp) that they were not detected as plasmids for many years until plasmid-handling methods became more sophisticated. This raises the following interesting point. It seems plausible that nodulation was present in the progenitor to rhizobia and its non-nodulating relatives and had been selectively lost over time. It is also possible that nodulation transferred into strains by way of this plasmid.

Certainly the presence of the genes on plasmids, rather than on the bacterial chromosome, makes it easier to understand how they might be lost. However, the plasmid-location suggests another alternative: perhaps the progenitor did not have this ability, but it evolved later on a plasmid. The ability of such plasmids to move among strains might also explain the presence in some but not all members of the larger family. But if this were the case, wouldnt you expect the plasmid to be found in relatively unrelated bacteria as well? Perhaps, but perhaps not.

Possibly, there are other metabolic features in this bacterial family that make them particularly good at metabolizing plants products, so that they are the only microbes that can use the information on the plasmid efficiently and are therefore the only ones to retain it. At least this story shows the complexity in trying to make such progenitor identification arguments. The slow-growing strains also have the genes for nitrogen fixation, but in this case they are in their chromosomes. It is possible that these microbes recombined the aforementioned plasmid into their chromosome and it has been retained there.

Rhizobia are called plant symbionts, rather than pathogens, because when they nodulate plants, they actually provide a benefit. They fix nitrogen and supply it to the plant, which provides them with carbon and energy in return. They are capable of forming relationships with a wide variety of legumes such as alfalfa, soybeans and peas. In nitrogen-poor soils, rhizobia give a competitive advantage to their hosts, allowing them to grow in nitrogen poor soil.

There has been substantial scientific interest in the rhizobia since many of the plants they nodulate are important crops around the world and the rhizobia contribute significantly to the overall fertility of the soil. A few years after rhizobia were first described and cultured in 1895, they were used for inoculating legumes by coating the seeds with culture or mixing soil, seeds and culture together. This improved the rate of nodulation of the plants and had a marked effect on their growth. However, the issue has become somewhat complicated as there are now clearly many fields where there is a substantial population of rhizobia in the soil that out-compete those added with the seeds.

In such cases, it is the indigenous bacteria that form nodules and many of these are not particularly effective at fixing nitrogen. Much of the current effort in the field is now directed toward making productive nitrogenfixing rhizobia more competitive in infecting plants. The other approach to improving the agricultural value of biological nitrogen fixation involves nitrogen-fixers other than the rhizobia. These so-called associative nitrogen-fixing bacteria do not form the involved symbiosis with plants and therefore might be more amendable to forming productive relationships with a variety of plants.

Dimorphic Prosthecate Bacteria Caulobacter

Most bacteria divide by binary fission, but prosthecate bacteria reproduce asymmetrically. Their name refers to the prostheca, which is a long appendage found on one of the two cell types. Caulobacter species are gram-negative, non-spore-forming rods. Phylogenetically the prosthecate bacteria are widely divergent, but are more closely related to each other than to non-prosthecate microorganisms.

They are ubiquitous in the environment and second only to the pseudomonads in their distribution. They specialize in aquatic environments, especially nutrient-poor ones, including drinking water. In short, if a site has been wet for any length of time, prosthecate bacteria will be present. They have not been isolated from hot environments, however. These bacteria tend to be harmless and with few exceptions, they are not found in association with animals. Prosthecate bacteria are, however, often found in association with phototrophic and heterotrophic diatoms and bound to algae.

In photosynthetic hosts this may be a mutualistic relationship. The photosynthetic microbe benefits because the Caulobacter cells remove the oxygen generated during photosynthesis, thus decreasing the effective oxygen concentration and the potential for oxidative damage. In return the Caulobacter cells obtains excess nutrients from the photosynthetic microbe.

They are chemoheteroorganotrophs, growing on a variety of carbon compounds with most species capable of catabolizing carbohydrates and amino acids. A few members can also attack other organic acids and primary alcohols. All species are obligate aerobes. Members of this groups tend to be mesophilic, but a few can grow at temperatures as low as 5°C. The genome of C. crescentus has been found to contain a very high number (105) of genes for two-component signal transduction proteins. Such systems are typically involved in environmental sensing and these presumably play a role in that process as well as the subsequent developmental life cycle of these microbes.

Caulobacter cells exist in two different forms during their life cycle. One form, the stationary cell, is non-motile and contains a cylindrical and relatively narrow prostheca, which is an outgrowth of the cell wall and cell membrane and serves as an anchor for attachment to surfaces. The other cell type, termed a swarmer, is motile with a single polar flagellum and does not go through cell division.

Stationary cells have already identified a reasonable environmental niche and use their prosthecae to maintain themselves there, but the organism wants its progeny to have the ability to move to new environments. The stationary cells therefore elongate and divide, creating a swarmer cell on the pole opposite of the prostheca. The swarmer cell synthesizes a flagellum and breaks away, swimming for a period of time without dividing. At some point the decision is made to stop and this is presumably due to systems that sense an attractive environment. The flagella fall off, the cell synthesizes a prostheca and adheres to a surface. The new stationary cell now increases in size and begins the cycle again.

These microbes have a high tolerance for prolonged nutrient scarcity and many species are markedly inhibited by rich medium. The large surface area provided by the prostheca is one reason they are able to grow in dilute environments, and. their habitation in such nutrient-poor situations explains why the number of these bacteria never exceeds 105 per ml. Indeed, this quality can be taken advantage of for their isolation. A typical isolation medium for them contains 0.1% peptone, 0.05% yeast extract and a few salts, prepared in tap water. This is a 10-fold dilution of more typical microbial media.

Prosthecate bacteria are very important in the mineralization of organic molecules from aquatic habitats. Other microorganisms act on organics when the concentration of the substrate is high, but the prosthecate bacteria finish degradation when the concentration of nutrients becomes more dilute. In the future these microbes may play a role in the bioremediation of areas contaminated with low concentrations of pollutants.

Methanotrophs

There are two major groups of methanotrophs. Type I consists of six genera: Methylococcus, Methylocaldum, Methylomonas, Methylobacter, Methylomicrobium and Methylosphaera that all belong to the a subgroup. Species of Methylocaldum are thermophilic and their relationship to the others in Type I is somewhat distant, but they are still their closet relatives. Type I methanotrophs route carbon for biosynthesis through formaldehyde. Type II methanotrophs actually belong to the ß subgroup of proteobacteria but will be mentioned briefly here. They include Methylocystis and Methylosinus and some species are capable of forming cysts or spores that can survive for months. Type II methanotrophs route carbon for biosynthesis through serine.

Methanotrophs are gram-negative rods and cocci that have a highly specialized metabolism restricted to the use of single-carbon compounds. These compounds are completely oxidized to H_2O and CO_2 using oxygen as the terminal electron acceptor. As bacteria, they are completely unrelated to the archaeal methanogens, though their complementary metabolism means that they are often found nearby in aerobic habitats, if an oxygen gradient is present. (In anaerobic habitats methane is attacked by a unique consortium that includes an archaeon and a sulfate reducer.)

Due to the widespread availability of methane, methanotrophs are ubiquitous in the environment and are the main prokaryotic consumers of methane. The largest populations of methanotrophs are found in areas where both oxygen and methane are continually available and they make up a large proportion of biomass in many fresh water aquatic habitats. These include rice paddies, muddy soils, marshes, rivers, ponds and lakes, meadows and deciduous forest soils. They are also found in sewage sludge, some peat bogs, coals mines and drainage waters. It is not known how common they are in marine environments, but they are thought to provide a food source for phytoplankton in some situations. Methanotrophs have generally not been isolated from extreme environments, even though the activity of methanogens in these environments results in significant concentrations of methane. A few species have been isolated from Antarctic lakes and soda lakes, suggesting that some are capable of growth in extreme cold and at high pH.

Several species of methanotrophs coexist with sulfur-oxidizing bacteria and form symbiotic relationships with various invertebrate species on the sea floor of the Pacific and Atlantic oceans. Relationships with deep-sea mussels and tubes worms have been demonstrated, in which the microbes live inside the tissues of the host. Several cold-water coral reefs also appear to use methanotrophs instead of algae as their symbiont in areas where hydrocarbons naturally seep into the local ocean. Carbonate ion is fixed into organic carbon and some of the resulting organic material is shared with the invertebrates. It has not been possible to cultivate these symbiotic microorganisms, but 16S rRNA analysis places them in Type I methanotrophs.

Methanotrophs are strict aerobes, but they can grow over a wide range of oxygen tensions. Most are limited to methane and methanol as substrates, but a few species are capable of utilizing methylamine and formate for their energy generation. Despite their strict reliance on single-carbon compounds for energy generation, some are capable of using complex organic molecules as a carbon source.

Methanogens, a major source of methane, are obligate anaerobes. This presents a bit of a problem for methanotrophs, a stable source of their electron donor (methane) is abundant in places where their terminal electron acceptor (oxygen) is not. They can solve this problem by growing in places near methanogens, but where oxygen is still available. This occurs at the surface of lakes and in the top layers of sediments where oxygen is present. Methane bubbles up from nearby anaerobic environments into the oxygen gradient and the methanotrophs are there to use it. However, while this is a common situation, methanotrophs are not restricted to this habitat. Methane is the most abundant organic gas in the atmosphere and is second only to CO_2 as a greenhouse gas.

Methane oxidation takes place in invaginations of the membrane, called intracytoplasmic membranes. The amount of intracytoplasmic membrane increases as the methane concentration becomes higher. This likely occurs because as more substrate is present to metabolize, the microbes create more enzymes for its catabolism. These are membrane proteins and as more are made, more membrane surface area is needed. Invagination of the membrane accommodates the elevated level of these proteins.

A wide variety of nitrogen sources can be used by methanotrophs including ammonia, nitrate, amino acids and complex mixtures such as yeast extract. Many are also capable of nitrogen fixation, but because of the oxygen-sensitivity of nitrogenase, most will only grow in nitrogen-free conditions at oxygen concentrations less than 10%.

Methane oxidation serves two purposes in methylotrophs, generation of energy and creation of cell carbon. Methane is first oxidized to methanol and then to formaldehyde.

From here formaldehyde can proceed down two pathways depending upon the cells needs. if energy is needed, further oxidation of formaldehyde can lead to formic acid and subsequently to CO_2, with all the electrons reducing NAD(P) to form NAD(P)H. These electrons are then passed to an electron transport chain that generates a proton gradient and finally ATP synthesis. If carbon is needed, formaldehyde can follow a different pathway, eventually leading to biosynthesis of necessary cell components.

A key enzyme for methane oxidation is methane monooxygenase (MMO), which catalyzes the first step of the oxidation of methane to methanol. All methanotrophs possess a copper-containing MMO bound to their ICM. Some methanotrophs also form a soluble form of MMO, which is of considerable interest because of its amazing lack of substrate specificity. It has been shown to be able to react with over 250 hydrocarbon compounds and will likely have great utility in the bioremediation industry. Soluble MMO does not contains copper and its synthesis is repressed in the presence of the element. It appears that it is a back-up system for the organisms if they find themselves in a copper-poor environment.

Soluble MMO has given methanotrophs a significant biotechnological potential that has been harnessed in applications including bioremediation and industrial processes. However, these bacteria grow slowly and require the presence of methane as substrate, which is potentially explosive. The repression by low concentrations of copper might also be a concern for bioremediation, though we can presumably circumvent this matter as a better understanding of the molecular basis of the regulation is understood. Recent cloning of the genes for soluble MMO into Pseudomonas putida F1 may have circumvented these problems. The enzyme is functional in Pseudomonas and degrades trichloroethylene, a major pollutant at a rate much faster than Pseudomonas that does not contain the plasmid.

Agrobacterium

Agrobacterium species are closely related to certain species of Rhizobium. In fact, when plasmids from Rhizobium phaseoli, which were known to carry genes for infecting beans, were introduced into A. tumefaciens, the resulting bacteria were able to form nitrogen-fixing nodules on bean roots. This result shows that the metabolic properties of the two organisms are rather similar and that the plant infection ability encoded by the plasmid was sufficient to convert the Agrobacterium strain to a different lifestyle. Many of the species of this genus are plant pathogens and A. tumefaciens, which causes Crown Gall tumors on a wide range of plants, is the best understood. Cells in the Agrobacterium genus are gram-negative, non-spore-forming short rods that grow by chemoheteroorganotrophic metabolism.

A. rhizogenes causes hairy root disease on a number of plants, while A. vitis causes tumors and necrotic lesions on grape vines and is commonly found in the xylem sap of infected plants. Nonpathogenic Agrobacterium species are common in the soil, and these have been designated as A. radiobacter. None of the A. radiobacter isolates contain the Ti plasmid. All Agrobacterium species are motile by flagella and for the pathogenic strains this ability is an important virulence factor.

They are widely distributed in soil and in association with plants roots, tubers, and underground stems, where they cause tumors. These microbes grow readily on complex or defined medium and have optimum temperature ranges from 24-28°C. A. tumerfaciens has an unusual genome, possessing a circular chromosome of 3 Mb and a linear one of 2.1 Mb. In addition to its chromosomes, A. tumefaciens carries a 200-kB plasmid, termed the Ti plasmid (for tumor-inducing). As described below, a potion of this plasmid is actually transferred by the bacterium into the plant cells genome and causes that plant to provide compounds specifically utilized by the pathogen. The transferred genes are involved in plant colonization, conjugation and utilization of the metabolic products of the plant tumor.

A. tumefaciens first senses the presence of the plant by detecting phenolic compounds that plants excrete and more precise recognition follows through a variety of surface interactions. These signals are transmitted by a two-component regulatory pathway and causes the production of a Type IV secretion system similar to that seen in human pathogens such as Helicobacter pylori and Vibrio cholerae. The system in A. tumefaciens can actually transfer both DNA and specific proteins into the host cell. The transferred DNA, termed T DNA, moves to the nucleus, and inserts into the plant cells chromosome.

Gene expression from the T DNA ultimately leads to the production of two types of compounds. The first type includes auxin, a plant growth hormone, and cytokinins, which together cause the uncontrolled growth of plants cells and the formation of tumors. This therefore increases the fraction of the plant material that has been taken over by the pathogen. The second set of compounds produced is opines, which are formed from the condensation of metabolites present in the plant cell cytoplasm. For example, octopine is formed from the combination of arginine and pyruvate. Opines are unusual compounds that are not easily degraded by most other bacteria, but Agrobacterium of course, does have such an ability, again encoded on its Ti plasmid.

Essentially the bacterium is converting the plant metabolism to produce a compound that only A. tumefaciens cells can utilize. Given the way microbes work, however, you wont be surprised to read that a few other microorganisms also have the ability to use opines as carbon and energy sources, but the majority goes to the Agrobacterium cells.

If you think through the above scenario, something should bother you a bit. The Agrobacterium cell caused the transfer of bacterial genes into a plant cell, but we have said repeatedly that bacterial and eukaryotic genes are rather different, with different transcriptional signals. How can these genes that reside in a bacteria be expressed? Remarkably, the transferred T DNA already has eukaryotic promoters. The presence of these eukaryotic signals in a microorganism, where they have no meaning, is curious. One wonders how these regulatory signals ever found their way into Agrobacterium.

There is another interesting signaling system that Agrobacterium, or more properly the Ti plasmid, employs. The Ti plasmid produces a homoserine lactone species as produced by many other quorum-sensing systems. When it detects an elevated population of like organisms, it turns on expression of the conjugation system that moves the plasmid to other bacteria, but this is not the same system that mobilizes the T DNA into plants. However, there is a paradox here: Why would the plasmid seek to conjugate itself (only) when there are already a number of other plasmid-containing cells around? There is no apparent advantage in transferring a plasmid to a cell that already has a copy, for example.

This paradox is unresolved, but may have to do with the fact that the Ti plasmid is unusually unstable for a naturally occurring bacterial plasmid (i.e. you see plasmid-free cells). In fact, a majority of Agrobacterium cells lack the plasmid. So the logic might be that the presence of other plasmid-containing cells implies the presence of many plasmid-free cells as well, which then explains the reason for the plasmid to try to conjugate and re-establish itself in these cells.

The ability of these microbes to transfer DNA from a plasmid to a plant has made them extremely useful in the genetic engineering of plants. Transfer and integration depend only upon the presence of two 24-bp regions flanking the transferred DNA. It is therefore possible to insert any gene of interest, carrying appropriate promoters and recognition sequences, and have it integrated into the plant genome. This transferred DNA can integrate into a variety of sites and can be used to either create mutations (rather like transposons) and/or to get expression of desired genes inside of plant cells. This system has been used to engineer a wide variety of plants.

Purple non-sulfur bacteria

Photosynthetic bacteria are found throughout the different phyla of microorganisms and not restricted to one branch on the tree. They fall into several broad categories: the cyanobacteria, the purple non-sulfur bacteria, the purple sulfur bacteria, green sulfur bacteria and Chloroflexus. It appears that while they all perform photosynthesis, other genetic characteristics can be quite different. For example, even the photosynthetic apparatus varies between the different species.

Green bacteria use a different photosystem and series of enzymes than do the purple bacteria, while cyanobacteria seem to use a combination of both of these and have a more plant-like photosynthesis system. Cyanobacteria, green sulfur bacteria and Chloroflexus form relatively tight phylogenetic groups, but the purple bacteria are distributed throughout the proteobacteria. It appears that the photosynthetic apparatus from the purple bacteria has been horizontally transferred between species in the proteobacteria resulting in very divergent members having similar photosynthetic abilities.

In fact recent work has discovered a purple type of photosynthetic apparatus operating in an endospore-forming, gram-positive bacterium. It is also possible that eh progenitor of the proteobacteria was photosynthetic, but this ability was lost in many of its decedents when they adapted to habitats where it was not required. In contrast to their name, broth cultures of the purple non-sulfur bacteria can be beige, olive green, red, orange, pink and even blue. The purple non-sulfur bacteria are a highly diverse and heterogeneous group of microorganisms. There are four phylogenetically distinct groups of purple non-sulfur bacteria, Rhodocyclus falls in the a subgroups of proteobacteria, while the Rhodospirillum, Rhodopseudomonas and Rhodobacter groups make up the other three divisions and are all located in the ß proteobacteria.

Purple non-sulfur bacteria can have very diverse lifestyles and forms of division. Species capable of budding division and binary fission are known. Many different morphologies including spirilla (Rhodospirillum), rods (Rhodopseudomonas and Rhodobacter), and even networks of cells have been isolated. One of the more interesting species morphologically is Rhodomicrobium vanielii. The microbe exists as motile swarmer cells that eventually settle down and begin to grow. During division, prosthecae grow out from the cells and new cells develop at the end of these appendages.

Each cell is able to grow prosthecae in several different directions. Growth proceeds in this manner until a tangled network of cells develops. Eventually, swarmer cells develop and leave the network, establishing new colonies of microbes in other places. In this way the microbe can spread throughout an environment. R. vannielii is also capable of forming polyhedral exospores that are resistant to various harsh conditions.

The photosynthetic apparatus of the purple bacteria dictates their ecological niche. Photosynthesis occurs under anaerobic conditions when light is present. Therefore, purple bacteria are often found in anoxic environments where a suitable electron donor, such as H_2S, and light is present. A common habitat where this occurs is in aquatic environments and their sediments, where light of sufficient quality and quantity can reach them. Since these conditions are easily met, it is not surprising to find purple non-sulfur bacteria in a wide array of aquatic habitats. They are present in most marine and fresh waters, including hypersaline waters.

Purple non-sulfur bacteria are found in highest numbers in mesophilic bodies of water, but have also been isolated from thermal springs and cold polar habitats. Fresh water eutrophic lakes can have numbers of purple non-sulfur bacteria reaching up to 108 cells/ml in flat shore areas that have good light penetration. Interestingly, purple non-sulfur bacteria are found in all stages of conventional sewage treatment. In these situations they are likely growing chemoheteroorganotrophically, but if the anaerobic sewage is incubated in the light, it will turn a red-brown color due to the photosynthetic growth of the purple non-sulfur bacteria.

Their metabolism is highly diverse and flexible. In fact they are some of the most metabolically capable microorganisms known, being able to grow photoautolithotrophically, photoheteroorganotrophically, chemoheteroorganotrophically and some species even chemoautolithotrophically. While photosynthesis is likely the major method of metabolism in the environment, the purple non-sulfur bacteria are not limited to it, presumably because not all environments are simultaneously anaerobic and lit by the sun. They tend to have the ability to utilize a variety of organic compounds using many of the same pathways found in other microorganisms.

Many species are also capable of using nitrate, nitrite and nitrous oxide as alternative electron acceptors and they reduce these compounds to nitrogen gas. Some species of purple non-sulfur bacteria are even capable of growth under chemoautolithotrophic conditions. For example, Rhodopseudomonas capsulata can grow in the dark using hydrogen as a source of electrons and oxygen as the terminal electron acceptor. In the absence of an acceptable terminal electron acceptor, a few species of purple non-sulfur bacteria are also capable of fermentation. Rhodospirillum rubrum can ferment fructose to produce succinate, acetate, propionate, formate, CO_2 and H_2. If grown on pyruvate, the organism forms acetate, formate, CO_2 and H_2.

Sulfur compounds can be important for these microorganisms, because they serve as an electron donor for their photosynthetic metabolism. Hydrogen sulfide is a common source of sulfur that can be reduced by these bacteria, but it can also be quite toxic. Tolerance to sulfide varies greatly between species and this affects their ability to live in certain habitats. Generally, marine isolates are capable of tolerating a much higher concentration of sulfide than are fresh water isolates. Due to the high activity of sulfate reducers, which produce sulfide in marine environments, it is not surprising that marine isolates would have a higher tolerance and readily use H2S in their metabolism.

Nitrogen can be obtained from a number of different sources including amino acids and ammonia and many species of purple non-sulfur bacteria are also capable of nitrogen fixation. Nitrogen fixation, as well as a variety of other metabolisms in these organisms, leads to the production of H_2. The microbes can then utilize this hydrogen for photoautolithotrophic growth, but conditions have been manipulated so that they produce H_2 for commercial purposes. As cars that run on hydrogen fuel cells become more common, these microorganisms may serve as a source of renewable fuel.

SAR11

Many microbes in the environment are unculturable. From microscopic and biochemical studies this phenomenon had been clear for many years, but little could be learned about these mysterious, recalcitrant microbes. With the advent of PCR, fluorescently labeled probes, sophisticated cloning techniques and methods to survey these microbes without amplification, it has become possible to search for bacterial DNA directly in the environment. These studies have revealed that unculturable species are often at high populations in many environments.

Surveys of microbial diversity, using culture independent techniques of aqueous environments, have shown that up to 25% of all rRNA genes that have been identified are unculturable microbes that are members of the a proteobacteria. This group of unculturable microbes clusters together to form what is called the SAR11 clade. The type species, SAR11, has been found in coastal and near shore waters and in the open ocean to depths of 3000 m.

Culturing SAR11 allowed the determination of a number of properties of these microbes. They are small, crescent shaped cells, having an average length of 0.6 m and a diameter of of 0.16 m. SAR11 is, therefore, one of the smallest microorganisms known that can autonomously replicate. The genome of SAR11 is estimated to be 1.5 Mb. When possible, it will be interesting to determine its entire DNA sequence and compare this to other organisms. From cultivation experiments, SAR11 appears to be a chemoheteroorganotroph that utilizes organic material in the sea.

ß subgroup

Chemoautolithotrophy is a type of metabolism that depends upon the use of inorganic compounds as a source of energy, electrons and carbon. Organisms that can perform this type of metabolism are found both in the Archaea and the Bacteria, but many bacteria with this property cluster in the ß subgroup of the proteobacteria. Chemoautolithotrophic bacteria are typically gram-negative and utilize inorganic substrates including H_2, NH_3, NO_2^-, H_2S, S, Fe^{2+}, Mn^{+2} and CO. For example two important groups of microbes that can grow chemoautolithotrophically, the ammonia oxidizers and Thiobacillus. Both are important in the cycling of inorganic nutrients in the environment.

Ammonia oxidizers

Winogradsky was the first to isolate organisms of this group and he proposed the revolutionary idea that they were living by a completely inorganic form of metabolism. The ammonia oxidizers are a physiologically distinct group of microorganisms that oxidize ammonia to nitrite as an energy source and use CO_2 as a carbon source. Most species cluster in the ß subdivision with only one species, Nitrosococcus oceanus, being found in the γ subdivision of the proteobacteria.

Many of these organisms have been found in diverse environments, from soils to fresh and marine waters, although some species do show a preference for certain habitats. Ammonia oxidizers have also been found in very odd environments, such as the stones of buildings and in boulders. In these places they can cause serious corrosion of the surrounding rock resulting from the production of nitrous and nitric acid.

Nutritionally these organisms are obligate autolithotrophs and attempts to grow them heteroorganotrophically have not been successful. Energy is generated by coupling the oxidation of ammonia to the creation of a proton gradient, which is then used for the formation of ATP. All known ammonia oxidizers are obligate aerobes, but they are capable of growth at less than atmospheric levels of oxygen. Adaptability to various oxygen tensions is likely important for growth in certain environments such as the soil-water interface of aquatic sediments. Ammonia oxidizers perform the following net reactions

$$2H^{+} + NH_3 + 2_e^- + O_2 \rightarrow NH_2OH + H_2O$$

$$NH_2OH + H_2O \rightarrow HNO_2 + 4H+ + 4_e$$

The first reaction is catalyzed by ammonia monooxygenase and the second by hydroxylamine oxidoreductase. The result is the removal of ammonia and the production of nitrous acid (HNO_2). The nitrous acid produced can be further oxidized by Nitrobacter and related species to nitric acid (HNO_3).

All carbon is assimilated using CO_2 through the Calvin cycle. The key enzyme of this cycle, ribulose bisphosphate carboxylase, is found in some species in remarkable structures called carboxysomes. Carboxysomes are polyhedral structures that look very much like phage heads and are composed of 5-6 proteins that form a shell around the ribulose bisphosphate carboxylase. It is thought that the carboxysomes serve to concentrate CO_2 inside the structure and thus increase the efficiency of ribulose bisphosphate carboxylase. Carboxysomes are thought to be especially useful in situations of low carbon dioxide concentration.

Most ammonia oxidizers are mesophilic and have remarkably similar growth requirements, needing a few salts and ammonia. While species have been isolated from cold and high acid environments, all such isolates are facultative psychrophiles and acidophiles. The ammonia oxidizers are of ecological importance because of their biological conversion of inorganic nitrogen compounds. Ammonia present in the soil is often inaccessible, due to its strong attachment to clay particles. It can however be converted into NO_3^-, a more soluble form of nitrogen that can be used by many groups of microorganisms. Ammonia oxidizers are often in close association with nitrite-oxidizing bacteria that take the nitrite product and use it for energy generation.

Ammonia oxidation is a membrane-bound process and it must be performed at a high level in order to generate enough energy for reasonable cell growth. Many species create invaginations in their membranes, thereby increasing the surface area of the membrane in a fashion similar to the purple non-sulfur bacteria. The larger membrane can then accommodate more ammonia oxidation complexes and these intracytoplasmic membranes are a distinctive characteristic of this group.

Thiobacillus

Thiobacilli are a second group of chemoautolithotrophic bacteria, but they use reduced sulfur compounds instead of ammonia as a source of energy. It is easy to isolate organisms capable of this mode of metabolism with a simple medium containing salts and a reduced sulfur compound and no organic carbon source. Because of their ease of enrichment and common physiology, a number of species were found and classified as Thiobacillus. However, molecular analysis has shown that this group is phylogenetically diverse with many strains actually belonging in the γ or a subgroup of proteobacteria. Nevertheless, we will treat them here due to their common metabolism and similar ecological niche.

There are over 30 known species of thiobacilli capable of oxidizing reduced sulfur compounds and growing autotrophically. One example genera is Thiobacillus. These species are gram-negative rods that are motile by flagella, and most species are obligate autotrophs. A second example of thiobacilli is the genus Thiomonas, a gram-negative rod-shaped microbe. Unlike Thiobacillus, most Thiomonas are facultatively autotrophic and are capable of growth on simple organic sources such as yeast extract, peptone and pyruvate.

These organisms are restricted to habitats where both an acceptable electron donor (reduced sulfur compounds or iron in some cases) and an electron acceptor (oxygen or nitrogen oxides) simultaneously exist. These requirements exist in narrow zones where gradients of hydrogen sulfide and oxygen overlap. One example is the sediments of stratified lakes where the overlaying water provides a source of oxygen, while hydrogen sulfide bubbles up from decomposing sediments. Appropriate microenvironments also exist in places that contain anaerobic pockets such as wet soils. In general, sulfur oxidizers are found in a range of habitats and can be isolated from soils, sediments, and fresh and marine waters. They grow over a wide range of pH values and temperatures.

There are both obligately autotrophic sulfur oxidizers and those that can grow on organic carbon sources. In environments where organic carbon is limiting the autotrophic species predominate, but if organic compounds are more abundant, sulfide oxidizers capable of using them are present in higher numbers. Marine thiobacilli have been isolated from hydrothermal vents and in these communities they may be at the bottom of the food chain and serve as a source of organic carbon for other animals.

All sulfur-oxidizing bacteria use compounds such as H_2S, S, and S_2O_{32}- to generate energy using oxygen as the terminal electron acceptor. As usual, this is coupled to a proton gradient that generates ATP. The complete oxidation of these compounds and the production of sulfuric acid

(H_2SO_4) is common to many thiobacilli, which lowers the pH of their surrounding environment. Because many of the species of sulfur oxidizers produce sulfuric acid or ferric iron as an end product, they are often associated with the corrosion of the environment in which they live.

Thiobacilli have been implicated in the destruction of pipes, concrete, and monuments. They are also responsible for acid run-off from abandoned mines where the water leaving the mine can have pH values as low as 2. To add to the destruction, the acid dissolves minerals in the surrounding area leading to the solubilization of many metals including aluminum, which can be toxic to aquatic organisms. The high concentrations of iron and other metals along with the low pH make the water unfit for human consumption or even for industrial purposes.

While the above activity of the thiobacilli can cause tremendous environmental harm, in controlled situations it can have a very beneficial role in mining. Many desirable metals exist in ores composed of highly insoluble sulfides and the concentration of the metal in the ore is so low that it is not economically feasible to extract it by conventional chemical methods. Under these conditions, microbial leaching, where a microbe is used to extract a desired chemical, is often useful. Leaching finds its greatest utility in the extraction of copper, but has also been employed to solubilize gold from ores. The ores attacked contain sulfur and Thiobacillus plays its role by using these reduced sufur compounds as electron donors. In the process the desired metal is released.

γ subgroup

Enteric bacteria

The most studied group of microorganisms is the Enterobacteriaceae. This intense analysis has led to the isolation of many different members, which in turn led to the naming of numerous distinct genera and species. Recent molecular analysis has shown that of many of these genera are actually very closely related, but they have not been renamed for practical reasons. Because of their high degree of similarity, identification of enteric isolates to specific species can be difficult. However, this is important in medical situations, since many of the Enterobacteriaceae are pathogens, and in water analysis, where enterics are used as a measure of bacteriological contamination.

The Enterobacteriaceae are a large group of gram-negative non-sporulating, short rods that are motile by peritrichous flagella or are non-motile. They have relatively simple nutritional requirements and are facultative anaerobes that ferment sugars to a number of acids under anaerobic conditions. Enterics are facultative anaerobes and are oxidase-negative, which distinguishes them from the otherwise similar Vibrio, Photobacterium and Pseudomonadaceae. The medical importance of many members of this family has resulted in intense study of the group. Because of their rapid growth rate, genetic tractability and simple nutritional requirements, the enterics (especially Escherichia coli and Salmonella enterica subspecies Typhimurium) have been the model systems for a large number of investigations into basic questions of biology.

E. coli is the type species of the group and the genus is found almost exclusively in the intestinal tract of humans and other warm-blooded animals, but they are not the dominant organisms in this habitat. They are part of normal flora in most cases and may even benefit the host by synthesizing vitamins K and B12. Escherichia and other facultative anaerobes in the gut also readily use up any oxygen, keeping the instestines anoxic.

Not all members of the Enterobacteriaceae are restricted to the intestines as their only habitat. Enterobacter aerogenes while found in the intestine, is also a common inhabitant of water and sewage. Proteus also exists in the environment and is a common saprophyte of decaying organic matter. The production of urease (an enzyme that degrades urea) is a distinctive trait of this organism and this trait probably enhances its ability to cause urinary tract infections. Proteus is also of note for its high degree of motility by flagella. When grown on a solid surface, the microbe rapidly spreads across the agar plate, forming a distinctive pattern of concentric rings. The rings are caused by differential motility in the mass of Proteus cells. Microbes near the edge of a colony are more motile than those in the center. They migrate a short distance away from the colony, settle down and begin to divide. When enough cells again build up, the Proteus at the edge again move away and create another concentric ring.

An important differentiating characteristic within the Enterobacteriaceae is the method used to ferment glucose. Mixed acid fermenters metabolize glucose anaerobically to lactic acid, succinic acid, acetic acid, formic acid, ethanol, CO_2, and H_2, but not to butanediol. The acids produced in this fermentation lower the pH of the medium less than 4.4. Equal amounts of CO_2 and H_2 are produced by the enzyme formic hydrogen lyase, which acts on formic acid.. Genera of Enterobacteriaceae that have this type of metabolism include Proteus, Citrobacter, Edwardsiella, Salmonella, Shigella, and Escherichia.

The other group, which includes Klebsiella, Serratia, and Enterobacter, employs butanediol fermentation where glucose is broken down into the products mentioned above plus several other neutral end products including butanediol and acetoin. Less net acid is produced because more neutral end products (i.e. ethanol, CO_2 and H_2) are formed, so the pH of the medium is less affected. Two simple tests have been developed to distinguish these two types of fermentations: the methyl red test and the Vogues-Proskauer test. Methyl red is a dye whose color changes as the pH changes, being red under acidic conditions and yellow when the pH rises above 6.0.

Microbes possessing a mixed acid fermentation pattern have a red color in the test while those producing butanediol are yellow. The Vogues-Proskauer test detects acetoin by oxidation with oxygen in the presence of KOH. The resulting product of this reaction, diacetyl, is a red color. A significant number of the Enterobacteriaceae are pathogens. Yersinia pestis causes bubonic plague, Salmonella species are known for diarrheal infections and typhoid fever and Shigella dysenteriae causes bacillary dysentery. Klebsiella pneumoniae can cause pneumonia in humans, but is best known to scientists for its ability to fix nitrogen. Erwinia species are pathogens of plants, causing various soft rots and are a significant cause of crop loss around the world. Many other members of the family are opportunistic pathogens of humans.

Unfortunately, many pathogens are transmitted through the water supply. Some of these disease-causing pests enter water from the feces of ill individuals and are then ingested and thereby transmitted to others. Diseases such as polio, typhoid, cholera, hepatitis, shigellosis, salmonellosis and others can spread in this manner. To assure a safe water supply, it is critical to monitor for the absence of these pathogens. However, it would be expensive and time consuming to check water supplies for all of them, and instead indicator organisms are used to assay for fecal contamination and coliforms are the standard indicator of biological pollution.

Coliforms are defined as non-spore forming, facultatively anaerobic, gram-negative rods, which ferment lactose to acid and gas within 48 hours at 35 °C. In practice, isolated coliforms are almost always Enterobacteriaceae from the genera Enterobacter, Klebsiella, Escherichia and lactose positive strains of Citrobacter. Because the sole natural habitat of E. coli and K. pneumoniae is the intestines of warm-blooded animals, these are good indicators pollution and are termed fecal coliforms. The EPA standards for safe water is based on their absence.

Vibrio and Photobacterium

Vibrio and Photobacterium are closely related bacteria, some of which have a distinct requirement for Na^+. Because Vibrio species can be pathogens, they were initially studied by clinical microbiologists, while Photobacterium species were noticed first for their bioluminescence and were the province of environmental microbiologists. These two groups of scientists have very different interests, and there was relatively little interaction between the two camps, as a result the general similarities of these two groups of organisms were largely ignored. Phylogenetic analysis has shown, however, that Vibrio and Photobacterium are closely related to one another and more distantly related to the enterics and the pseudomonads.

Vibrio species cluster phylogenetically with other Vibrio species and the genus Photobacterium. However, close examination by DNA-DNA analysis reveals that within the Vibrio there are several distinct groups. This is not surprising, since the criteria for being placed into the genus were easily met by many marine isolates (i.e. gram-negative short rods, oxidase-positive, ferment glucose to acid and have a requirement for sea salts).

Photobacterium isolates were first identified because of their bioluminescence, a phenomenon that has been observed in the oceans since antiquity. Interestingly, several Vibrio species are also bioluminescent. The microbial nature of bioluminescence was only understood in the last 100 years and has now been clearly associated with a number of Vibrio and Photobacterium species. The genus Photobacterium was originally identified by the great environmental microbiologist Beijerinck, with its only major criterion being the ability to produce light. As above, this led to many divergent microbes being lumped together in this genus. As has happened with many other genera, the application of molecular phylogeny is helping to make sense of the microbes and the genus has recently been reorganized with most of the members moved to other genera. Presently there are only three species: P. phosphoreum, P. leiognathi, and P. angustum.

Both Vibrio and Photobacterium are widely distributed in aquatic environments and they are some of the most common microorganisms cultured from the open ocean. Some species will infect various hosts including marine animals and humans and Vibrio infections often result in disease. However, photobacterial associations with higher eukaryotes often result in a symbiotic relationship. Some hosts have a light organ that becomes infected with a pure culture of a specific species of Photobacterium and a few Vibrio species are also capable of these symbiotic associations.

Pseudomonads

There are a large number of bacteria that fit the description of the pseudomonads and many were originally grouped together in the genus Pseudomonas. Studies of the phylogeny of these organisms soon made it clear that there were several distinct phylogenetic groups, and these have now been split off into separate genera. This section describes three common genera, Pseudomonas, Burkholderia and Ralstonia. The specific genus names will be used when describing unique traits of these microbes. When referring to general characteristics, we will use the term pseudomonads, but this term can be applied to a number of genera.

The pseudomonads are a large group of gram-negative, polarly flagellated rods that inhabit a wide variety of environments. All grow chemoheteroorganotrophically, relying on respiration for the catabolism of compounds.

Pseudomonads are usually motile and capable of growth in simple minimal medium at the expense of a large variety of low-molecular-weight organic compounds. Organic growth factors are typically not required.

Pseudomonads are ubiquitous in the environment and often constitute a substantial fraction of the microflora in any given area. They are present in soils, fresh and seawater and sewage. They can also be isolated from items present in laboratories, including distilled water and solutions of antiseptics. There are even reports of them growing in extraordinary sites such as oil spills, in clay suspended in kerosene and contaminated paint vats. Pseudomonads are also found in food industry wastes, flowers, fruits, vegetables, diseased plants and animals.

Saprophytic pseudomonads, those that are non-pathogenic and grow on decaying organic matter, are found everywhere, while pathogens are often associated with their hosts. Pseudomonads are also important agents of food spoilage, especially at low temperatures and are often the cause of slime formation on meats and some vegetables.

P. aeruginosa is an important pathogen of humans, being the major cause of nosocomial infections and the leading cause of death in cystic fibrosis patients. This microbe is particularly troubling because of its resistance to many antibiotics. Different pathovars of P. syringae cause a number of important diseases in plants including: bacterial speck (tomatoes), brown spot (bean) and halo blight (bean). Each of the interactions between a pathovar and a host plant are specific, much like the interaction between certain rhizobia and their host plants. The genomes of several of these pathovars have been sequenced and it will be interesting to compare them and determine what genes dictate host interaction and the presentation of disease symptoms. Many other Pseudomonas species are non-pathogenic. These species, along with other pseudomonads play an important role in the carbon and nitrogen cycles.

They also attack small, monomeric organic compounds and they are important for the mineralization of molecules liberated from lignin by wood-degrading fungi. Some Pseudomonas species are also capable of denitrification, a process by which NO3- is reduce to N2 and released into the atmosphere.

Burkholderia are capable of growing in very different habitats, including free in the soil, in commensal, mutualistic and pathogenic relationships with plants and as pathogens of animals. Burkholderia species that are plant pathogens can infect many different kinds of plants and cause various blights and rots. Other species develop intimate relationships with plants. B. tuberum and B. phymatom nodulate tropical legumes and fix nitrogen for their plant hosts, in a fashion similar to the rhizobia. B. mallei and B. pseudomallei that cause the diseases glanders and melioidosis, respectively. B. mallei was the first microbe to be developed into a biological weapon by Germany during World War I.

Some of the most versatile Burkholderia are a group closely related microbes called the Burkholderia cepacia complex. These microbes were initially classified as one species, but further analysis has shown that they are different enough to warrant separate identification. Some B. cepacia complex strains are pathogens of humans, especially those with underlying illness. They are an important cause of infection in cystic fibrosis patients and can also cause nosocomial infections. Once a cystic fibrosis patient is infected with B. cepacia, it is very difficult to rid a patient of the microbe, and it is can sometimes lead to serious illness and death. The pathogenesis of this microbe is still unclear.

While certain strains of B. cepacia are plant pathogens, others are important as biocontrol agents for important soil borne plant pathogens. It appears that B. cepacia, when growing in the rhizosphere of plants, inhibits pathogenic bacteria and fungi from damaging the plant. The most promising results have come by introducing Burkholderia species along with the planting material. B. cepacia strains have been able to control root disease in corn, rice, peas, sunflowers and radishes, greatly increasing plant health and yield. B. cepacia strains were found to be as effective as chemical pesticides in protecting the health of the plant.

Exceptional metabolic diversity is also found in B. cepacia strains as well as other Burkholderia and these microbes can utilize an impressively wide array of small organic molecules. For example, B. cepacia is able to use over 100 carbon sources including organic acids, alcohols, aromatics, and hydrocarbons. This large collection of potential carbon sources makes them important in the environment for the mineralization of organics. They have found great utility in the bioremediation of sites polluted with man-made organic chemicals and seem capable of readily adapting to degrade many pollutants. However, they are usually unable to degrade biopolymers and they have no significant role in anaerobic degradation.

Several genomes of Burkholderia species have been sequenced and contain an unaually complex genome for a bacteria. They contain 2-4 circular replicons of >500 Kb each. Genomes sizes vary widely from 4 Mb to 9 Mb and this accounts for the wide degree of capabilities of these microbes. Many of the traits described above are carried on plasmids that can be lost, thus explaining the observed instability of these phenotypes. Some species have an extensive array of insertion sequences, which may be important in genome rearrangements or regulation of gene expression.

Ralstonia solanacearum is an important plant pathogen that causes a lethal wilting disease in more than 200 different plants. The microbe enters plants from the rhizosphere, moving into the root. It then invades the xylem and from there spreads through the vascular system. Here it produces an extracellular slime that clogs the xylem, thus interfering with water transport throughout the plant. An array of virulence factors are necessary to accomplish this pathogenesis with the two most important known factors being plant cell wall-degrading enzymes and the extracellular polysaccharide slime. Another interesting Ralstonia species is the heavy metal resistant R. metallidurans. The microbe carries a number of plasmid borne genes for resistance to a wide array of metal ions including, zinc, mercury, cadmium, cobalt and nickel. There is great interest in understanding the mechanisms of this resistance and in using these microbes to decontaminate sites polluted by heavy metals.

SAR86

Molecular microbial ecology is beginning to uncover interesting properties of microbes in the environment that are still unculturable. One such microbe, named SAR86, was found to be very common in aquatic marine habitats.

δ Subgroup

Sulfate-reducing bacteria

Desulfovibrio was the first member of the group to be isolated, by Beijerinck in 1895, but many phylogenetically diverse species capable of dissimulatory sulfate reduction have been isolated since. All of them perform these reactions under anoxic conditions. Many sulfate-reducing bacteria are members of the d-proteobacteria, but have significant phylogenetic diversity. Despite this diversity, analysis of their 16S rRNA has revealed that those in the d-proteobacteria are more related to one another than to other bacteria.

Sulfate-reducing bacteria fall into over 20 separate genera and these can be classified by the types of substrates that are utilized. A convenient division is by the ability to utilize acetate as a source of electrons. Group I sulfate reducers, such as Desulfovibrio, Desulfobacula and Desulfomicrobium are not capable of utilizing acetate. In fact these species only partially oxidize other organic substrates to acetate and excrete it into the medium. Those species in Group II can utilize acetate and other fatty acids, oxidizing them completely, and include Desulfosarcina, Desulfobacterium and Desulfobacter.

A third group of sulfur-reducing organisms are unable to utilize sulfate, but can reduce sulfur to sulfide. These include genera such as Desulfuromonas and Desulfurella. They utilize substrates such as acetate or ethanol and couple this to the reduction of sulfur or other electrons acceptors such as thiosulfate, sulfite or dimethyl sulfoxide. This ability is not unique to these bacteria, but is widespread among chemoheteroorganotrophic bacteria. For example, Salmonella, Campylobacter, and Proteus are all capable of this type of reduction.

In contrast to these chemoheteroorganotrophs, the sulfur reducers are anaerobes and only use sulfur compounds as their terminal electron acceptors. Interestingly, sulfur reducers often form associations with certain H_2S-producing photosynthetic bacteria such as green sulfur bacteria. In this situation, the H_2S produced by the sulfur reducers is used as a source of electrons by the green sulfur bacteria, which reduce it to sulfur. The sulfur then serves as a terminal electron acceptor for the sulfur reducers to form H_2S, thus completing a very abbreviated sulfur cycle.

Sulfate reducers have a wide range of cellular morphologies, including rods, vibrios, ovals, spheres and even tear-dropped or onion shaped cells. Some are motile: others are not. Most sulfate-reducing bacteria are mesophilic, but a few thermophiles are known. Mesophilic species appear to be the most widespread collection of sulfate reducers in the environment. The major habitat appears to be the aquatic part of waters that have turned anoxic and sulfate reduction by these species is a major part of the sulfur cycle in these areas. A great variety of species have been isolated from marine sediments where sulfate is plentiful. However, they are also found in freshwater environments such as lakes, ponds, rice paddies and anaerobic sewage digesters.

Sulfate reducers can spread from anaerobic sediments into oil refineries and industrial sites where they can cause oil souring (an increase in the concentration of sulfide) and corrosion, both significant problems in the oil industry. Strains present in fresh water habitats are often inhibited by salt water, but marine strains may require NaCl and Mg^{2+} in order to grow. Many sulfate reducers have rapid growth rates when H_2 serves as electron donor. When there are sufficient concentrations of sulfate present in an environment, they are very efficient scavengers of H2 and out-compete methanogenic bacteria for the substrate, thus dominating the specific niche.

Microorganisms of this group are capable of dissimulatory sulfate reduction, a process where organic compounds or hydrogen are oxidized, with sulfate or sulfur serving as the terminal electron acceptor in catabolism. In this process, the sulfur compounds are reduced to hydrogen sulfide. This is in contrast to assimilatory sulfate reduction, an energy-requiring process where the goal is to use the sulfur for biosynthetic processes.

A wide number of electron donors are used for sulfate reduction including H_2, alcohols, fatty acids, other organic acids, some amino acids, a few sugars and some aromatic compounds. Certain species are capable of chemoautolithotrophic growth using H2 as electron donor and CO_2 as a source of carbon. Growth on aromatic compounds that have been found to be pollutants has sparked interest in understanding these microbes for their bioremediation potential. Many species of sulfate reducers are also capable of utilizing sulfur, nitrate and other sulfur compounds as electron acceptors. Also, in the absence of any suitable electron acceptor, several of species can also grow by fermentation, with pyruvate being the most common fermentable substrate. It is converted to acetate, CO_2 and H_2.

For many years sulfate reducers were thought to be strict anaerobes exclusively, but recent experimentation has shown that certain isolates are quite tolerant to oxygen. These are often obtained from microbial mats where cyanobacteria generate oxygen during photosynthesis. It seems as though sulfate reducers in these habitats have developed mechanisms to tolerate oxygen evolving from the cyanobacteria. However, these mechanisms appear to be only protective and the microbes are not able to grow with oxygen as a terminal electron acceptor.

ε Subclass

Campylobacter

In 1889 Theodore Escherich was the first to describe this genus from an infant who died from gastrointestinal disease. In 1913 McFadyean and Stockman first isolated the microbe from the fetus of an aborted lamb. Analysis soon made it clear that these pathogens were different than other species and they were assigned to a new genus named Campylobacter. The campylobacteria are a large group of gram-negative bacteria that form both commensal and pathogenic associations with animals.

The 15 known Campylobacter species have a number of common traits: optimal growth temperatures between 30-42 °C, non-spore-forming, sensitive to 3% or more NaCl and reduction of fumarate to succinate. Most species are oxidase-positive and indole-negative. Microscopic observation reveals bacterial cells that are slender, helical or curved rods of 0.2-0.8 μm wide and 0.5-5.0 μm long.

sometimes being found in chains. When put under stress, such as exposure to atmospheric oxygen, the rods form coccoid shapes. Most strains are motile by a single polar flagella and have a characteristic corkscrew, darting motility.

Campylobacter species colonize the digestive tracts and urogenital tracts of a wide range of animals. An interesting example is C. jejuni, which lives as a commensal organism in the cecum, of birds (temperature 42 °C). It is frequently found in poultry and contaminates processed chicken. When present in the human digestive tract at 37 °C, it turns pathogenic and causes diarrhea. Several campylobacter species colonize the oral cavity including C. concisus, C. curvus and C. showae, where they are part of the normal flora. The microaerophillic nature of these organisms precludes their growth in other habitats outside of their hosts, however they are found in material that has been contaminated with feces of infected animals.

All campylobacters are microaerophiles, growing best at 5-10% oxygen and 3-5% CO_2. Some are even capable of growing in the absence of oxygen using an alternative terminal electron acceptor, but all strains grow using a respiratory chain. The microbes have fastidious growth requirements and only grow on complex medium. Their strict growth requirements and microaerophilic oxygen relationship is somewhat surprising since they have to survive the harsh conditions of the digestive system in order to cause illness in the host. It is also surprising that they often survive food processing procedures. Whether they have mechanisms that protect then under these conditions is unknown.

Gastroenteritis caused by C. jejuni and C. coli is probably the most common form of food borne illness worldwide. In industrialized countries these organisms cause an acute watery diarrheal illness that lasts for several days. In the immunocompromised, the organisms can spread systemically and cause serious illness. Due to their importance in causing illness in humans, isolation and detection of campylobacter is of great interest. Because of their microaerophilic nature, these organisms can be difficult to grow and specialized incubators are necessary. This may result in an underreporting of the incidence of this illness. However, PCR detection methods have been developed for Campylobacter and these should help speed diagnosis. PCR does have a number of challenges to overcome, however. Many foods have substances that inhibition good PCR amplification and must be removed, adding extra steps to the analysis. Also, damaged Campylobacter cells are still detectable by PCR, but scientists believe that these are not relevant as a health hazard.

High-GC gram-positive bacteria

Gram-positive bacteria fall into two major phylogenetic divisions, "low-GC" and "high-GC." GC content is a abbreviation for the percentage of GC base pairs in an organisms DNA. Those that have a low GC content, have more AT base pairs in their DNA. GC content is a crude measure of the relatedness of microorganisms, but is still useful for differentiating large phylogenetic divisions. In this section we describe some of the better-known species and their importance. Again, these descriptions of the various groups of gram-positive bacteria are by no means exhaustive; the goal is to give the student an appreciation of the types of microbes that are present.

Low GC gram-positive bacteria

The staphylococci have spherical cells often found in groups resembling clusters of grapes. Bacteria of this genus were originally grouped with other spherical microorganisms, especially of the genus Micrococcus, since these two genera often shared similar habitats. However, physiological studies and phylogenetic analysis have shown that these two genera are very different from one another.

They are common parasites of animals and some strains cause serious disease. Their major habitats seem to be on skin, skin glands and mucous membranes of mammals and birds. However, staphylococci have also been isolated from oil contaminated tropical soil, and in this habitat they were found to be growing on naphthalene. Staphylococci are facultative anaerobes capable of metabolizing a number of different sugars. Under anaerobic conditions the major end product is lactic acid, but acetate and a small amount of pyruvate are also formed. Catabolism of sugars is by the Emden-Meyerhoff-Parnas pathway to pyruvate. Respiration occurs through the typical enzymes and pathways when oxygen is used as a terminal electron acceptor. A curious observation is their ability to reduce nitrate to nitrite, but only under conditions where some oxygen is available. It is not clear what the significance of nitrate reduction has for the organism, but it cannot use it as a sole terminal electron acceptor under the conditions tested. Staphylococci are fastidious, requiring some amino acids and vitamins to be able to grow on minimal medium and given their habitat, this is not surprising.

Mycoplasma

Mycoplasmas are distinguished by their minute size and lack of a cell wall. The total lack of a cell wall explains many of the unique properties of these organisms, including their great sensitivity to detergents and osmotic shock and their resistance to penicillin and other cell-wall antibiotics. The species that can be grown on agar tend to be easy to identify by their unusual fried-egg shaped colonies. There are a number of different genera collectively referred to by the trivial term mycoplasmas, such as Mycoplasma,

Ureaplasma, Spiroplasma, Anaeroplasma, Phytoplasma and several others. Molecular phylogeny places the mycoplasmas among the gram-positive bacteria of low G+C content. It is likely that they were originally gram-positive bacteria and through constant association with a host went through degenerate evolution. Many abilities were lost in this process, including cell wall synthesis and biosynthetic capabilities.

The cell morphology of mycoplasmas is often amorphous, but predominately spherical. However, some species can have more distinctive shapes, such as filaments of various length and helical and branching forms. Most mycoplasmas are non-motile although a few species, including the human pathogen M. pneumoniae, exhibit a poorly understood type of gliding motility. Motile species can be chemotactic, but the chemotactic systems are likely unique, since no apparent homology to known chemotaxis systems is evident in their genomes.

Cyanobacteria

Cyanobacteria are some of the only prokaryotic microorganisms capable of oxygenic photosynthesis (Prochloroaceae species are the others). They form a tight phylogenetic group and their reaction centers are highly conserved. However, the light-harvesting complexes are diverse, having different structures, proteins and pigments. Cyanobacteria are also capable of anaerobic metabolism and can perform anoxic photosynthesis using reduced electron donors.

The morphological diversity of the cyanobacteria is considerable. Cyanobacteria are divided into five morphological groups: unicellular, dividing by binary fission; unicellular, dividing by multiple fission; filamentous, containing differentiated cells such as heterocysts; filamentous, with no differentiated cells; and branching, filamentous forms. Some of these form multicellular communities that are often held together by sheaths or envelopes produced by the organisms. Cyanobacteria range in size from that typical for bacteria (0.5-1 μm in diameter) to giants that are 60 μm in diameter. The cell wall structure of cyanobacteria is gram-negative and their cell walls contain peptidoglycan.

Spirochetes and Planctomyces

Spirochetes are defined by their unique morphology and mode of movement. Spirochetes cluster together phylogentically into a large order that is distantly related to other organisms. In contrast to many other microorganisms the cellular morphology of these microbes is a good marker for their phylogeny. They can be divided into three distinct families, the Spirochaetaceae consist of the genera Borrelia, Brevinema, Cristispira, Spirochaeta, Spironema, and Treponema. The second family is the Sperpulinaceae and contains the genus Brachyspira and the third family is the Leptospiraceae consiting of the species Leptonema and Leptospira.

Despite their overall cell wall structure being that of gram-negative bacteria, spirochetes have a unique cell morphology. The outer member is typical of gram-negative bacteria, but the arrangement of structures inside this membrane is unique to the spirochetes. Inside of the outer membrane is a helical cell body containing the peptidoglycan-cell membrane complex, the cytoplasm and the nuclear region. The helical body wraps around a central axis that is filled by proteinaceous filaments, which resemble flagella and are called axial filaments or endoflagella. In most spirochetes the two sets of endoflagella are inserted into opposite poles of the helical cell and they overlap in the middle.

Spirochetes are common in a wide range of aqueous environments: both marine and freshwater, high and low salt, and low to high temperatures. In general, free-living spirochetes tend to be found in environments rich in decaying plant material, where they probably ferment sugars released by the action of other microbes. There is some evidence that they even form cooperative arrangements with cellulolytic bacteria. Spirochetes are not apparently widely distributed in the deep sea, though they have been successfully isolated from some samples. Most are mesophiles, but a few species are able to grow at thermophilic temperatures. For example, Spirochaeta thermophila and Spirochaeta caldaria, both from thermal springs, have optimum growth temperatures of 67 and 50 °C, respectively.

Spirochetes have a limited metabolism and can only ferment a few types of organic molecules. They ferment carbohydrates to acetate, ethanol, CO_2, and H_2 as major end products. All spirochetes so far examined use the Embden-Meyerhoff-Parnas pathway to take glucose to pyruvate. Under anaerobic conditions this is converted to acetate and ethanol using common fermentative pathways. Interestingly, the facultative anaerobes in the group use both oxidative phosphorylation and substrate level phosphorylation in the presence of air and seem to be dependent on at least some fermentation.

Planctomyces, Piurella, Gemmata and Isosphaera form a phylogenetically related group of microorganisms that have many unusual properties. They are the only bacteria, other than the confusing case of the Chlamydia, whose cells walls appear to lack peptidoglycan. Cells of this group divide by budding and their cell surface contains many circular structures of unknown significance. Some members of the group produce long appendages, called stalks, and new cells are motile, developing stalks as they mature. Despite these similarities, there is not an obvious phylogenetic relationship to the prosthecate bacteria in the a proteobacteria.

Cells of this group can be pigmented (light rose, bright red, or yellow to ochre) or non-pigmented. An example species is Planctomyces limnophilus, which is ovoid, has a diameter of 1.5 μm and forms red pigmented colonies. It grows slowly at temperatures between 17-39°C and takes at least a week to form colonies. Stalks of the organism are very thin and cannot be seen by light microscopy. These stalks appear to be made of thin fibers twisted into a bundle that emanates from one pole of the ovoid cell. Cells multiply by budding and new cells are motile and stalkless, but eventually grow stalks as part of a maturation process similar to that seen for Caulobacter.

These microbes are common inhabitants of freshwater lakes, marine habitats and salt ponds, but most have been difficult to isolate in pure culture. For example, three of the four species in Planctomyces have only been observed in lake water and never isolated. Single-cell forms are often found attached to other bacteria by their stalks and might actually be living off substances produced by the bound microbe. These bacteria are at highest populations in the summer to late fall particularly in eutrophic lakes (lakes high in organic content). One of their most striking features is the formation of rosettes, but the functional significance of these structures is unclear.

8

Viral Pathogens

Viruses have a large impact on the human condition, causing everything from mild debilitation to severe disease and sometimes death. This coverage is by no means comprehensive. The criteria for picking viruses were based on the importance of the virus to human health, the amount of information known about the virus and the usefulness of the virus as a learning example.

Rhinovirus

Rhinoviruses cause the common cold, which probably causes infectious disease. Colds are economically a bane to most employers, but a boon to those companies hawking the latest remedy. Cold symptoms usually begin two to three days after infection and often include nasal discharge and headache among others. Most symptoms experienced during a cold are actually the bodys response to the viral invasion. Infection of the nasal cavity causes the recruitment of macrophage and neutrophils to the site of infection. These in turn send out lymphokines and cytokines invoking an immune response in the area. These chemicals lead to the symptoms of the common cold by causing inflammation of the nasal membranes, leakage of proteins and fluid from capillaries and lymph vessels and the increased production of mucus.

Diagnosis of colds is usually done by observation of symptoms, with very few people seeking medical attention. Only symptomatic treatment is available for uncomplicated cases of the common cold. Due to the large amount of basic research being done, scientists know more about the rhinovirus than almost any other virus. This knowledge base is beginning to bear fruit with the possible introduction of the first effective antiviral drugs against the common cold.

Many people extol the virtues of taking large doses of vitamin C to help prevent or shorten the duration of a cold. To date, no evidence has been presented to show that vitamin C has any benefit in preventing or shortening the duration of a cold or in relieving cold symptoms. It appears the benefit that many people feel from taking these remedies has more to do with their minds than with any curative effect.

The successful development of a vaccine to prevent the common cold is highly unlikely due to the number of viruses that can cause cold symptoms. There are over 110 different distinct rhinovirus types alone and several other virus families have been implicated in upper respiratory tract infections as well. As our immune systems are exposed to cold viruses, we develop immunity, but this immunity is likely only effective against a few types of cold viruses. The RNA genome of the rhinoviruses also mutates rapidly, creating new variants that then circumvent any immunity that may have built up.

Rhinovirus is part of the Picornaviridae family ("Pico" meaning small and "RNA" signifying that these are RNA viruses). The rhinoviral genome is composed of a single strand of positive-sense RNA (meaning it can be translated directly by the ribosome) enclosed in a small tetrahedral capsid. The single-stranded RNA is translated into a large polyprotein that is subsequently digested into about 10 proteins.

The majority of rhinoviruses find their host by attaching to the Icam receptor and entering the endosome. The drop in pH of the endosome causes uncoating of the virus and movement of the single-stranded RNA into the cytoplasm. The exact molecular events of this interaction are unknown, but likely resemble those proposed for poliovirus the best studied model system. Poliovirus enters the cell by having the viral capsid punch a hole in the cell membrane. Binding of receptor causes a conformational shift in the VP1 protein, a capsid protein that is near each vertex. This conformational shift causes VP1 to create a pore in the membrane. Once this pore is created, the viral RNA then moves through this channel from the capsid to the cytoplasm. The intact (+) single-stranded RNA looks enough like an mRNA to fool the ribosome into translating it into the polyprotein precursor. The polyprotein is initially digested into three pieces, P1, P2 and P3, some of which are then further processed.

Rhinovirus replication is independent of the host, so the rhinovirus has to code for its own replicase, since the hosts machinery is not going to recognize RNA as a template for polymerization. Viral RNA replication takes place on the surface of membrane vesicles and the proteins that participate in this process are transported there. Interestingly, replication begins with a viral priming protein, Vpg that is covalently attached to the end of the RNA genome. Replication proteins copy the (+) single-stranded RNA to make a (-) single-stranded RNA strand. The negative strand is then replicated to form further (+) strands. Some of these lose their attached Vpg and migrate back to the ribosome to serve as templates for translation. After several rounds of amplification, (+) single-stranded RNA that still retains its Vpg assembles with other structural proteins to form progeny virus. Progeny virus is then released by lysis of the cell.

Interestingly, the virus needs much more P1 proteins (viral capsids) than P2 or P3, but they are made in equal amounts. Despite this wasteful behavior, the virus successfully replicates. In a host cell this kind of wastefulness would likely be strongly selected against, but viruses live by different rules. It is obviously not too important for the virus to reach optimum efficiency and it may be constrained by its chosen lifestyle, since it only has one reading frame that can be translated. Inefficiency is a common theme in eukaryotic viruses and they often leave a cell littered with unused viral parts and create large numbers of defective viral particles (assembled viruses that for some reason are not infectious). In many cases, the defective particles outnumber correct viruses. The only thing that seems to be critical is that enough viruses get created so that they can infect another host and continue the spread of the pathogen.

Adenovirus

The adenoviruses infect the mucosal linings of the respiratory tract, intestines and urinary tract. The signs and symptoms of the diseases they cause vary depending upon the area of the body infected. Diseases of the respiratory tract are the most common outcome of an adenoviral infection. Sufferers experience standard cold symptoms and swollen glands. In children under three, infections of the lower respiratory tract are possible, causing bronchitis, croup and viral pneumonia. Infections of the eyes can cause discharge, tearing, sore throat and itching eyes. Finally, gastroenteritis can be caused by adenovirus resulting in watery diarrhea, fever, vomiting, headache and abdominal cramps.

Adenovirus infections occur much more frequently in children than adults and the virus causes 3 - 5% of all acute respiratory infections. The disease is highly contagious and symptoms appear in 2-12 days after infection and last a few days to a week. Diagnosis is based on the symptoms presented, but the diseases caused by adenovirus often resemble bacterial infections. Treatment with antibiotics has no effect and there is no known treatment for adenoviral infections. Almost all cases are self-limiting and need no intervention. The biggest worry is dehydration in young children if vomiting and/or diarrhea are present.

Infection with the virus induces immunity to that specific type of adenovirus. Since there are a limited number of types, it is possible to develop immunity to most of them by the time one reaches adulthood and this may explain why these infections are typically found in children. A live, attenuated adenovirus vaccine is available, but its use is restricted to military recruits.

The genome is a single copy of a linear double-stranded DNA molecule. It is 36 kbp long and contains a covalently linked terminal protein that promotes efficient transcription and also plays a role in replication. The origins of replication are at the ends of the genome.

The receptor for the virus is different for the different subtypes of adenovirus, but they all attach by a reaction between the host receptor and the viral fiber protein. Endocytosis of the viral particle occurs when a penton base interacts with integrin, a second cell receptor. Adenoviruses then have the problem of getting their genome to the nucleus for replication. The first barrier is the membrane in the endosome. Soon after the capsid enters the endosome, the fibers fall off. The drop in pH of the endosome then causes the release of the penton bases on that capsid and their release causes lysis of the endosome. The capsid is now devoid of most of its components except viral DNA, core proteins and hexon proteins. It migrates to the nucleus and docks into the nuclear pore complex, where the DNA is delivered into the nucleus.

The adenovirus replication cycle is a good example of sequential gene expression. There are several different sets of transcripts and only the first, EIA, is expressed without viral transcription factors. Each subsequent set of transcripts is dependent upon the production of a transcription factor provided from the previously expressed set of genes. In this way, the virus controls the timing of each transcripts expression as shown in the animation below. This kind of sequential expression is common in all types of viruses, especially those that have a large number of genes involved in their replication. Early genes function to create copies of the viral genome, while later genes are involved in virion assembly.

Inside the nucleus, capsids are assembled from the hexons, pentons, fibers and core proteins and these are then combined with viral genomes to form non-infectious virions. The virus becomes infectious by the action of the viral protease that cleaves several precursor proteins within the viral core into their mature forms. Similar to the case of rhinovirus, progeny virions are released upon destruction of the host cell.

Influenza Virus

There are three types of influenza virus (A, B and C), but C does not cause classic flu disease and will not be discussed further. Influenza A is organized into several types based upon serological typing of the major outer envelope proteins of the virus, hemagglutinin (HA) and neuraminidase (NA). Influenza B contains only one recognized serological type and causes a less severe disease than influenza A.

Influenza is common, causing widespread epidemic respiratory illness during the fall and winter in temperate climates. Prevalence is highest in school-age children. After infection, the virus incubates for 48 hours, replicating in the respiratory tract. In mild cases, when the infected person is partially immune, symptoms of the common cold may be observed, and then the illness subsides. In unprotected individuals, chills and fever begin suddenly, accompanied by generalized aches and pains. Later, lower respiratory illness becomes dominant accompanied by a persistent cough. After 2 to 3 days, acute symptoms rapidly subside and fever ends. Rarely, pulmonary congestion and edema may end with death in as little as 48 hours after onset. Such severe diseases most likely occur during pandemics caused by a new influenza A serotype and in persons with underlying cardiac or pulmonary diseases.

Severe aches, malaise and fever differentiate influenza from the common cold. The incidence of flu in the community can also influence the diagnosis. In rare cases, or at the outbreak of flu season, a specific diagnosis can be done by isolating virus and demonstrating infected cells in secretions. Alternatively, there are immunological and molecular tests for the presence of virus. The immunological tests use antibodies against the HA and NA proteins that then classify influenza into several different isolates.

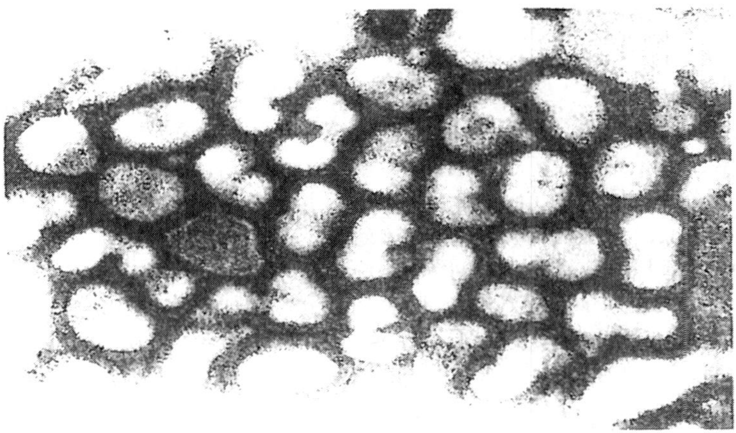

An electron micrograph of the influenza virus

There are 15 separate immunological H types known, but only three subtypes of HA (H1, H2, H3) and two of NA (N1, N2) circulate in the human population. Common strains that currently circulate in the United States are H1N1 and H3N2. Molecular tests to detect influenza involve reverse transcriptase and PCR amplification using probes against the influenza genome. These tests provide public health organizations with information on what strains of flu are present in the community. Monitoring flu strains is useful for tracking epidemics and preparing vaccines.

Recently, antiviral drugs against influenza have begun to appear. Amantadine and rimantadine are effective against influenza A, but not influenza B. These drugs inhibit uncoating of the virus once inside the cell. Ribavirin is a synthetic nucleoside and inhibits viral replication by being incorporated into the RNA. It has shown promise in reducing fever and shortening the duration of both A and B influenza. NA is required for the release of virus from infected cells and the neuraminidase inhibitor drugs cause new virus to stick to the cell, preventing infection of other cells. All these antiviral drugs must be administered early in infection to have their beneficial effect.

Recovery from the flu creates immunity to that particular strain of influenza, but the frequent genetic variation of the virus prevents life-long immunity. Vaccines that include prevalent strains circulating in the population reduce the incidence and severity of infection, if the HA and NA of the virus used for immunization match the infecting strain. Current vaccine consists of 3 strains, influenza A (H1N1) influenza A (H3N2) and influenza B.

A new nasal vaccine (coined FluMist) is under development has shown promise, being 93% effective at preventing illness in one study; it even shows protection against flu strains that it was not specifically designed to stop. This vaccine uses live attenuated virus, in contrast to the traditional injected vaccine that uses dead virus. It is now approved for use in the United States

On the outside surface of the influenza virus is a lipid bilayer with HA, NA and M2 proteins inserted into it. Inside the bilayer are eight separate, linear RNA segments that make up the viral genome.

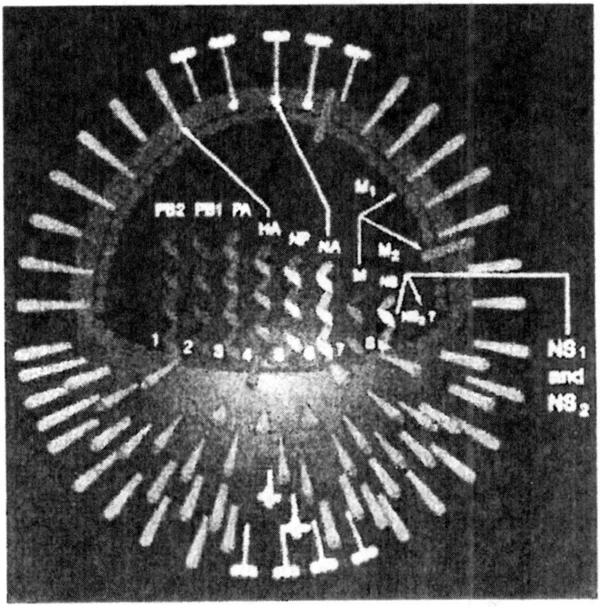

A representation of the flu virus

The figure shows the outer shell of the flu virus and a cutaway revealing the 8 RNA pieces that compromise the genome of the virus. The outer shell is composes of lipids obtained from the last host cell. This is decorated with hemagglutinin and neuraminidase. H is necessary for entrance into cells, while N is needed for release from cells. NP is the viral polymerase. This copies the RNA genome into mRNA for protein synthesis and later in the life cycle makes copies of each RNA for new viral particles. NP is very error prone and creates many mutation in the viral genome. HA and NA therefore change rapidly, and eventually change enough that our immune system no longer recognizes them. Image taken from Herlocher

The genome of the virus is composed of eight (-) single-stranded RNAs (these (-) strands cannot be translated into protein) with each segment being complementary to one mRNA. Six of the eight mRNAs code for single proteins, while the remaining two code for two proteins by differential splicing of the RNA. Each mRNA segment is associated with multiple copies of the nucleocapsid protein (NP) and an RNA polymerase (made from the viral proteins PB1, PB2 and PA).

The HA on the outer membrane of the virus binds to any one of the numerous sialic acid-containing proteins or lipids on the membrane of the cell. The virus is taken in by receptor-mediated endocytosis. A pH drop inside the endosome causes a conformational change in the HA protein, which then fuses with the endosome membrane. This results in the release of the genome segments into the cell. HA is critical to the entry of the virus into the cytoplasm and one would think that mutations in this gene would certainly be detrimental to the virus. However, this protein is a major target for the immune system, and the virus has shown the ability to change the HA sequence without affecting its function.

Replication and Translation

Influenza virus has two problems to overcome if it is to replicate. First, the genomic RNAs of the virus are not mRNA and cannot be translated by the ribosome. Each influenza virus RNA must, therefore, first create a complementary mRNA strand before protein can by synthesized. The host cell lacks a protein capable of doing this, so the virus needs a replicase activity to be present before expression of its own genome. Influenza solves this by carrying its own replicase within each virion.

Immediately after entering the nucleus of the cell, the replicase goes to work making copies of the RNAs to create mRNA.

It makes sense that a DNA virus might replicate in the nucleus so that it can borrow host replication machinery, but why would this RNA virus do so? It is in response to a second problem. The copied (+) RNA strands need to look like mRNA; they need 5' caps and polyadenylated tails. These 5' caps are readily available in the nucleus, and the replicase snatches caps from cellular mRNA during synthesis of the (+) strand. Polyadenylation is added by the replicase after copying the strand. The finished viral (+) RNA strand now looks like an mRNA to the cell and is dutifully translated after transport to the ribosome.

Viral membrane proteins have signals similar to those of host membrane proteins. This is yet another example of a virus taking advantage of host traits. The virus attaches a short leader peptide to viral proteins that it wants to migrate to certain places. Depending upon the signal sequence the viral protein can be directed to the endoplasmic reticulum, the Golgi apparatus or the nucleus. During this migration, the viral protein can take advantage of all the host machinery for membrane protein maturation. HA and NA have the appropriate signals, and after translation, they wind their way through the Golgi apparatus, undergoing glycosylation, and eventually end up in the host cell membrane.

All other mRNAs are translated in the cytoplasm. mRNA is responsible for the replication of the genomes. Early in infection, the replicase uses the (-) strand viral RNAs to make mRNA. The shift to packaging RNA into viral particles is controlled by protein M1. As mRNA is translated, newly made M1 is transported back to the nucleus. As the concentration of M1 protein increases, it binds to newly synthesized (-) strand viral RNA and causes viral replication to end. M1 together with NS2 induce export of progeny viral nucleocapsids (NP, RNA polymerase plus the viral RNA) to the cellular membrane.

The viral nucleocapsids converge in areas of the cytoplasm adjacent to regions of the membrane where HA, NA and M2 are accumulating. Assembly of the viral particle is complete when the membrane containing HA, NA and M2, together with the eight viral RNAs, buds from the cell. The assembly of influenza virus is especially interesting since it has to place eight separate RNA genomes into each head to make an infective particle. It appears that this is accomplished by short unique nucleotide sequences on the 5' end of each RNA. By analogy to other viruses, each of these segments might cause a base-pairing with another of the RNAs, eventually creating a complex containing all eight.

The details of such a complex formation and its subsequent packaging remain unknown. Despite such a mechanism (or, perhaps, because of the complexity of it), influenza creates large numbers of defective virions lacking one or more of the essential RNA strands. This again emphasizes that the virus is willing to waste the host's energy with the only goal being the successful infection of a future host. As long as the virus is successful in this, it can tolerate large numbers of errors.

If two different influenza viruses happen to infect one cell, both sets of viral genomes will replicate in the nucleus and be transported to the membrane. Upon packaging, there will be extensive mixing of the viral RNAs causing the creation of potentially novel flu strains. This process is especially common in pigs that are capable of picking up many different strains of flu virus. With the right combination, these jumbled viruses can dramatically alter their antigenic properties, making them capable of infecting large numbers of hosts. If the strain is especially virulent, it can cause worldwide pandemics that can kill millions of people.

Human Immunodeficiency virus (AIDS virus)

Human Immunodeficiency virus (HIV), the cause of acquired immunodeficiency syndrome (AIDS), is a cause of a devastating pandemic with about 34 million people infected with the virus as of 2000. More people died from AIDS in 1999 (over 2.6 million) than ever before. In the African continent, infection rates have risen to such levels that the disease is threatening to tear apart the social fabric of many countries. In southern Africa, where the life expectancy had risen to nearly 60 years, it is expected to be just 45 for a child born in 2005.

The disease AIDS is caused by infection with HIV, one of a large family of retroviruses that infect mammals. They get their name because of their ability to transcribe RNA into DNA as part of their replication cycle, and this is the reverse of the transcription observed normally in cells. HIV cannot attack cells on the skin or epithelium and must have access to the bloodstream to spread from one individual to another. This limits transmission to blood-to-blood contact, which occurs during behaviors that damage blood barriers.

After entry into the bloodstream, the virus attaches to cells containing the CD4 receptor on their surface. These are primarily cells involved in the immune system (T cells, macrophages, monocytes and some dendric cells). Most importantly, HIV attacks the regulators of immune function, T helper cells. Destruction of these cells is particularly debilitating, because they normally direct the rest of the immune system against foreign invaders and cancer cells. The loss of these cells virtually eliminates the cell-mediated arm of the immune system. This allows the invasion of numerous pathogens as well as the proliferation of rare cancers that normally would be handled by the immune system of a healthy individual.

For the first 3-8 weeks, HIV replicates in its host and releases large numbers of virions into the bloodstream that then attack other cells. This builds up to a point that the immune system begins to fight back and symptoms of the disease begin to appear. Eventually, a period of viral latency begins, lasting an average of 10 years. During this time, the virus inserts into the host cell's genome and does not replicate. Latency can vary widely, but in most individuals, a rapid drop in CD4+ T cells eventually begins. This is accompanied by a variety of symptoms, including fever, weight loss, pain and especially swollen lymph nodes.

If the level of CD4+ T cells drops low enough, the patient is susceptible to the debilitating opportunistic illnesses characteristic of the disease. AIDS is the disease manifestation of HIV infection. The types of secondary illnesses include problems with various organs, bacterial, viral and yeast infections, intestinal parasites and rare cancers. Some of the more serious maladies are tuberculosis, Pneumocystis carinii pneumonia and Karposi sarcoma, often resulting in the death of the patient. The average life expectancy for people who have progressed to AIDS is two years.

Diagnosis of HIV infection is normally done with a blood test (ELISA) for antibodies to the virus. The test has a low rate of false positives, so an HIV-positive diagnosis is usually confirmed by a Western blot that detects the presence of HIV, by reacting with antibodies the body raises against HIV proteins. Treatment of HIV infection consists controlling replication of the virus and managing the opportunistic infections that arise. Recent work has lead to the development of an arsenal of antiviral drugs against HIV that attack two general targets, reverse transcriptase and the HIV protease. Both of these proteins are pivotal enzymes in the viral life cycle, to which humans have no analogous functions. This fact limits the side effects of the drugs.

Drugs that inhibit reverse transcriptase are of two types, those that mimic nucleosides and those that do not.

Nucleoside analogs affect viral replication by fooling reverse transcriptase into inserting incorrect bases. At some frequency, these substitutions damage critical viral genes and kill the virus. Other inhibitors, which are not nucleoside analogs, inhibit reverse transcriptase directly, which prevents replication of the RNA. Finally, protease inhibitors inactivate the HIV protease that is necessary for processing of the translated viral protein precursor to its functional parts.

RNA viruses such as HIV mutate rapidly and viruses resistant to these drugs are known. Combination therapy that uses three or more of the drugs together greatly decreases the likelihood that a resistant strain will arise and has improved the potency of these drugs. High mutation rates and variation due to recombination can even change the v iral population within an individual. Early in infection, a person will appear to be infected with a single variant of HIV, but once HIV infection becomes established, the virus continually undergoes changes and many variants may arise in just one individual. These pseudo-species allow HIV to potentially avoid the immune system.

The second phase of treatment deals with the numerous afflictions of an immunocompromised individual. While this has been rather successful, the treatment can run into thousands of dollars a year and some of the side effects of the drugs can be debilitating. Carrying the burden of these health care costs is an impossible task for most developing nations, and help from the industrialized world is needed to lessen the human catastrophe that is brewing in these countries. Fortunately, the world has begun to respond and is providing funding to fight the AIDS epidemic.

There is no known cure for HIV nor is one very likely. Infection with the virus almost always results in death of the individual. The surest way to prevent HIV infection is to avoid contact with the virus. HIV is not easily transmissible and the avoidance of high-risk behavior eliminates the possibility of contracting the disease. While this seems like a simple thing to do, changing behavior can be difficult, even when ignoring this advice can carry the possibility of a death sentence.

Development of a vaccine against HIV has been problematic. This is due to the nature of the virus and a lack of information about how our body's immune system responds to it. The best way to design an effective vaccine is to know which aspect of the immune response protects against the pathogen and then create a vaccine that stimulates that response, but these have not been precisely identified for HIV. Perhaps the most difficult challenge in making a vaccine is reflected in the fact that the major target of HIV is the immune system itself. However, there are resistant individuals in the population and the analysis of the basis of that resistance may help in designing a vaccine.

There are three areas of vaccine development. Using live attenuated HIV is understandably not a method most scientists favor due to the risk of creating the very disease you are trying to prevent. In the absence of a live virus, component vaccines, containing proteins from membrane of the virus, were the first to be created and tested. Unfortunately, these vaccines do not elicit a strong immune response and have been found not to be protective. Another, more promising, technique may be the prime-boost method where HIV proteins are added to a live vaccinia virus vaccine by genetic engineering.

The vaccinia virus, which was once used to immunize against small pox, then infects host cells and expresses the HIV proteins. A strong memory T cell response is generated, but few antibodies. Later booster shots of a different vaccine containing the same HIV proteins generate an antibody response and hopefully provide more complete protection. A recent interesting development is the use of plasmid DNA vaccines, which involve direct injection of DNA containing HIV genes. Some of these get into cells where they are expressed and an immune response is elicited against the proteins produced.

HIV is one of a large family of retroviruses that cause similar diseases in cats, horses, monkeys and other mammals. The virus is a lentivirus or slow virus, so named because the disease is characterized by a long latency period before symptoms appear. HIV is spherical in shape, with a diameter of about 100 nm. The envelope of the virus contains a surface glycoprotein known as Env, which is composed of two parts. Glycoprotein 41 (gp41) forms the stem of Env and serves to anchor it in the envelop of the virus. The cap of the Env protein consists of gp120 that sticks out into the environment and is important in the invasion of susceptible cells. Much of the research to develop a vaccine against HIV has focused on gp120 and gp41.

Immediately inside the envelope of a mature HIV particle is a matrix protein (p17) and within this is a cylindrical core made of 2000 copies of p24. Inside this capsid are two copies of the single-stranded (+)RNA HIV genome, each containing the viruss nine genes. The core of the virus also contains integrase (IN), a protein that integrates a DNA copy of the viral genome into the host cells chromosome.

The nucleic acid of HIV is used efficiently, packing nine genes into a genome of only 9749 bp. The coding regions are flanked by long terminal repeats (LTR) that are important in the replication of the virus. HIV mRNA transcripts fall into three classes: the complete mRNA transcript; singly spliced mRNAs that form Vif, Vpr, Vpu and Env; and multiply spiced mRNAs responsible for Tat, Rev and Nef.

HIV attaches to the cell by specific binding to the CD4 receptor, but entry into the cell is dependent upon the presence of a chemokine coreceptor (19-24). It is thought that some HIV-resistant individuals may have a mutant coreceptor that does not allow entry of the virus into the cell. Uncoating of HIV occurs at the cell surface, with fusion of the cell and viral envelopes. The viral core is then deposited into the cytoplasm.

Making copies of the HIV virus is complex, but a brief summary will give you an idea of the process. Upon entry into the cell, the two viral (+) single-stranded RNAs are copied by RT. This process involves switching of RT from one template to the other several times until a double-stranded DNA copy of the RNA templates is made. The linear double-stranded DNA product of RT forms a looping structure and now migrates to the nucleus. By the action of IN, this DNA inserts randomly into the genome of the host.

This process is very similar to that used by mobile genetic elements in bacteria and they have served as a valuable tool in understanding the integration of HIV. The integrated state of the viral DNA is called the provirus and is somewhat reminiscent of the lysogenic state of some bacteriophage. At this point, the virus can lay dormant inside the host cell for many years or can immediately begin to produce viral mRNA transcripts.

Transcription of proviral DNA by RNA polymerase results in the formation of a full-length RNA product. The newly formed HIV RNA can take several paths. A full transcript can exit the nucleus and serve as mRNA for Gag and Gag-Pol polyproteins precursors. Other full length RNAs serve as viral genomes and are assembled into viral cores in the cytoplasm. Still other RNAs are spliced to form Env mRNAs that encode the envelope proteins.

Env mRNA is translated at the endoplasmic reticulum and moves through the Golgi apparatus. Inside the Golgi apparatus glycosylation and proteolysis result in the formation of gp120 and gp41, the mature proteins found on the envelope of the virus. After processing, gp120 and gp41 finish their journey at the cellular membrane. Viral cores (containing two copies of viral RNA, Gag, and Gag-Pol precursors) assemble at viral budding sites where gp120 and gp41 have accumulated. By a number of interactions between the viral proteins, the virus buds from the cell. Maturation of the viral particle occurs by the action of the viral protease that is itself part of the Gag-Pol precursor. RT, IN, viral protease and other proteins are released from the Gag-Pol precursor and the particle is now infective.

Hepatitis Viruses

Hepatitis is an inflammation of the liver most often caused by an infection. There are various causes of hepatitis, but a subset of viruses, hepatitis viruses A-G, cause most liver disease. Besides infecting the liver, the hepatitis viruses show few similarities and none of them are closely related at the level of nucleic acid or protein. All the viruses will cause changes in liver function and this can lead to various symptoms including; fatigue, jaundice, abdominal pain, loss of appetite, nausea, diarrhea and vomiting. The prevalence of these symptoms is dependent upon the virus that is causing the hepatitis and asymptomatic infections are common. Infection can be acute or chornic, with chronic infections potentially leading to serious liver disease such as cirrhosis (destruction of the cells and anatomy of the liver) and possibly liver cancer.

Hepatitis is a common viral infection and causes most of the serious infectious liver disease in the United States. The Centers of Disease Control and Prevention estimates there were 93,000 new infections with Hepatitis A virus (HAV), 78,000 with Hepatitis B virus (HBV) and 25,000 with Hepatitis C virus (HCV) in 2001. Chronic infection with HBV and HCV viruses is possible and there are an estimated 1.25 million chronic hepatitis B infections and 2.7 million chronic hepatitis C infections.

HAV causes an acute infection of the liver. A person infected with HAV will shed large amounts of virus in their feces and the virus then spreads to others by contact with feces, either person-to-person or from fecally contaminated food. Severe cases of illness are rare and subclinical infections, especially in children, are common. From serum antibody studies, it is estimated that 31% of the general population has antibodies against HAV and presumably had the disease at one time. In epidemics of hepatitis A the most common source is oysters and clams from water polluted with human sewage.

Hepatitis E virus (HEV) was identified as an acute hepatitis that was not caused by HAV. It is a single-stranded RNA virus that is unrelated to HAV. Chronic infection with hepatitis E is not observed and mortality is usually low (< 0.6%). However, it can cause rapid destruction of the liver in 15-25% of pregnant women infected with the virus. The reason that pregnant women are at greater risk for complications is not known. HEV is spread through the fecal-to-oral route by consuming contaminated drinking water and there is little person-to-person transmission. It is endemic in Asia, Mexico and parts of Africa where it periodically causes epidemics. HEV can be prevented by maintenance of clean drinking water supplies.

HBV is a double-stranded DNA virus that can cause both acute and chronic infections of the liver. It is transmitted by exchange of blood or bodily fluids during sex, while sharing needles during intravenous drug use, or from mother to child during birth. The likelihood of chronic infection decreases with age: Infants have a 90% chance of chronic infection, children have a 30% chance and adults have a 6% chance. Of those chronically infected with the virus, 15-25% will suffer serious complications that will result in death. Because of the high rate of chronic infection in children, mothers are routinely screened for HBV infection and steps are taken to prevent transmission to children.

Hepatitis D virus (HDV) is a defective virus that cannot replicate on its own, but instead is dependent upon HBV for successful propagation. This is very different from the incomplete viral particles that are a bi-product of the infection of many viruses, and that we also sometimes refer to as defective viruses. This latter case refers to the simple problem of poor assembly, so that some virus-like particles simply do not have all the parts to function in another round of infection.

However HDV is a virus that has evolved in such a way that it does not carry all of the information it needs for its own propagation and requires functions found only in HBV. Rather remarkably, the two viruses are very different. HBV is a double-stranded DNA virus, while HDV is a single-stranded RNA virus. HDV codes for a protein to copy its own genome, but lacks genes necessary to make the protein coat of the virus. These it borrows from HBV. Since HDV is dependent upon HBV, it is only observed in patients who are also infected with HBV. Understandably, the transmission pattern for HDV is similar for that seen for HBV, however transmission from mother to child is rare.

Infection with HDV can follow two paths. Coinfection is the term used when HBV and HDV infect at the same time. In these cases, severe, acute disease develops, but there is a very low risk of chronic infection. Superinfection describes the case when HDV infects after HBV is already present. In this situation, chronic infection with HDV occurs 85% of the time and the likelihood of serious illness increases when both HDV and HBV are present. Complications for HDV infection are similar to those found for HBV and include cirrhosis of the liver and cancer. These illnesses can take several decades to develop after infection with HDV.

Hepatitis C is the most common blood-borne infection in the United States. Over 80% of those initially infected have no signs or symptoms, and the illness is often not diagnosed until serious complications occur from chronic infection. Chronic infection occurs in 70% percent of cases, with about 3% progressing to severe liver disease. Despite the low frequency of serious illness, HCV infection is prevalent enough in the population that it is the leading reason for liver transplantation.

Hepatitis is initially diagnosed by disease symptoms, but because the symptoms of hepatitis for each of the viruses can be so similar, blood tests have to be carried out to discern which virus is causing the illness. Most of the tests are based upon virus-specific immunoassays that look for antibodies directed against viral proteins present in the blood. Other tests detect the presence of viral nucleic acids in the blood and these methodologies are based upon the polymerase chain reaction. Once the causative agent of illness is discerned, courses of treatment vary.

There are effective vaccines for hepatitis A and B and these have caused dramatic decreases in the incidence of both diseases. Due to the potential for serious illness, hepatitis B vaccine is part of the recommended vaccination schedule for children and is also given to all those in the health care field. Immunoglobulin that reacts against HAV has also been found to be protective if given to patients within two weeks of exposure to the virus.

Hepatitis B can be treated with antivirual drugs, such as adefovir dipivoxil, interferon, and lamivudine, that block the HBV replication cycle. However, they do not rid the patient of the virus. At present there are no vaccines for hepatitis C, D or E. However, the significant decrease in intravenous drug use since 1990 has caused a drop in the incidence of hepatitis C. Hepatitis C can be treated with a combination of interferon and ribavirin. This treatment eliminates the virus in up to 80% of cases. There are no treatments for hepatitis E or D.

The life cycles and viral structure of the hepatitis viruses are each unique. HAV is similar to other picornaviruses and replicates in a manner similar to rhinovirus and poliovirus. HCV has marked similarities to the flaviviruses, such as West Nile Virus and has a similar replication cycle.

HBV is an enveloped, double-stranded DNA virus and has a genome of only 3,200 bp, the smallest known DNA virus. The genome is circular, but is only partially double-stranded, containing gaps of single-stranded DNA. A polymerase is in the core of the virus, and is associated with the genome. The life cycle of HBV is unique. After entry into liver cells, the viral DNA migrates to the nucleus and once there is converted into a covalently closed circular DNA by the polymerase. Inside the nucleus, viral transcription of the DNA leads to four RNA transcripts that code for various viral proteins, which then migrates to the cytoplasm, where the RNA is translated into viral proteins. The longest RNA of 3.5 kb can also associate with viral proteins to form a pregenomic RNA. This serves as a target for viral polymerase that now works as a reverse transcriptase and makes a DNA copy of the RNA template. This is an amazing enzyme in that it can act both as a DNA polymerase (DNA-dependent DNA polymerization) and as a reverse transcriptase (RNA-dependent DNA polymerization). The DNA is then made double-stranded and associates with envelope proteins, when it is finally being exported from the cell.

HDV is a single-stranded, RNA virus with a genome of 1,679 bp. The HDV capsid is composed of the proteins of the HBV virus. It is remarkable that this virus not only utilizes the functions of the host, but also the functions of another virus. Once inside the cytoplasm, the HDV genome is copied to form an antigenome. Further rounds of replication result in formation of copies of the viral genome. A third RNA species is also made that serves as an mRNA for the production of the small delta protein, a protein that is essential for HDV viral replication. The host provides all other proteins necessary for viral replication. This means that somehow the RNA polymerase of the host is modified such that it now uses RNA as a template instead of DNA! Replicated, genomic RNA is packaged into viral proteins and escapes from the cell in a manner similar to that of HBV.

HEV is a single-stranded, positive sense RNA virus of approximately 7,500 bp. Sixty copies of a single protein form the capsid of the virus. The genome encodes three open reading frames, ORF 1, ORF 2 and ORF 3. ORF 1 is proposed to be a viral polymerase with other activities that maybe important in viral replication, ORF 2 encodes the viral capsid protein and ORF 3 may interact with the host cytoskeleton. Replication of this virus is not well understood.

Herpes

Herpes virus is the causative agent of cold sores. More than 80 percent of the adult population in the United States endure oral herpes infections and the CDC estimates that over 45 million people in the United States have genital herpes. While in most cases infections with these viruses are mild, there can be severe illnesses in infants and the immunocompromised. Two similar herpesviruses cause disease in humans: herpes simplex virus type 1 (HSV-1) and type 2 (HSV-2). HSV-1 is most often associated with oral infections, causing fever blisters or cold sores, while HSV-2 typically causes genital herpes.

Initial HSV infection is most often mild, especially in children, being either asymptomatic or causing localized infections. These manifest themselves as vesicles filled with fluid from virus-damaged cells, cell debris and inflammatory cells, but heal in 2-3 weeks without scarring.

After initial infection, the virus retreats to sensory neurons in the ganglia of the nervous system where the viral DNA becomes nearly dormant in the nucleus of the cell. Reactivation of the infection can occur spontaneously or by a variety of changes in the host such as fever, stress or trauma. After reactivation, the virus retraces its steps down the nerve axon to epithelial cells and causes a recurrent lesion, almost always at the initial site of infection.

Recurrent infections are smaller, shed fewer viruses, elicit a stronger immune response and heal more quickly than primary lesions. As the immune systems humoral and cellular immunities increase, the body becomes better at suppressing breakouts of HSV. Successive lesions often become milder until they finally cease after a few episodes, but there are individuals who are plagued with lesions throughout their lives.

Of great concern is neonatal herpes that is contracted by newborns from mothers infected with HSV-2 or from the hospital environment. HSV infection in infants begins with a skin lesion that disseminates in 70% of cases, causing severe disease. The infants rapidly deteriorate and often die with 10 days, but with early diagnosis and treatment, the chances for survival greatly increase. Most people treat cold sores with over-the-counter medications, but genital herpes normally causes the patient to seek medical attention.

HSV-1 reactivations are rarely recurrent, while HSV-2 symptoms recur more frequently. Genital herpes can be effectively treated with several antiviral drugs including Acyclovir, Famciclovir and Valacylovir. These drugs are nucleoside analogs and interfere with viral DNA polymerase. There is no known cure for HSV infection. Even individuals not showing symptoms likely have the virus in a latent state. A vaccine against HSV, consisting of viral surface protein glycoprotein D, is under development and recent findings have produced the curious result that it is protective for women, but not for men. This is a novel finding for a vaccine and further investigation may reveal some interesting physiology. The vaccine also seems to only produce protection in women who have never been exposed to HSV-1 or HSV-2. Previous exposure to one of these viruses seems to generate an immune response similar to that of vaccination and additional challenge by the vaccine does not improve protection.

Virions first bind to the extracellular matrix on the outside of cells using envelope proteins. Another viral membrane protein, gD, then interacts specifically with one of several molecules on the cell surface. Interestingly, gD does not have a single target, but can bind to HvA, herpesvirus entry mediator, members of the nectin family of proteins or 3-O-sulphated heparan. This recognition of multiple targets accounts for the ability of the herpes virus to infect many different cells throughout the body. Virus binding to the secondary receptor then initiates fusion between the viral envelope and the cell membrane. Uncoating of the virus into the cytoplasm releases the tegument proteins and the capsid into the cell.

The tegument proteins begin affecting cellular metabolism in various ways. Some proteins help to shut off host functions while others activate transcription of viral genome in the nucleus. The capsid itself attaches to microtubules and is transported to the nucleus where it docks at a nuclear pore and releases the double-stranded DNA into the nucleus. The DNA circularizes, and with the help of viral proteins, begins transcription of the immediate-early genes. The mRNAs of the immediate-early genes are spliced and transported to the ribosomes for translation. Some of these proteins make their way back to the nucleus where they stimulate transcription of the early genes and shut down the expression of the immediate-early genes.

Some proteins of the early genes function in the cytoplasm to help control the cells physiology, while others go back to the nucleus to initiate replication of the circular viral DNA. This consists of the synthesis of concatameric DNA, which are similar to phage P22 and T4. These concatamers are templates for late gene expression. Proteins synthesized now consist of the envelope proteins, the tegument proteins and the capsid proteins. The envelope proteins are synthesized at the rough endoplasmic reticulum and modified by glycosylation as they make their way through the Golgi apparatus. Mature viral glycoproteins eventually end up at the plasma membrane of the infected cell. The tegument proteins and the capsid proteins are transported to the nucleus.

Newly replicated viral DNA is cut into genome-length pieces from the concatamers and packaged into the already assembled capsids. A genome length is recognized by the packaging enzymes using the certain sequences on the genome. The completed nucleocapsid, along with tegument proteins, then assembles at the nuclear membrane and buds into the lumen of the endoplasmic reticulum (ER). Passage from the ER to the cell surface is not well understood. One model suggests that the virus loses its membrane as it passes from the surface of the ER into the cytoplasm.

More tegument proteins are added and then re-envelopment takes place at a nearby Golgi compartment that contains mature viral membrane proteins. The finished virion is then transported to the cellular membrane for release by exocytosis. Latent infection by HSV occurs primarily in neurons. The virus enters the cell and then the nucleus in a similar manner to active infection, but then the transcription cascade is blocked by an unknown mechanism. The viral DNA circularizes, but only produces a single mRNA that contains two open reading frames, which are translated into protein. How latency is regulated and the identity of the players is not well understood. As noted before, physiological changes in the host can initiate a productive cycle and new virus is made.

West Nile Virus

West Nile virus (WNV) burst onto the consciousness of the American public when seven residents of New York City died of encephalitis (an inflammation of the brain) caused by the virus and 62 others became seriously ill. WNV is part of the flavivirus family, many of which are capable of causing serious illness in humans. WNV was first isolated in Uganda in 1931 and is commonly found in humans, birds and other vertebrates in Africa, Eastern Europe, West Asia and the Middle East. However, it had not found its way to the Western Hemisphere until 1999.

The WNV disease is initiated with a bite from a mosquito and symptoms appear 3 to 15 days after infection. In most cases, the disease is asymptomatic or mild with fever, headache, and other symptoms. About 1% of cases turn severe with high fever, coma and paralysis. Fifteen percent of severe cases result in death.

WNV seems to be a much more dangerous agent for birds with at least 70 species of birds dying of it in the United States. Birds are also the primary reservoir for WNV. The disease is not contagious, but is transmitted from birds to animals and humans by mosquitoes, primarily those of the Culex species. After feeding on the blood of an infected bird, the virus survives in the salivary glands of the mosquito. During subsequent blood meals the mosquito may inject the virus into animals or humans.

The symptoms of WNV disease are similar to those of many viral infections that can lead to encephalitis, and laboratory testing is necessary to determine the cause. Since no commercial kit is yet available to test for the presence of WNV, a test that detects antibodies against the virus is available from the CDC. If this test comes up positive, a second analysis is done to verify the existence of the specific flavivirus antibodies. Alternatively, polymerase chain reaction (PCR) tests are available to detect viral RNA directly in specimens. There is no known treatment for WNV infection. WNV illness seems to provide life-long protection against the virus and several companies are working on a vaccine that may be available in the near future.

WNV is enveloped and spherical, with a diameter of 40-50 nm, similar to all other flaviviruses. The viral membrane appears rough and contains surface projections probably caused by the two envelope proteins, E and M, found in the mature virion. Inside the membrane is an icosahedral shell composed of the C protein. C is synthesized as a precursor, containing a hydrophobic tail that anchors into a membrane until assembly of the virus.

WNV is a (+) single-stranded RNA virus of 10,290 bp The entire genome of the virus has been sequenced, revealing a single open reading frame. The nucleic acid serves as mRNA and is translated into one polypeptide that is subsequently processed by cellular and viral proteases into structural and nonstructural proteins. At either end of the virus are untranslated regions (UTR) that seem to be important for viral replication.

The WNV attaches to cells at an unknown host receptor and gains entry to the cell by clathrin-mediated endocytosis. Once inside the lysosome, a drop in pH is thought to cause a conformational change in a surface protein exposing a hydrophobic domain that then inserts in the lysosome membrane. This causes fusion between the viral and host membranes and deposits the nucleocapsid in the cytoplasm of the cell. Unlike rhinovirus, WNV solves the problem of entry by using the cells normal absorption mechanism (endocytosis) and then fusing with the lysosomal membrane. By fusing after entering the lysosome, the virus has a signal that it is inside a cell.

The (+) single-stranded RNA dissociates from its capsid and is translated into the viral polyprotein. The amino terminal end of the polyprotein includes the 3 structural components of the virus, while the rest becomes the 7 different nonstructural proteins. Translation of the polyprotein occurs at the ER with the envelope proteins being translocated across the membrane and into the ER lumen. The internal C protein and others end up in the cytoplasm of the cell. In this process, the virus takes a single polyprotein containing both membrane and cytoplasmic proteins and is able to get the host cell to direct each protein to its correct destination. However, because they are all made on a single polyprotein, the levels of each of these proteins is similar and this leads to waste, since structural proteins are required at greater concentrations. In another interesting feature, the virus uses protein N3 for three separate activities: a viral protease, a nucleic acid helicase and an RNA triphosphatase activity. No doubt this saves valuable coding space, which is at a premium in a relatively small virus.

Immediately after the RNA-dependent RNA polymerase and helicase are made and released from the polyprotein, RNA replication begins with synthesis of (-) strands from the (+) RNA template. All replication takes place in the cytoplasm of the cell. The (-) strand is again copied to form (+) strands that can serve either as templates for further rounds of replication or move to the ribosome to produce more polyprotein. (+) RNA strands are replicated at a greater rate with the ratio of (+) RNA to (-) RNA being 10:1. This makes sense since the only role for the (-) strands is to serve as template for making (+) strands. After enough capsid proteins have accumulated, the nucleic acid associates with them to form nucleocapsid.

The envelope proteins accumulate in the membrane and assemble in such a way as to mask the surface protein that originally allowed the membranes to fuse upon viral entry. This prevents the protein from catalyzing a membrane fusion reaction that would cause reentry into the cell during assembly. This approach is a common strategy used by many viruses with the same problem. The nucleocapsid precursor then associates with ER membrane containing the surface proteins and then an assembled virion buds into the ER lumen. The virus then exits the cell using the host secretory pathway with protein processing, activating the membrane-fusion protein that had previously been masked.

9

Archael Diversity

The archaea were recognized about a century after the culture of microorganisms began. Understandably our knowledge of them is less than that of bacteria, but is rapidly increasing. There are three subdivisions within the Archaea: Euryarchaeota, Crenarchaeota and Korarchaeota.

A common habitat for some of the most unusual archaea are hot sulfide containing environments so we will now pause here to describe these environments. One such environment is called a solfatara, which is a hot sulfur-rich environment such as a hot spring, fumarole, mud pot, or steam heated soil. These are found throughout the world although certain areas have high concentrations of solfataras including Italy, Iceland, New Zealand and Yellowstone National Park in the United States. The pH of these hot environments depends upon the surrounding geology, with some being close to neutral (pH 5-8) and others being highly acidic (pH 1 or lower).

Solfataras tend to be the domain of hyperthermophilic microorganisms. Another favorable environment for hyperthermophilic microbes is hydrothermal vents. These habitats are below the surface of the oceans at any depth up to 4,000 meters, but always near the places where the earth's crust is emerging from the underlying magma. Heat is released by the magma and even deep sea hydrothermal vents can reach temperatures well above 100°C. All of the record-setting thermophiles have been obtained from these habitats.

As with many archaeal groups, Crenarchaeota cells were originally cultured from extremely hot environments such as solfataras and hydrothermal vents. After characterization of these hyperthermophiles it was possible to make DNA probes that were complementary to their unique 16S rRNA sequences. By attaching fluorescent dyes to these probes and adding them to smears of microbes on slides, the Crenarchaeota became distinguishable in a fluorescence microscope. These and other experiments have demonstrated Crenarchaeota species in not only hot environments, but also in marine waters worldwide including the oceans of the Antarctic where temperatures of water can be as low as 2°C.

Crenarchaeota cells have also been found in mesophilic environments in association with plants roots. This calls into question the notion that these archaea are restricted to extreme habitats and suggests that they may have escaped detection in less exotic habitats due to competition with other bacteria. It may turn out that Crenarchaeota, and archaea in general, are much more common than we realize and our poor knowledge of them is caused more by the culture techniques we have been employing than by their absence from many environments. Once brought into culture, it will be intriguing to understand the physiology of the mesophilic and psychrophilic representatives and to learn the relationship between the plant-associated Crenarchaeota cells and their hosts.

Euryarchaeota

Microbes share many basic properties, but despite these commonalities, the Euryarchaeota are have a great deal of metabolic diversity. They can be divided neatly into four catabolic subgroups: methanogens, halophiles, thermoacidophilic archaea and hyperthermophiles.

Methanogens

Many members of the Euryarchaeota produce methane (CH_4) as an end product of their metabolism and are called methanogens. As judged by 16S rRNA analysis, methanogens cluster together in a deep and ancient branch of the Archaea and are quite diverse. Methanogenesis is only possible under strictly anaerobic conditions due to the oxygen lability of a number of cofactors and enzymes present in the microorganisms. Despite their oxygen sensitivity they are found in a wide variety of habitats.

The sediments of many bodies of water, especially anaerobic sediments of marshes, swamps and rice fields serve as excellent habitats for these organisms. Areas that collect and process human waste, such as moist landfills and anaerobic sewage digesters, also have high numbers of methanogenic bacteria. In addition, methanogens are common residents of the digestive tracts of various types of animals including ruminants (cattle, sheep, buffalo and goats), the large intestine of humans, dogs, and swine and in the hindgut of cellulose-utilizing insects (termites).

In these relationships, the methanogens can be detrimental or beneficial. In the absence of methanogens, microbes in the rumen would quickly become inhibited by high concentrations of H_2 and cease degrading cellulose. However, the methanogens also create CH_4 from acetate, thus removing utilizable carbon (acetate) and creating CH_4 that the ruminant cannot absorb. In the termite hindgut, methanogens resembling Methanobacterium and Methanobrevibacter are present inside trichomonal protozoa.

The protozoans degrade cellulose to glucose and this is then broken down to acids and H_2. Methanogens aid their host by consuming excess H2 and driving the cellulolytic reaction forward. Methanogens can also be found in high temperature habitats including hydrothermal vents, hot springs and areas of volcanic activity.

The commonality among all these habitats is an anaerobic environment that contains CO_2 and a highly reduced substrate. Common substrates include H_2, several one-carbon compounds and acetate. If CO_2 is the source of carbon, H_2 is necessary as a source of energy because CO_2 is no a very good terminal electron acceptor. High-energy electrons need to be used to reduce CO_2 and H_2 is one of a few compounds that contains such electrons and is abundant in anaerobic habitats. For methanogens to be prevalent, the concentration of SO_4^{2-} must also be low. High concentrations of sulfate encourage the growth of sulfate-reducing bacteria and they are able to out compete the methanogens for H_2.

Coupling the oxidation of H_2 to SO_4 yields more energy than the reduction of CO_2 by H_2. Thus, if all other parameters are neutral, sulfidogens will prevail over methanogens. A key feature of methanogens, and one that explains their ability to process vast amounts of carbon, is that the end product of their reaction is a volatile gas. As a consequence, there is little problem with the end product building up and interfering with the energetics of the process.

Reactions of methanogenesis

Methanogens are common in areas where decomposition of organic material is occurring. Under these conditions H_2 and acetate are present and are readily used. When growing on H_2 methanogens convert CO_2 to CH_4 and also release water in the following reaction.

$$CO_2 + 4H_2 \text{->} CH_4 + 2H_2O$$

The ΔG of this reaction is -131 kJ and an identical amount of energy is released when methanol and H_2 are used:

$$CH_3OH + H_2 \rightarrow CH_4 + H_2O$$

In contrast a subset of methanogens are capable of growth on methanol alone. In the absence of H_2 the the amount of energy that can be extracted is only about -20 kJ per methanol catabolized:

$$4CH_3OH \rightarrow 3CH_4 + CO_2 + 2H_2O$$

Finally, growth on acetate is also performed by a small subset of methanogens. Acetate oxidation is more energetically favorable than methanol oxidation and yields -31 kJ:

$$CH_3COO^- + H_2O \rightarrow CH_4 + HCO_3^-$$

Methanogens are extremely adept at coupling the energy gained in substrate oxidation to ATP synthesis achieving almost 100% efficiency. In comparison, aerobic microbes growing on glucose only convert 50% of the energy released from their catabolism into ATP.

Despite the limited number of methanogenic species that can grow on acetate, those that perform this metabolism are critical for carbon cycling in the environment. Methanogens capable of utilizing acetate readily degrade it and fully 2/3 of the methane generated in the environment originates from the metabolism of acetate.

Methanogens run a unique series of reactions containing a number of distinctive cofactors that are essential to the process. Reduction of CO_2 to CH_4 is dependent upon high-energy electrons that are most often derived from H_2 gas, but CO, formate and several alcohols can also serve as electron donors. CO_2 is first activated by a methanofuran-containing enzyme and reduced to the formyl level (HCO). Methanofuran is one of the unique cofactors of methanogenesis. It contains an amino nitrogen atom capable of binding CO_2.

The formyl group now bound to methanofuran is transferred to another enzyme containing a second unique cofactor, methanopterin. Methanopterin is also a carrier of one-carbon units, but is capable of holding onto its carbon through a series of reductive steps. Its chemical structure resembles that of the vitamin folic acid. After transfer to methanopterin, two reductions follow where the formyl group is converted first to a methylene (CH_2) and then a methyl group (CH_3). The electrons for this process are obtained from coenzyme F420, a unique electron carrier in methanogenesis.

Coenzyme F420 is a flavin derivative, resembling flavin mononucleotide, a common electron carrier in many organisms. It also is used as a diagnostic test for methanogenesis, since the coenzyme absorbs light at 420 nm and will then fluoresce a blue-green light. The reduced methyl group is then transferred to coenzyme M (CoM) forming methyl-CoM. Finally, this is reduced to methane by the methyl reductase system, a complex of several polypeptides that involves the action of coenzyme F430 and coenzyme B (CoB). Coenzyme F430 is a nickel-containing tetrapyrrole similar in structure to heme. In this reaction the methyl group is first transferred to the Ni in coenzyme F430 and then CoB reduces it to methane. Oxidized CoB then reacts with CoM, forming a complex that is subsequently reduced with H_2 to regenerate both coenzymes. These are then ready for another round of the pathway.

Energy generation is achieved at the last step in methanogenesis. The formation of the CoB-CoM complex is reduced by the enzyme heterodisulfide reductase. The electrons for this process come from H_2 and pass through coenzyme F420 and methanophenazine, the latter being a unique hydrophobic electron carrier present in the membrane. Methanophenazine then reduces heterodisulfide reductase, but this enzyme will only accept electrons and not protons. We have seen this game before and the protons are released and passed to the outside of the membrane, creating a proton motive force. The electrons on heterodisulfide reductase then reduce the CoB-CoM complex.

Alternative substrates such as methanol and acetate involve the use of preliminary reactions that extract a methyl group from the substrate. Methanol reacts with a corrinoid-containing protein, forming methyl corrinoid. Corrinoids are coenzymes (such as vitamins B12) that contain cobalt and have a porphyrin-like structure. The methyl group is then donated to CoM, forming CH_3-CoM, from which energy is generated in a manner identical to that described previously for the case of CO_2 reduction. If hydrogen gas is not present, electrons for the methyl reductase system are generated by reversing the steps of methanogenesis, which results in the oxidation of a portion of CH_3-CoM to CO_2. This explains why the energy yield when growing on methanol along is lower.

The acetate pathway is a bit more involved. Acetate is first activated by addition of coenzyme-A, forming acetyl-CoA. This in turn reacts with the enzyme carbon monoxide dehydrogenase. The methyl group of acetyl-CoA is donated to the corrinoid-containing protein as in the case of methanol and this then passes through the final step of methanogenesis. The carbonyl group is oxidized to CO_2 and the electrons obtained are donated to the methyl reductase system.

Methanogens produce most of the methane in the Earth's atmosphere and methane is a significant greenhouse gas and is a cause of global warming. Much of this methane production is associated with activities for which humans are at least partially responsible. This includes the flooding of rice paddies and the raising of domestic cattle, both of which create habitats for methanogens. It is clear that these microbes are having a significant impact on the earths atmosphere.

Methanobacterium thermoautotrophicum and Methanococcus jannaschii.

Two examples of methanogens are Methanobacterium thermoautotrophicum and Methanococcus jannaschii. M. thermoautotrophicum is often found in flooded soils, sewage digesters and manure piles. Cells stain gram-negative, but they do not have a classic gram-negative cell wall structure. The cell wall contains pseudopeptidoglycan as its major constituent instead of peptidoglycan. As one would expect from its name, M. thermoautotrophicum will grow at temperatures of up to 70°C, but it is also capable of growth at mesophilic temperatures down to 35°C. It forms rod-shaped cells.

The microbe is capable of using H_2 and formate as substrates for growth. M. jannaschii has been isolated from deep-sea hydrothermal vents in the ocean. It is a methanogen and a thermophile, living at temperatures near 85°C and growing primarily on H_2 and CO_2. The cells are spherical with a diameter of about 1 m. Both microbes are able to synthesize all necessary biosynthetic compounds from only CO_2.

These are two of the first methanogens to have their genomes sequenced. The genome of M. thermoautotrophicum contains 1.75 Mb and 1873 proposed genes, while that of M. jannaschii contains 1.66 Mb and 1729 proposed genes. Studies of the genomes have identified genes for methanogenesis in both species and they are highly conserved between them. Gene products involved in anabolic processes such as amino acid biosynthesis share homology with their bacterial counterparts. However, those involved in central cellular processes such as DNA replication and RNA transcription are more closely related their eukaryotic homologues. This supports placement of these Archaea on the tree of life between the Bacteria and the Eukarya.

Interestingly, 50% of identified ORFs in these organisms have no known counterpart. They likely play a role in the many unique reactions of methanogens and it is clear there is much to learn about these amazing organisms and their way of life. Comparison of their genomes reveals that the two methanogens are very different, 20% of M. thermoautotrophicum genes are not found in M. jannaschii and 15% of M. jannaschii genes are not found in M. thermoautotrophicum. Methanogens are strict anaerobes that make their living by converting CO_2 into CH_4, yet they are related to at least two separate aerobic groups: the extreme halophiles and the thermoacidophiles.

Archaea and Bacteria do not seem very diverse when observed from a morphological point of view. There are rods and spheres, spirals and curved cells, and for major excitement there are a few that form complex fruiting structures as part of their developmental life cycle. In comparison to the breadth of interesting morphological constructs formed in macroorganisms, microorganisms seem rather bland. However, the diversity in microorganisms comes from their almost endless creativity in metabolic processes, specifically catabolic reactions, and in the extreme conditions under which they can thrive.

Extreme Halophiles

Extreme halophiles are a diverse group of archaea that inhabit highly saline environments and are the most salt tolerant organisms known. They have invented a form of light-based energy generation that does not use chlorophyll as the major antenna. In fact the light-capturing protein they use, bacteriorhodopsin, has as its cofactor retinal, a compound very similar to the light-sensitive molecules in the rods of our eyes.

There are about 20 known species of extreme halophiles with diverse cell morphologies and cell structures, but they do share some things in common. They stain gram-negative (although their cell wall structure is unlike gram-negative bacteria), divide by binary fission and contain no resting stages (i.e. spores or cysts). Most are non-motile and obligate aerobes. Many extreme halophiles actually require salt to grow and are not viable in low-salt medium. They are chemoorganotrophs, using organic acids and amino acids as energy sources, and they require some growth factors.

A relative few of the extreme halophiles are capable of catabolizing carbohydrates, which are handled by the TCA cycle and generate reduced electron carriers. The electrons then travel an electron transport chain containing membrane proteins with a-, b- and c-type cytochromes similar to those found in many bacteria. As is typical, this electron transport generates a proton motive force that drives ATP synthase. A few halophilic archaea are capable of anaerobic growth. In some cases this involves sugar fermentation, while in others substrate oxidation is linked to anaerobic respiration with nitrate or fumarate as the terminal electron acceptor.

Habitats

Extreme halophiles are obviously limited to areas containing high concentrations of salt; at least 1.5 M (8.8%) NaCl with an optimum between 2-4 M (11.7-23.4%)NaCl and a maximum at 5.5 M (32%) NaCl. Amazingly, saturated solutions of salt will still support the growth of some extreme halophiles. Highly saline environments are rather rare, usually being found in hot dry areas of the world where water coming into a lake has no exit except by evaporation. This causes an accumulation of minerals and salts that were brought there by the running water as it passed over land to the lake. Saline lakes often have a similar array of salts as that found in seawater, but the concentration is much higher. However, the composition of each specific lake depends upon the surrounding land and the minerals available for erosion. For example, the Great Salt Lake in Utah has Na^+ and Cl^- as the dominant ions, while the Dead Sea has high concentrations of Mg^{2+}. Soda lakes have a similar salt composition to other salt lakes, but have a pH near 11 due to high concentrations of carbonate ion.

These harsh conditions exclude the growth of most microorganisms, but certain archaea are able to thrive due to their unique metabolism. In addition to archaea, eukaryotic microorganism are also present and high-salt lakes are one of the few extreme environments that eukaryotic microbes have been able to adapt to. Dunaliella is a eukaryotic algae found in salt lakes and is likely the only oxygenic photosynthetic microbe present in these environments. In highly alkaline soda lakes where Dunaliella will not grow, anoxygenic phototrophs predominate, such as the purple non-sulfur bacteria Ectothiorhodospira and Halorhodospira. These primary producers create organic matter that can then be used by halophilic chemoorganotrophic archaea such as Haloanaerobium and Halobacteroides.

Salt tolerance mechanisms

One of the main problems associated with high salt environments is that osmosis will pull most of the water out of the cell, literally dehydrating the cell if nothing is done to prevent it. Adaptation to relatively high salt concentrations by microbes that are not extreme halophiles involves the manufacture of small organic molecules called compatible solutes that sit in the periplasmic space and cytoplasm and balance the osmotic pressure outside the cell. Extreme halophiles employ a variation of this type of strategy. Instead of synthesizing organic compounds, they accumulate inorganic ions inside the cell at concentrations that match the salt concentration outside the cell.

In Halobacterium, a pump transports high amounts of potassium inside the cell such that the concentration of potassium is greater inside the cell than the sodium concentration outside the cell. In this case potassium serves as the compatible solute. The macromolecular constituents of the cytoplasm have been altered such that they still function in the presence of high potassium concentrations. With these adaptations the extreme halophiles are able to live in environments where most other organisms die and they therefore take advantage of a niche that is rich in nutrients.

Many of the molecular adaptations that allow growth in high salt also restrict microbes to this habitat. One of these involves the cell wall. It is composed of glycoproteins that contain an unusually high concentration of the acidic amino acids aspartate and glutamate. These negative charges are neutralized by sodium ions present in the surrounding environment and likely enable the microbe to attract water to its surface. However, if the concentration of sodium ions becomes too low, they can no longer shield the negative charges on the glycoproteins and the electrostatic repulsion between the negative charges on aspartate and glutamate destabilizes the cell wall and causes lysis.

The cytoplasmic proteins of these bacteria as well as their ribosomes are also very acidic and require positive charges for stability. Since the dominant ion inside the cells is potassium, the proteins have evolved to require potassium, rather than sodium as a counter ion. In addition, many of the proteins of halophiles contain fewer hydrophobic amino acids than do non-halophilic species. This is likely another adaptation to life in high salt. Ions in solution interact with surrounding water molecules to create spheres of hydration. The binding of these water molecules is what allows these ions to become soluble. Any water bound to an ion in this way is unavailable to proteins of the cell.

Proteins also need spheres of hydration to prevent them from aggregating and to enable their enzymatic activity. As the concentration of ions in the cell increases, the amount of available water becomes scarce. At the high salt concentrations present in extreme halophiles (5.3 M K^+) there is frantic competition for water molecules. Proteins that function in this environment have to compete with the K^+ for the water. Halophiles increase the competitiveness by decreasing the number of hydrophobic amino acids on their surface and increasing the number of hydrophilic amino acids.

Halophile energetics

Certain species of extremely halophilic bacteria are capable of a form of light-mediated energy generation that uses distinctive light-harvesting proteins and pigments. The microbes have a purple color due to the production of red and orange carotenoids called bacteriorubrins and other pigments of energy metabolism. Under oxygen-limiting conditions, Halobacterium cells contain the protein bacteriorhodopsin in their membranes. This hydrophobic barrel-shaped protein spans the membrane and contains at its center a molecule of retinal, a long carbon molecule with many double bonds and a nitrogen atom at its end. The double bonds allow the molecule to absorb light and the nitrogen on its end can accept and release protons.

Retinal, is normally in a straight conformation with the nitrogen atom facing the cytoplasm from which it picks up a proton. When light strikes the retinal it causes a conformational shift such that the nitrogen is rotated about 180 and now faces the outside of the cell. Amino acids on the protein near the nitrogen atom of retinal now cause the proton to be released into the environment. The retinal eventually loses its energy and falls back to the ground state and the nitrogen rotates to its original position. It is again protonated from the cytoplasm, completing the cycle. In this way the retinal serves as a pump, pushing one proton across the membrane for every photon it absorbs.

The net effect is the creation of a proton gradient across the membrane, which of course leads to the formation of ATP via ATP synthase. In contrast to the other types of photosynthesis we have covered, this mechanism only establishes a proton gradient and does not result in the formation of reducing power. While bacteriorhodosin does provide energy to Halobacterium, these microbes are still dependent upon organic compounds for their source of carbon and are therefore incapable of autotrophic growth.

The reactions associated with rhodopsins contribute to cell metabolism in other ways. The proton gradient generated by bacteriorhodopsin allows a Na^+/H^+ antiporter to pump Na^+ out of the cell, keeping concentrations of this ion relatively low in the cytoplasm. The resulting Na^+ gradient is then used to pump amino acids into the cell using Na^+/amino acid symporters and to uptake K^+ ions that are necessary for maintaining osmotic balance.

A second rhodopsin, halorhodopsin, is responsible for using light to pump Cl^- ions into the cell as a counter ion for K^+. There are also two sensory rhodopsins that control phototaxis (movement toward light) in Halobacterium. The state of the sensory rhodopsins control flagellar rotation in a manner analogous to that observed for chemotaxis. The result is a migration of the microbe toward light and the energy it provides.

Thermoacidophillic Archaea

This branch of the Euryarchaeota contains thermophilic and

acidophilic organisms that thrive in the most acidic environments known to support life. Three genera are known: Thermoplasma, Picrophilus and Ferroplasma.

Thermoplasma

Two species of Thermoplasma have been isolated, T. acidophilum from coal refuse piles and T. volcanii from sites of volcanism. Both organisms are chemoheteroorganotrophs, growing on organic compounds present in their environments, and fastidious, requiring a number of growth factors to multiply. Thermoplasma can use oxygen and sulfur compounds as terminal electron acceptors. T. acidophilum is a thermophile with a temperature range of 4567C, while T. volcanium is capable of growth at mesophilic temperatures (33°C), yet can still grow at 67°C. Both organisms thrive in acidic conditions and can grow at pH values as low as 0.5.

Coal refuse piles contain coal, pyrite and organic material and often undergo spontaneous combustion to produce very high temperatures. T. acidophilum uses available organic compounds and grows in these piles by respiration either aerobically or anaerobically using sulfur as the terminal electron acceptor. Because coal piles are of distinctly human origin, it is unlikely that the organisms evolved for this habitat. Instead, their metabolism probably evolved in anaerobic zones of continental solfataras and these are probably their natural habitats.

A unique feature of Thermoplasma species is that they lack a cell wall, which is even more amazing given the harsh environment in which they exist. Detailed examination of the cell membrane has revealed the presence of LPS-like molecules consisting of mannose and glucose units attached to abundant tetra-ether lipids in the membrane. An unusual mannose-rich, 152-kDa glycoprotein is also located in the cell membrane and is thought to form a hydroskeleton via a network of sugar residues surrounding the cell, thus contributing to the remarkable rigidity of the membrane. These membranes are extremely impermeable to acid and heat and allow the organism's survival in its habitat.

Amazingly, even in extremely acidic environments the microbe maintains a neutral cytoplasmic pH. This is achieved by the presence of pumps in the membrane that actively remove protons from the cell. This method of protection for acidophiles is common and suggests that some critical biological reactions cannot occur under highly acidic conditions.

The genomes of both T. acidophilum and T. volcanii have been sequenced and have a reasonably high degree of sequence similarity. The genomes have sizes of only 1,565 kb (T. acidophilum) and 1,585 kb (T. volcanium) and are some of the smallest of free-living organisms. This might reflect the absence of the genes necessary for synthesis and maintenance of a cell wall, though it probably also suggests the absence of very many catabolic pathways as well. Examination of the genome of T. acidophilum also reveals that there has been a high degree of lateral gene transfer (17%) between it and Sulfolobus solfataricus, a distantly related Crenarcheaota that shares the same habitat. This suggests that the habitat of a microbe is much more important in determining gene transfer partners than phylogenetic relatedness.

Picrophilus

Picrophilus species are some of the most acid-tolerant organisms known and are common in terrestrial solfataras. Their pH optimum is an astounding 0.7 and they are capable of growth at 0.06! This is equivalent to a 1.15 M solution of hydrochloric acid, something capable of dissolving metal. Picrophilus species are obligate aerobes that grow by oxidative phosphorylation of organic compounds. They are also thermophilic and grow only between 40°C and 69°C. Unlike Thermoplasma cells, those of Picrophilus contain a cell wall made of a protein S layer. The extreme acid-tolerance of the microbe is of great interest and early experiments have shown that its membrane is extremely acid impermeable, but the molecular mechanism that causes this is still unknown.

Ferroplasma

The first isolates of this genus were made from a bioreactor in Kazakhstan and an abandoned mine in the U.S.. Since both isolated organisms grow at temperatures around 37°C and have been isolated from highly distant locations, they may occur in many sulfidic ore-containing mines and heaps on earth. Ferroplasma cells are chemolithotrophic, oxidizing ferrous iron or pyrite for energy and autotrophic, using CO_2 as a carbon source. Ferric ion (Fe^{3+}) is the end product of the oxidation, although Mn^{2+} can also be oxidized. The organism grow optimally at a pH of 1.2 and has a range of pH 0.1-2.5. The isolate from the US mine (Ferroplasma acidarmanus) has been shown to be the dominant species in acid mine drainage, making up fully 85% of the microbial community. They are similar to Thermoplasma in that they lack a membrane, yet are able to survive low pH and heavy metals that would kill most normal microorganisms. How they accomplish this is of great interest, but is not yet clear.

The oxidation of metal sulfides, especially pyrite (FeS_2) is important because one of the major end products of this reaction is protons, which results in extremely acidic water. These acidic solutions are able to hold high concentration of metal ions including Fe^{2+}, Cd^{2+}, Cu^{2+}, and Zn^{2+}. Ferroplasma will often exist in abandoned mines and drainage from these areas is extremely toxic due to the acidity and high concentrations of heavy metals.

The final branch of the Euryarchaeota that contains a group of thermophiles capable of growing at temperature up to 113°C. Many species from this group have been isolated at sofataras and hydrothermal vents, so their temperature tolerance is not surprising.

Thermococcales

All species of the Thermococcales known to date are thermophiles, and their optimal growth temperatures ranges from 75°C to 104°C. They are strict anaerobes, thriving in marine or terrestrial solfataras. Themococcales species are organotrophs that can utilize yeast extract, peptides and amino acids as carbon and energy sources. They seem to be capable of a respiratory as well as fermentative metabolism, although the details are not clear. Species of this group have some of the most rapid growth rates among the archaea, with the shortest generation times being 35 minutes for Pyrococcus and 120 min for Thermococcus.

Pyrococcus cells are spherical with a diameter of 0.8-2.5 m and grows optimally at 95C. They are motile because of a tuft of flagella at one end and contain a circular chromosome of about 2 Mbp. Thermococcus cells are also coccoid with a diameter of 0.5-3.0 m. Both of these organisms are capable of growth on peptides and carbohydrates and these fermentative pathways depend upon tungsten-containing enzymes. This is unusual because tungsten is seldomly used in biological systems. There also appear to be some unique characteristics to the catabolic pathways used to degrade these substrates.

For example, P. furiosis produces a tungsten-containing glyceraldehyde-3-phosphate ferredoxin oxidoreductase that replaces glyceraldehyde-3-phosphate dehydrogenase in the Emden-Meyerhof-Parnas pathway. It remains to be seen what the purpose of tungsten is in these enzymes and what advantage it gives to thermophiles.

Organisms in both of these genera are of considerable interest as a source of thermostable enzymes. In contrast to many of the hyperthermophiles, these microbes grow without the reduction of elemental sulfur to hydrogen sulfide. This is important because hydrogen sulfide is poisonous and highly corrosive to stainless steel fermentors, the most common type in industrial settings. In the near future a number of enzymes from these microbes may have industrial applications.

Archaeoglobales

Archaeoglobus is another hyperthermophile and is the only genus of its group. Its 16S rRNA sequence is very different from any other known microorganisms. Its requirements for high salt and high temperature restrict Archaeoglobus to marine solfataras and the vicinity of hydrothermal sea vents. They are strict anaerobes that can grow using inorganic or organic chemicals. Archaeoglobus is the only known thermophilic, archaeal, sulfate reducer and can growth at 60-95C. As with all sulfate reducers, growth depends on use of sulfate as a terminal electron acceptor and reducing it to H_2S. The microbe can grow on H_2 as electron donor for sulfate reduction, but can also use a number of organic compounds such as sugars organic acids (lactate), starch and peptides.

Interestingly, this organism seems to have some metabolic similarity to the methanogens in that it contains small amounts of several coenzymes otherwise unique to methanogens. It also produces small amounts of methane during its metabolism, but cannot grow on typical methanogen substrates such as H_2 and CO_2 unless sulfate is present. The complete genome sequence of Archaeoglobus has revealed genes for many of the enzymes of methanogenesis, but the organism lacks a key enzyme of the process, methyl-CoM-reductase. One hypothesis is that these methanogenesis-like enzymes serve in a pathway that uses lactate and forms CO_2 rather and methanogenesis per se. Archaeoglobus may even be an intermediate step on the way to the evolution of methanogens.

Crenarchaeota

The Crenarchaeota group is composed of thermoacidophiles and hyperthermophiles that are phylogenetically distinct from physiologically similar Euryarchaeota. The hyperthermophiles of this kingdom can grow at the highest temperatures ever recorded for life. Crenarchaeota species are defined more by what they cannot do than by what they can. They lack eukaryotic histones, their DNA polymerase is unlike the Euryarchaeota, and they do not contain the cell division proteins MinD and FtsZ that are common to bacteria as well as eukaryotes.

Future research will certainly reveal better descriptions of the common capabilities of these microbes. Hyperthermophilic Crenarchaeota species form a tight cluster, with short branches on the phylogenetic tree. Since they have probably been around for billions of years, this suggests that these microbes have low mutation rates and slow evolutionary clocks, though it is possible that their environments put specific demands on the 16S rRNA function and therefore sequence.

Hyperthermophilic Crenarchaeota

The best studied members of this groups tend to be the hyperthermophiles and they are all found near volcanic habitats either on land or in the sea. Sulfolobus species grow in hot, sulfur-rich, acidic springs with pH values of 1 to 5 and temperatures up to 90°C. Given the low solubility of oxygen in hot water, Sulfolobus species may have systems to increase the rate of oxygen uptake. Sulfolobus is a strict aerobe and can grow chemolithotrophically by oxidizing H_2S or So to H_2SO_4 and using oxygen as the terminal electron acceptor. The microbe is capable of CO_2 fixation by a modified 3-hydroxypropionate pathway, but also utilizes organic compounds present in the environment for its carbon source. Sulfolobus cells have a somewhat irregular lobate morphology.

Another species of Crenarchaeota found in these hot springs has a potentially interesting metabolism. The genus is Acidianus, and includes facultative anaerobes that use elemental sulfur under both aerobic and anaerobic conditions. This microbe is capable of using sulfur at either end of its catabolic processes, either as an electron donor or as a terminal electron acceptor. In the presence of oxygen, sulfur is oxidized to sulfuric acid, and the electrons added to oxygen. Under anoxic conditions hydrogen gas is reduced and sulfur is oxidized, with the two elements combining to form hydrogen sulfide. Acidianus cells are more or less spherical and not as irregular as those of Sulfolobus. They can grow at temperatures from 60 to 95°C and have an optimum pH of 2.

Sulfolobus DNA is about 37% GC and that of Acidianus is even lower at 31% GC. This might be a bit surprising because high-GC DNA is more thermostable than in low-GC DNA when melting curves are done in a test tube. However, under physiological salt conditions and in the presence of proteins that associate with DNA, even low-GC is stable at these growth temperature. This explanation only shows that low-GC is tolerated by thermophiles, but not how such an unusual GC content was not arrived at. Indeed, we really do not know how the GC content of any organism evolved.

Hydrothermal vents under the ocean are also excellent habitats for Crenarchaeota cells and they harbor the most thermophilic of all known microorganisms. Pyrodictium species have an optimum growth temperature of 105°C, but are also notable because of their remarkable cell morphology. Irregular disk-shaped cells are bound together in a mycelium-like matrix that is attached to sulfur crystals. The matrix is made of fibers that are hollow and consist of protein arranged in a helix like-fashion, reminiscent of that of flagella. These fibers bind cells together and also serve as anchors onto the sulfur crystals present. Pyrodictium cells generate energy by the oxidation of H_2, using elemental S as a terminal electron acceptor. Carbon can be obtained through CO_2 fixation or by the use of organic compounds.

Pyrolobus fumarii currently holds the record as the most thermophilic organism, having a temperature maximum for growth of 113°C. Its growth optimum is also the highest know at 106°C and it will not grow below temperatures of 90 C! These temperatures make sense when you consider its habitat is the walls of black smoker hydrothermal vents. In this environment H_2 is available and Pyrolobus cells are obligate H_2 chemoautolithotrophs. The electrons are coupled to the reduction of NO_3-, S_2O_3-, or O_2, forming NH^{4+}, H_2S and H_2O, respectively. The microbe is also extremely thermotolerant and is able to survive autoclaving (121°C) for over an hour. This capability is likely useful in the ever shifting environment of the hydrothermal vent where the organism may have to withstand periodic increases in temperature.

The sulfate-reducing archaea of both the Euryarchaeota and Crenarchaeota are now known to be widespread. One of the reasons that this group has begun to receive attention is that sulfate-reducing organisms are responsible for "souring" oil wells (they metabolize sulfate to hydrogen sulfide, which is highly soluble in oil). In addition to increasing the sulfur emissions when the oil is burned or increasing the cost of refining it, sulfide attacks the metal in well casings and pipelines, causing leaks and corrosion.

Kornarchaeota

Direct isolation 16S rRNA genes from an unusual hot spring

in Yellowstone revealed one candidate that did not fit into any other phylogenetic kingdom. This new sequence was placed into its own kingdom, the Kornarchaeota, and since that time several other related species, including culturable isolates, have also been found. These isolates split very early in the phylogenetic tree of life and their properties may be similar to those of the earliest microbes on earth.

10

Antimicrobial Drugs

An antimicrobial drug is a chemical substance that destroys disease-causing microorganisms with minimal damage to host tissues. Antibacterial drugs affect many targets in a prokaryotic cell.

Action of Antimicrobial Drugs

1. General action is either by directly killing microorganisms (bactericidal) or by inhibiting their growth (bacteriostatic).
2. Some agents, such as penicillin, inhibit cell wall synthesis in bacteria.
3. Other agents, such as chloramphenicol, erythromycin, tetracyclines, and streptomycin, inhibit protein synthesis by acting on 70S ribosomes.
4. Agents such as polyrnyxin B cause injury to plasma membranes.
5. Rifampin and the quinolones inhibit nucleic acid synthesis.
6. Agents such as sulfanilamide act as antimetabolites by competitively inhibiting enzyme activity.

Inhibitors of Cell Wall Synthesis

1. All penicillins contain a b-lactam ring. Penicillins inhibit peptidoglycan synthesis.
2. Natural penicillins produced by *Penicillium* are effective against gram-positive cocci and spirochetes.
3. Penicillinases (b-lactamases) are bacterial enzymes that destroy natural penicillins.
4. Semisynthetic penicillins are made in the laboratory by adding different side chains onto the b -lactam ring made by the fungus.
5. Semisynthetic penicillins are resistant to penicillinases and have a broader spectrum of activity than natural penicillins.
6. The monobactam aztreonam affects only gram-negative bacteria.
7. Cephalosporins inhibit cell wall synthesis and are used against penicillin-resistant strains.
8. Carbapenems are broad-spectrum antibiotics that inhibit cell wall synthesis.
9. Polypeptides such as bacitracin and polymyxin B are applied topically to treat superficial infections.
10. Bacitracin inhibits cell wall synthesis primarily in gram-positive bacteria.
11. Vancomycin inhibits cell wall synthesis and may be used to kill penicillinase-producing staphylococci.
12. Isoniazid (INH) inhibits mycolic acid synthesis in mycobacteria. INH is administered with rifampin or ethambutol to treat tuberculosis.
13. The antimetabolite ethambutol is used with other drugs to treat tuberculosis.

Inhibitors of Protein Synthesis

Aminoglycosides, tetracyclines, chloramphenicol, and macrolides inhibit protein synthesis at 70S ribosomes.

Injury to plasma membrane

Polymyxin B and bacitracin cause damage to plasma membranes.

Inhibitors of Nucleic Acid (DNA/RNA) Synthesis

1. Rifamycin inhibits mRNA synthesis; it is used to treat tuberculosis.
2. Quinolones and fluoroquinolones inhibit DNA gyrase for treatment of urinary tract infections.

Competitive inhibitors of the synthesis of essential metabolites

1. Sulfonamides competitively inhibit folic acid synthesis.
2. TMP-SMX (trimethoprim-sulfamethoxazole) competitively inhibits dihydrofolic acid synthesis for treatment of urinary tract and intestinal infections.

Antifungal Drugs

1. Polyenes, such as nystatin and amphotericin B, combine with plasma membrane sterols and are fungicidal.
2. Azoles interfere with sterol synthesis and are used to treat cutaneous and systemic mycoses.
3. Griseofulvin interferes with eukaryotic cell division and is used primarily to treat skin infections caused by fungi.

Antiviral Drugs

1. Amantadine blocks penetration or uncoating of influenza A virus.

2. Nucleoside and nucleotide analogs such as acyclovir, AZT, ddI, and ddC inhibit DNA or RNA synthesis.
3. Protease inhibitors, such as indinavir and saquinavir, block activity of an HIV enzyme essential for assembly of a new viral coat.
4. Alpha-interferons inhibit the spread of viruses to new cells.

Antiprotozoan and Antihelminthic Drugs

1. Chloroquine, quinacrine, diiodohydroxyquine, pentamidine, and metronidazole are used to treat protozoan infections.
2. Chloroquine and quinacrine stop DNA synthesis by intercalation between base pairs.
3. Antihelminthic drugs include niclosamide, mebendazole, praziquantel, and piperazine.
4. Mebendazole disrupts microtubules; pyantel pamoate paralyzes intestinal roundworms.

Antimicrobial Chemotherapy

The earliest evidence of successful chemotherapy is from ancient Peru, where the Indians used bark from the cinchona tree to treat malaria. Other substances were used in ancient China, and we now know that many of the poultices used by primitive peoples contained antibacterial and antifungal substances. Modern chemotherapy has been dated to the work of Paul Ehrlich in Germany, who sought systematically to discover effective agents to treat trypanosomiasis and syphilis. He discovered p-rosaniline, which has antitrypanosomal effects, and arsphenamine, which is effective against syphilis. Ehrlich postulated that it would be possible to find chemicals that were selectively toxic for parasites but not toxic to humans. This idea has been called the "magic bullet" concept. It had little success until the 1930s, when Gerhard Domagk discovered the protective effects of prontosil, the forerunner of sulfonamide.

Ironically, penicillin G was discovered fortuitously in 1929 by Fleming, who did not initially appreciate the magnitude of his discovery. In 1939 Florey and colleagues at Oxford University again isolated penicillin. In 1944 Waksman isolated streptomycin and subsequently found agents such as chloramphenicol, tetracyclines, and erythromycin in soil samples. By the 1960s, improvements in fermentation techniques and advances in medicinal chemistry permitted the synthesis of many new chemotherapeutic agents by molecular modification of existing compounds.

Progress in the development of novel antibacterial agents has been great, but the development of effective, nontoxic antifungal and antiviral agents has been slow. Amphotericin B, isolated in the 1950s, remains an effective antifungal agent, although newer agents such as fluconazole are now widely used. Nucleoside analogs such as acyclovir have proved effective in the chemotherapy of selected viral infections.

Biochemical Basis

Bacterial cells grow and divide, replicating repeatedly to reach the large numbers present during an infection or on the surfaces of the body. To grow and divide, organisms must synthesize or take up many types of biomolecules. Antimicrobial agents interfere with specific processes that are essential for growth and/or division (Fig. 1). They can be separated into groups such as inhibitors of bacterial and fungal cell walls, inhibitors of cytoplasmic membranes, inhibitors of nucleic acid synthesis, and inhibitors of ribosome function (Table 1). Antimicrobial agents may be

Table 1: Mechanisms of action of antimicrobial agents

Inhibitors of Bacterial Cell Wall Synthesis
- Drugs that inhibit biosynthetic enzymes
  - Fosfomycin
  - Cycloserine
- Drugs that combine with carrier molecules
  - Bacitracin
- Drugs that combine with cell wall substrates
  - Vancomycin
- Drugs that inhibit polymerization and attachment of new pepidoglycan to cell wall
  - Penicillins
  - Cephalosporins
  - Carbapenems
  - Monobactams

Inhibitors of Cytoplasmic Membranes
- Drugs that disorganize the cytoplasmic membrane
  - Tyrocidins
  - Polymyxins
- Drugs that produce pores in membranes
  - Gramicidins
- Drugs that alter structure of fungi
  - Polyenes (amphotericin)
  - Imidazoles (kotoconazole, fluconazole)

Inhibitors of Nucleic Acid Synthesis
- Inhibitors of nucleotide metabolism
  - Adenosine arabinoside (viruses)
  - Acyclovir (viruses)
  - Flucytosine (fungi)
- Agents that impair DNA template function
  - Intercalating agents
  - Chloroquine (parasites)
- Inhibitors of DNA replication
  - Quinolones
  - Nitroimidazoles
- Inhibitors of RNA polymerase
  - Rifampin

Inhibitors of Ribosome Function
- Inhibitors of 30S units
  - Streptomycin
  - Kanamycin, gentamicin, amikacin
  - Spectinomycin
  - Tetracyclines
- Inhibitors of 50S units
  - Chloramphenicol
  - Clindamycin
  - Erythromycin
  - Fusidic acid

Inhibitors of Folate Metabolism
- Inhibitor of pteroic acid synthetase
  - Sulfonamides
- Inhibitor of dihydrofolate reductase
  - Trimephoprim

either bactericidal, killing the target bacterium or fungus, or bacteriostatic, inhibiting its growth. Bactericidal agents are more effective, but bacteriostatic agents can be extremely beneficial since they permit the normal defenses of the host to destroy the microorganisms.

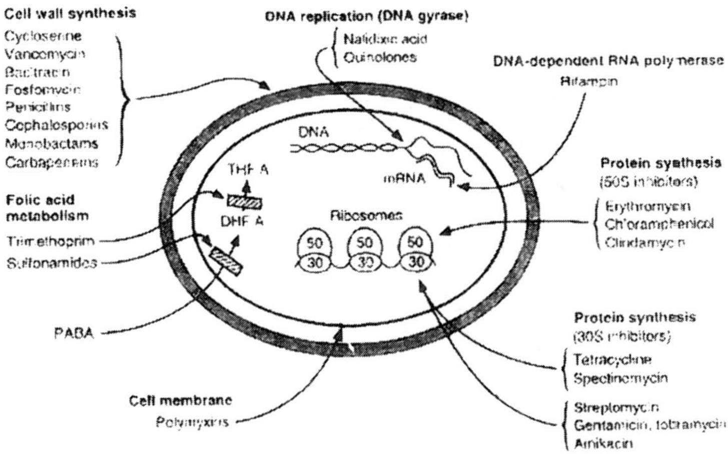

Figure 1: Sites of action of different antimicrobial agents. PABA, paraminobenzoic acid; DHFA, dihydrofolic acid; THFA, tetrahydrofolic acid.

Bacterial Cell Wall Synthesis

Bacteria are classified as Gram-positive and Gram-negative organisms on the basis of staining characteristics. Gram-positive bacterial cell walls contain peptidoglycan and teichoic or teichuronic acid, and the bacterium may or may not be surrounded by a protein or polysaccharide envelope. Gram-negative bacterial cell walls contain peptidoglycan, lipopolysaccharide, lipoprotein, phospholipid, and protein

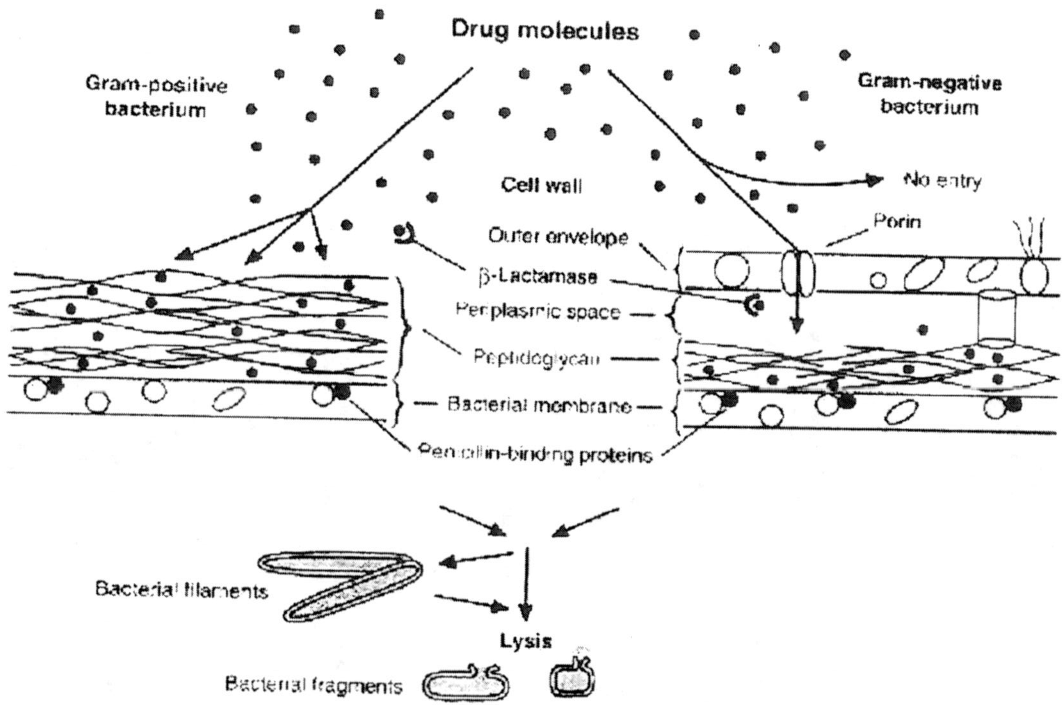

Figure 2: Outer wall of Gram-positive and Gram-negative species and deail of porin channels of Gram-negative bacteria.

(Fig. 2). The critical attack site of anti-cell-wall agents is the peptidoglycan layer. This layer is essential for the survival of bacteria in hypotonic environments; loss or damage of this layer destroys the rigidity of the bacterial cell wall, resulting in death.

Peptidoglycan synthesis occurs in three stages. The first stage takes place in the cytoplasm, where the low-molecular-weight precursors UDP-GlcAc and UDP-MurNAc-L-Ala-D-Glu-meso-Dap-D-Ala-D-Ala are synthesized. A number of antimicrobial agents interfere with these early steps in cell wall biosynthesis. UTP and N-acetylglucosamine alpha-1-P are converted to UDP-N-acetylglucosamine, which is subsequently converted by the enzyme phosphoenolpyruvate: UDP-GIcNAc-3-enol-pyruvyltransferase. Fosfomycins block this transfer by a direct nucleophilic attack on the enzyme.

Because mammalian enzymes such as enolase, pyruvate kinase, carboxykinases, and the shikimate enlaces are not inhibited by these compounds, fosfomycins have no effect on the host. Three amino acids are added to the muramyl peptide to yield a tripeptide to which two more amino acids will be linked. The dipeptide D-alanyl-D-alanine is synthesized from two molecules of D-alanine by the enzyme D-alanyl-D-alanine synthetase. D-Alanine is produced from L-alanine by an alanine racemase. Cycloserine inhibits both alanine racemase and D-alanyl-D-alanine synthetase owing to the structural similarity of cycloserine and D-alanine and to the fact that cycloserine actually binds to the enzymes better than the D-alanine.

The second stage of cell wall synthesis is catalyzed by membrane-bound enzymes. The nonnucleotide portion of the precursor molecules previously made are transferred sequentially to a carrier in the cytoplasmic membrane. This carrier is a phosphorylated undecaprenyl alcohol. The lipid carrier functions as a point of attachment to the membrane for the precursors and allows for transport of the subunits across the hydrophobic interior of the cytoplasmic membrane to the outside surface. Bacitracin is a peptide antibiotic that specifically interacts with the pyrophosphate derivate of the undecaprenyl alcohol, preventing further transfer of the muramylpentapeptide from the precursor nucleotide to the nascent peptidoglycan.

The third stage of cell wall synthesis involves polymerization of the subunits and the attachment of nascent peptidoglycan to the cell wall. Polymerization occurs by transfer of the new peptidoglycan chain from its carrier in the membrane to the nonreducing N-acetylglucosamine of the new saccharide-peptide that is attached to the membrane. The new peptidoglycan is attached to preexisting cell wall peptidoglycan by a transpeptidase reaction that involves peptide chains in both polymers, one of which must possess a D-alanyl-D-alanine terminus. It is believed that the transpeptidase enzyme cleaves the peptide bond between two D-alanyl residues in the pentapeptide and become acylated via the carbonyl group of the penultimate D-alanine residue.

This final reaction is inhibited by ß-lactam antibiotics. These antibiotics contain a critical four-membered ring, which undergoes an acylation reaction with the transpeptidases that cross-link the polymers mentioned above. The ß-lactam antibiotics are the penicillins (penams), cephalosporins (including oxacephems and cephamycins), penems, thienamycins (carbapenems), and aztreonam (monobactams) (Fig. 3). The enzymes involved in this final process of cell wall formation are called penicillin-binding proteins since they were discovered by labeling with radioactive penicillin G.

The enzymes are different in Gram-positive and Gram-negative bacteria and in anaerobic species. Differences in the penicillin-binding proteins explain, to some extent, differences in antibacterial activity of the ß-lactam antibiotics. The penicillin-binding protein, to which a particular ß-lactam antibiotic binds, affects the morphologic response of the bacterium to the agent. For example, some antibiotics bind to a penicillin-binding protein that is involved in forming the septum between dividing cells; as a result, the bacteria continue to grow into long filaments, which eventually die.

Binding to another penicillin-binding protein results in rapid lysis of a bacterium because the wall bulges and the bacterium bursts. ß-Lactams such as mecillinam (an amidino penicillin) do not bind to the penicillin-binding proteins of Gram-positive bacteria and therefore do not affect these bacteria. Aztreonam binds only to Gram-negative penicillin-binding proteins and does not inhibit Gram-positive or anaerobic species.

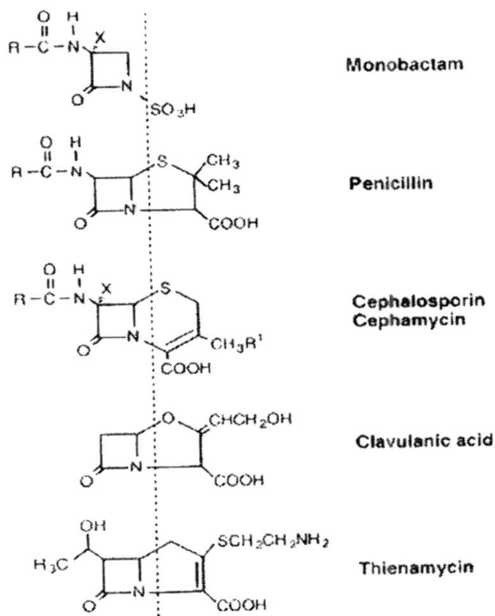

Figure 3: Basic structures of ß-lactam antibiotics.

Vancomycin interrupts cell wall synthesis by forming a complex with the C-terminal D-alanine residues of peptidoglycan precursors. Complex formation at the outer surface of the cytoplasmic membrane prevents the transfer of the precursors from a lipid carrier to the growing peptidoglycan wall by transglycosidases.

Biochemical reactions in the cell wall catalyzed by transpeptidases and D,D-carboxypeptidases are also inhibited by vancomycin and other glycopeptide antimicrobials. Because of its large size and complex structure (Fig. 4), vancomycin does not penetrate the outer membrane of gram-negative organisms. With resistance to beta-lactams increasing in frequency among staphylococci and enterococci, glycopeptides such as vancomycin remain important therapeutic agents against such bacteria.

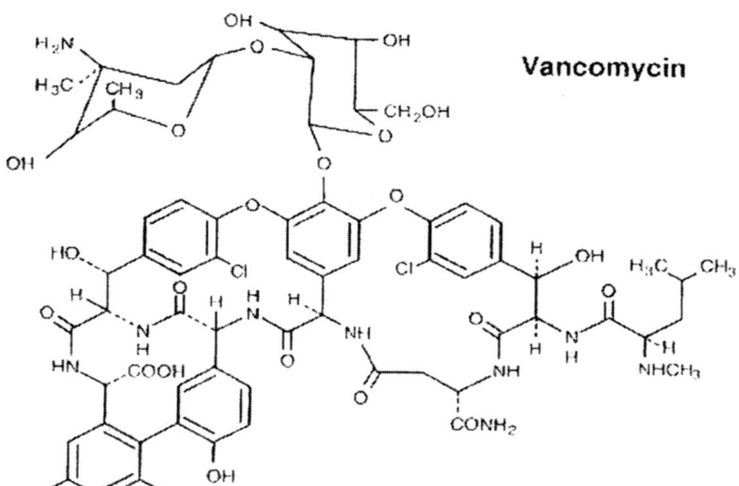

Figure 4: Structure of vancomycin

Cytoplasmic Membranes

Biologic membranes are composed basically of lipid, protein, and lipoprotein. The cytoplasmic membrane acts as a diffusion barrier for water, ions, nutrients, and transport systems. Most workers now believe that membranes are a lipid matrix with globular proteins randomly distributed to penetrate through the lipid bilayer. A number of antimicrobial agents can cause disorganization of the membrane. These agents can be divided into cationic, anionic, and neutral agents.

The best-known compounds are polymyxin B and colistemethate (polymyxin E). These high-molecular-weight octapeptides inhibit Gram-negative bacteria that have negatively charged lipids at the surface. Since the activity of the polymyxins is antagonized by Mg^{2+} and Ca^{2+}, they probably competitively displace Mg^{2+} or Ca^{2+} from the negatively charged phosphate groups on membrane lipids. Basically, polymyxins disorganize membrane permeability so that nucleic acids and cations leak out and the cell dies. The polymyxins are of virtually no use as systemic agents since they bind to various ligands in body tissues and are potent toxins for the kidney and nervous system. Gramicidins are also membrane-active antibiotics that appear to act by producing aqueous pores in the membranes. They also are used only topically.

Fungal Membranes

Fungal membranes contain sterols, whereas bacterial membranes do not. The polyene antibiotics, which apparently act by binding to membrane sterols, contain a rigid hydrophobic center and a flexible hydrophilic section. Structurally, polyenes are tightly packed rods held in rigid extension by the polyene portion. They interact with fungal cells to produce a membrane-polyene complex that alters the membrane permeability, resulting in internal acidification of the fungus with exchange of K^+ and sugars; loss of phosphate esters, organic acids, nucleotides; and eventual leakage of cell protein.

In effect, the polyene makes a pore in the fungal membrane and the contents of the fungus leak out. Prokaryotic cells neither bind to nor are inhibited by polyenes. Although numerous polyene antibiotics have been isolated, only amphotericin B is used systemically (Fig. 5). Nystatin is used as a topical agent and primaricin as an ophthalmic preparation.

A number of other agents interfere with the synthesis of fungal lipid membranes. These agents belong to a class of compounds referred to as imidazoles: miconazole, ketoconazole, clotrimazole, and fluconazole. These compounds inhibit the incorporation of subunits into ergosterol and may also directly damage the membrane.

Figure 5: Structure of amphotericin B.

Nucleic Acid Synthesis

Antimicrobial agents can interfere with nucleic acid synthesis at several different levels. They can inhibit nucleotide synthesis or interconversion; they can prevent DNA from functioning as a proper template; and they can interfere with the polymerases involved in the replication and transcription of DNA.

Interference with Nucleotide Synthesis

A large number of agents interfere with purine and pyrimidine synthesis or with the interconversion or utilization of nucleotides. Other agents act as nucleotide analogs that are incorporated into polynucleotides. Flucytosine (5-fluorocytosine) is an antifungal agent that inhibits yeast species. It is converted in the fungal cell to 5-fluorouracfl, which inhibits thymidylate synthetase resulting in a deficit of thymine nucleotides and impaired DNA synthesis. Adenosine arabinoside inhibits viruses.

It is phosphorylated in virus-infected cells and acts as a competitive analog of DATP, inhibiting the incorporation of DATP into DNA. Acyclovir is a nucleoside analog that, after being converted to a triphosphate, inhibits the thymidine kinase and DNA polymerase of herpes viruses. Zidovudine (AZT) inhibits human immunodeficiency virus (HM replication by interfering with viral RNA-dependent DNA polymerase (reverse transcriptase).

Template Function of DNA

A number of substances bind to DNA by intercalation. None of them is useful as an antibacterial agent; however, chloroquine and miracil D (lucanthone) inhibit plasmodia and schistosomes, respectively. These agents are thought to intercalate into the DNA and thereby to inhibit further nucleic acid synthesis. Acridine dyes such as proflavine act by this intercalation mechanism, but because they are toxic and carcinogenic in mammals they cannot be used as antibacterial agents.

Inhibition of DNA-Directed DNA Polymerase

Rifamycins are a class of antibiotics that inhibit DNA-directed RNA polymerase (Fig. 6). Polypeptide chains in RNA polymerase attach to a factor that confers specificity for the recognition of promoter sites that initiate transcription of the DNA. Rifampin binds noncovalently but strongly to a subunit of RNA polymerase and interferes specifically with the initiation process. However, it has no effect once polymerization has begun.

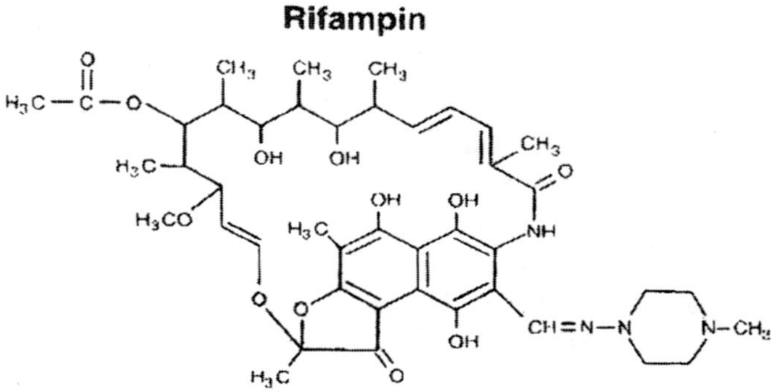

Figure 6: Structure of rifamphin, which inhibits the DNA-directed RNA polymerase.

Inhibition of DNA Replication

DNA gyrase and topoisomerase I act in concert to maintain an optimum supercoiling state of DNA in the cell. In this capacity, DNA gyrase is essential for relieving torsional strain during replication of circular chromosomes in bacteria. The enzyme is a tetrameric protein composed of two A and two B subunits. A transient, covalent bond between the A subunit and DNA occurs during the double strand passage reaction catalyzed by gyrase. Quinolones such as nalidixic acid (Fig. 7), bind to the cleavage complex composed of DNA and gyrase during this strand passage. This interaction of quinolone acts to stabilize the cleavage intermediate which has a detrimental effect on the normal DNA replication process. The effects of this inhibition result in the death of the bacterial cell. The newer fluoroquinolones such as ciprofloxacin, norfloxacin, and ofloxacin also interact with DNA gyrase and possess a broad spectrum of antimicrobial activity.

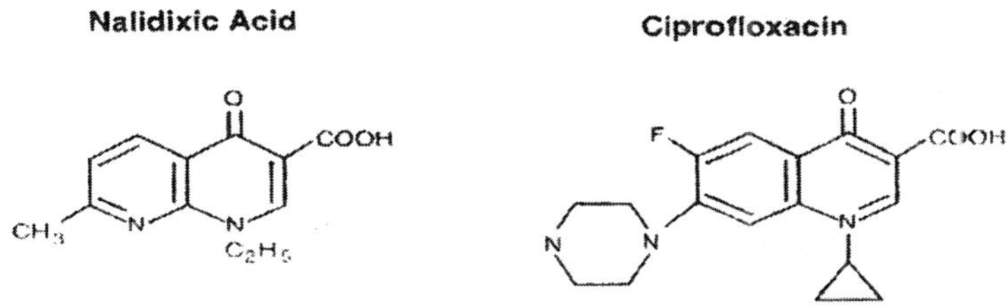

Figure 7: Structure of quinolone antibiotica.

Nitroimidazoles such as metronidazole inhibit anaerobic bacteria and protozoa. The nitro group of the nitrosohydroxyl amino moiety is reduced by an electron transport protein in anaerobic bacteria (Fig. 8). The reduced drug causes strand breaks in the DNA. Mammalian cells are unharmed because they lack enzymes to reduce the nitro group of these agents.

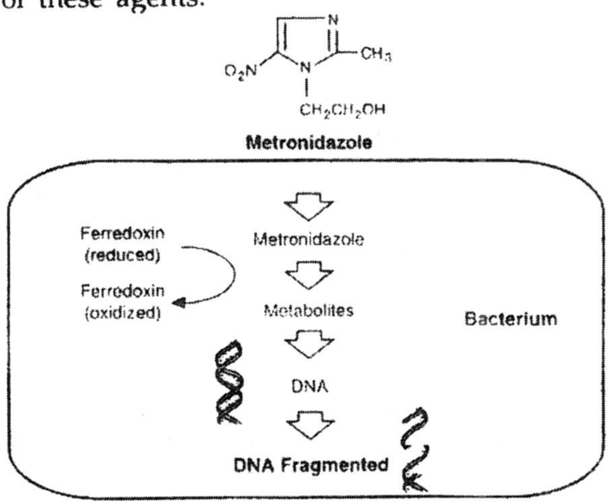

Figure 8: Structure of metronidazole and its mechanism of action

Ribosome Function

The basic structure and function of ribosomes are presented in Fig. 1. A number of antibacterial agents act by inhibiting ribosome function. Bacterial ribosomes contain two subunits, the 50S and 30S subunits, and it is possible to localize the action of antibiotics to one or both subunits. It is also possible to isolate the specific ribosomal proteins to which an agent binds and to isolate bacterial mutants that lack a specific ribosomal protein and therefore show resistance to a particular agent.

Aminoglycosides act by binding to specific ribosomal subunits. Aminoglycosides are complex sugars connected in glycosidic linkage (Fig. 9). They differ both in the molecular nucleus, which can be streptidine or 2-deoxystreptidine, and in the aminohexoses linked to the nucleus. Essential to the activity of these agents are free NH, and OH groups by which aminoglycosides bind to specific ribosomal proteins.

Streptomycin, the first aminoglycoside studied, was a useful too] in elucidating protein synthesis. However, it is rarely used clinically today except to treat tuberculosis, and its mode of action differs to some extent from that of the other clinically useful aminoglycosides, which are 2-deoxystreptidine derivatives such as gentamicin, tobramycin, and amikacin. Streptomycin binds to a specific S12 protein in the 30S ribosomal subunit (Fig. 10) and causes the ribosome to misread the genetic code.

Other aminoglycosides bind not only to the S12 protein of the 30S ribosome, but also to some extent to the L6 protein of the 50S ribosome. This latter binding is quite important in terms of the resistance of bacteria to aminoglycosides. Indeed, the aminoglycoside-type drugs can combine with other binding sites on 30S ribosomes, and they kill bacteria by inducing the formation of aberrant, nonfunctional complexes as well as by causing misreading (Fig. 11).

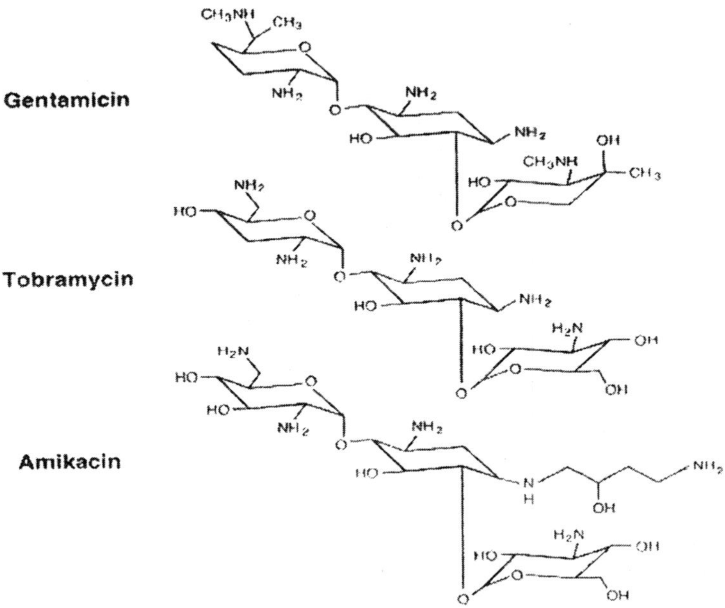

Figure 9: Structures of three aminoglycoside antibiotics used clinically

Spectinomycin is an aminocylitol antibiotic that is closely related to the aminoglycosides. It binds to a different protein in the ribosome and is bacteriostatic but not bactericidal. It is used to treat penicillin-resistant gonorrhea.

Other agents that bind to 30S ribosomes are the tetracyclines (Fig. 12). These agents appear to inhibit the binding of aminoacyl-tRNA into the A site of the bacterial ribosome. Tetracycline binding is transient, so these agents are bacteriostatic. Nonetheless, they inhibit a wide variety of bacteria, chlamydias, and mycoplasmas and are extremely useful antibiotics.

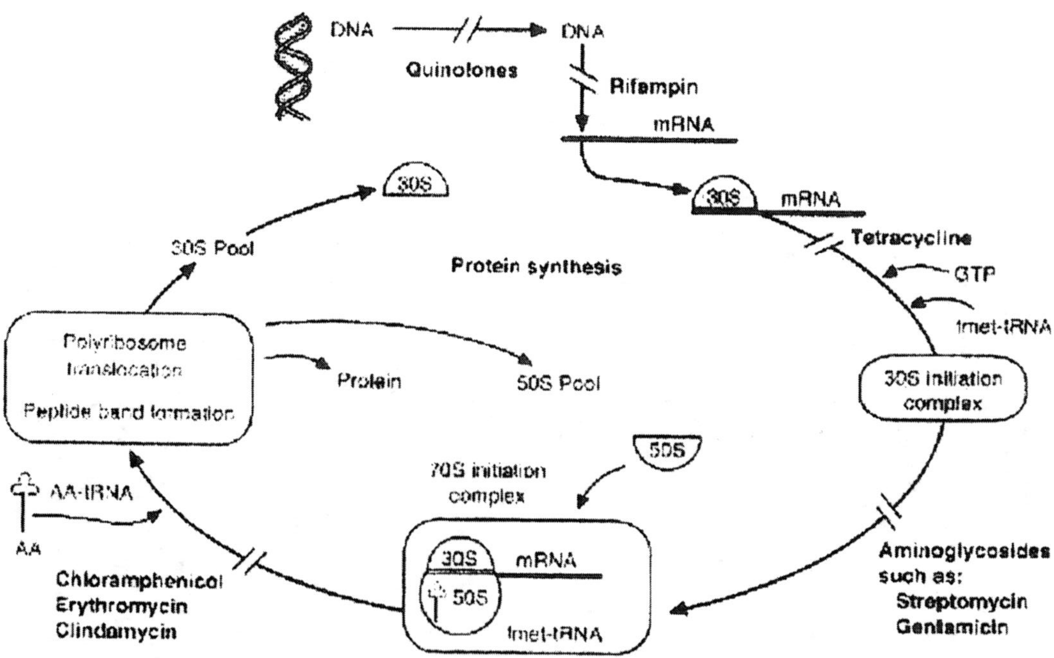

Figure 10: Diagrammatic representation of inhibition sites of protein biosynthesis by various antibiotics that bind to the 30S and 50S ribosomes.

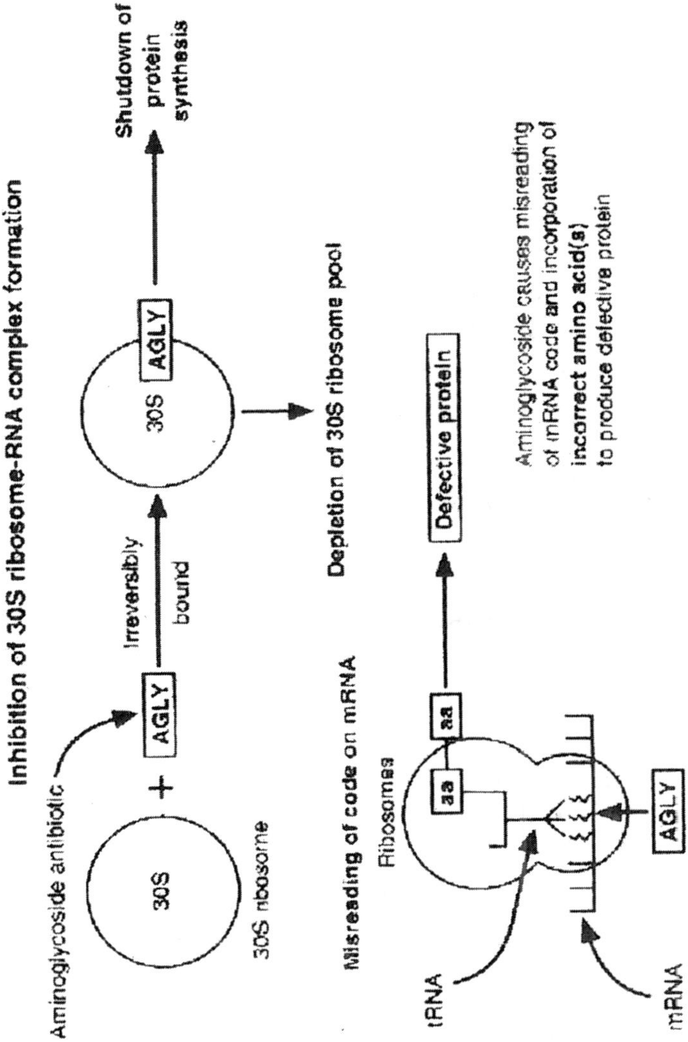

Figure 11: Inhibition of protein biosynthesis by aminoglycosides

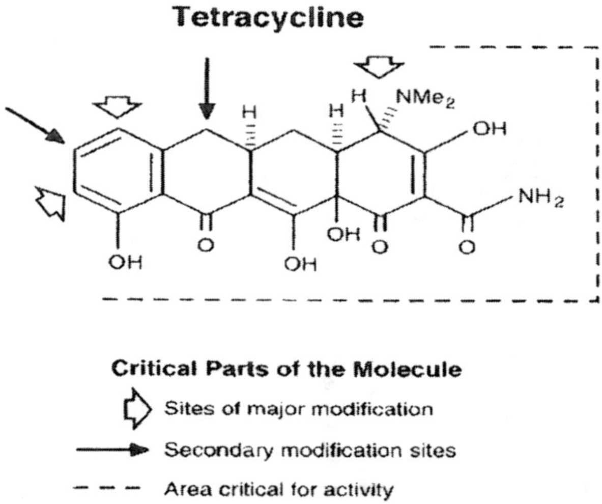

Figure 12: Structure of tetracycline showing the area critical for activity and major and minor points of modification

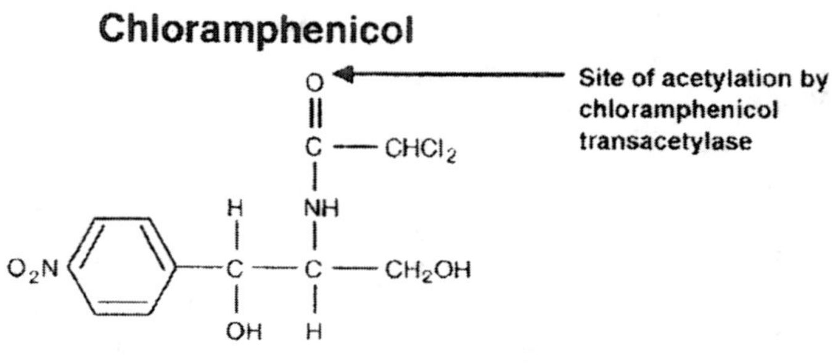

Figure 13: Structure of chloranphenicol

There are three important classes of drugs that inhibit the 50S ribosomal subunit. Chloramphenicol (Fig. 13) is a bacteriostatic agent that inhibits both Gram-positive and

Gram-negative bacteria. It inhibits peptide bond formation by binding to a peptidyltransferase enzyme on the 50S ribosome. Macrolides are large lactone ring compounds that bind to 50S ribosomes and appear to impair a peptidyltransferase reaction or translocation, or both. The most important macrolide is erythromycin, which inhibits Gram-positive species and a few Gram-negative species such as *Haemophilus, Mycoplasma, Chlamydia, and Legionella.*

New molecules such as azithromycin and clarithromycin have greater activity than erythromycin against many of these pathogens. Lincinoids, of which the most important is clindamycin, have a similar site of activity (Fig. 14). Both macrolides and lincinoids are generally bacteriostatic. inhibiting only the formation of new peptide chains.

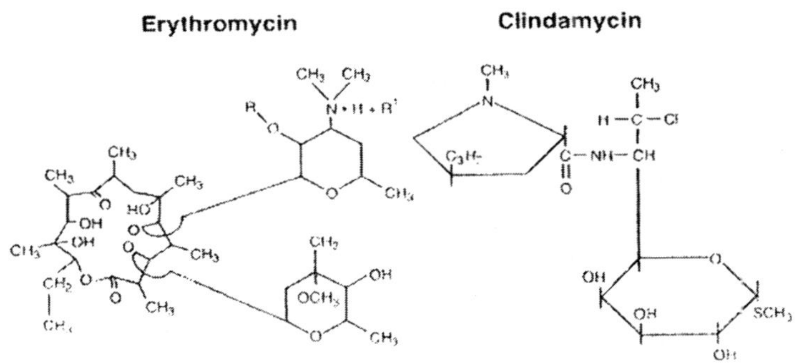

Figure 14: Structure of erythromycin (prototype or macrolide) and clindamycin

Biochemical Targets

Both trimethoprim and the sulfonamides interfere with folate metabolism in the bacterial cell by competitively blocking the biosynthesis of tetrahydrofolate, which acts as a carrier of one-carbon fragments and is necessary for the ultimate synthesis of DNA, RNA and bacterial cell wall proteins (Fig. 15). Unlike mammals, bacteria and protozoan parasites usually lack a transport system to take up preformed folic acid from their environment. Most of these organisms must synthesize folates, although some are capable of using exogenous thymidine, circumventing the need for folate metabolism.

Sulfonamides competitively block the conversion of pteridine and p-aminobenzoic acid (PABA) to dihydrofolic acid by the enzyme pteridine synthetase. Sulfonamides have a greater affinity than p-aminobenzoic acid for pteridine synthetase. Trimethoprim has a tremendous affinity for bacterial dihydrofolate reductase (10,000 to 100,000 times higher than for the mammalian enzyme); when bound to this enzyme, it inhibits the synthesis of tetrahydrofolate.

Antibacterial agents that affect mvcobacteria

Isoniazid is a nicotinamide derivative that inhibits mycobacteria. Its precise mode of action is not known, but it affects the synthesis of lipids, nucleic acids, and the mycolic acid of the cell walls of these species. Ethambutol is also an antimycobacterial agent whose mechanism of action is unknown. It is mycostatic, whereas isoniazid is mycocidal. The other antituberculosis drugs, rifampin and streptomycin, affect mycobacteria in the same manner that they inhibit bacteria. Pyrazinamide is a synthetic analog of nicotinamide. It is bactericidal, but its exact mechanism is unknown

Bacterial Resistance

Bacteria have proved adept at developing resistance to new antimicrobial agents. There are a number of ways in which bacteria can become resistant (Table 2). Most of the early studies of bacterial resistance focused on single-step mutational events of chromosomal origin. Resistance to the

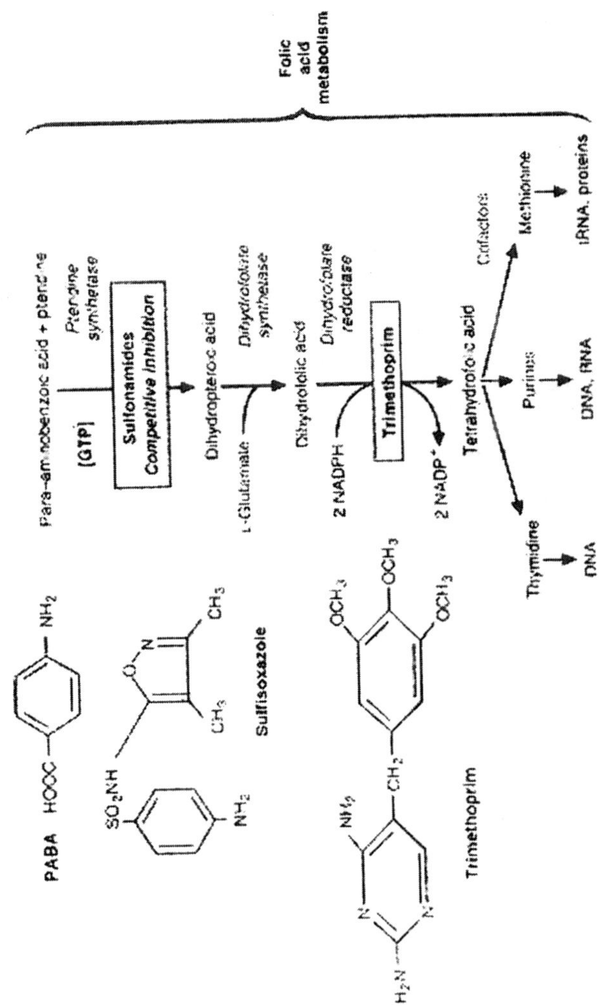

Figure 15: Structure of sulfonamide and trimethoprim with sites of inhibition of folic metabolism.

early sulfonamides, for example, was the result of a single amino acid change in the enzyme pteridine synthetase that caused sulfonamides to bind less well than p-aminobenzoic acid. Similarly, a single step mutation that altered a ribosomal protein conferred resistance to streptomycin.

In the late 1950s, Japanese workers found that enteric bacteria such as Shigella dysenteriae had become resistant not only to sulfonamides but also to the tetracyclines and chloramphenicol. This resistance was due not to a chromosomal change, but rather to the presence of extrachromosomal DNA that was transmissible. This type of resistance is called plasmid-mediated resistance.

Table 2. Mechanisms of resistance

Alteration of target
- Modification to insensitivity to inhibitor
- Reduction in physiologic importance of target
- Synthesis of new target enzyme that duplicates function of inhibited target

Prevention of access to target
- Efflux of more drug than enters cell
- Failure of modified drug to enter cell

Inactivation of agent
- Destruction of the agent
- Modification of the agent so it fails to bind to target

Failure to convert an inactive precursor agent to its active form

Resistance-conferring plasmids are present in virtually all bacteria (Table 3). For example, resistance to ampicillin appeared in *Haemophilus influenzae* in 1974 and in Neisseria gonorrhoeae in 1976. In the last several years, organisms such as enterococci have been shown to contain plasmids that confer resistance to drugs such as ampicillin and aminoglycosides.

Bacteria also contain transposons, which can insert into plasmids and also into the chromosome. Transposon-mediated resistance to most of the major antibiotics has been found in the past few years.

Table 3: R-Plasmid-Mediated-Resistance

Antibiotic	Mechanism	Organisms
Penicillin, ampicillin, carbenicillin, etc.	β-Lactamase hydrolysis	Staphylococci, enterococci (rare). Entero-bacteriaceae, pseudomonads. bacteroides
Oxacillin, methicillin, etc.	β-Lactamase hydrolysis	Enterobacteriaceae. pseudomonads
Cephalosporins	β-Lactamase	Staphylococci. Enterobacteriaceae, pseudomonads, bacteroides
Chloramphenicol	Acetylation	Staphylococci, enterococci, streptococci, Enterobacteriaceae, pseudomonads
Tetracyclines	Permeability block	Staphylococci, enterococci, streptococci, Enterobacteriaceae, pseudomonads, bacteroides
Aminoglycosides Streptomycin Neomycin Kanamycin	Acetylation Phosphorylation Adenylation (alters binding to ribosomes and uptake of drug)	Staphylococci, enterococci, Entero-bacteriaceae, pseudomonads
Tobramycin Amikacin		

Contd . . .

Contd . . .

Macrolides-Lincinoids		
Erythromycin	Altered 23S RNA	Staphylococci, enterococci, streptococci, bacteroides
Clindamycin		
Trimethoprim	Altered dihydrofolate reductase	Staphylococci, Enterobacteriaceae
Sulfonamides	Altered tetraphydro-pteroic synthetase	Staphylococci, enterococci, streptococci, Enterobacteriaceae, pseudomonads
Fostomycin	Altered glucose	Staphylococci, Enterobacteriaceae
Vancomycin	New protein	Enterococci

Antimicrobial agents exert a strong selective pressure on the development of both chromosomal and plasmid-mediated resistance, as discussed below. Administration of an antibiotic destroys the susceptible bacteria in a population, but may permit resistant ones to proliferate. From an epidemiologic viewpoint, plasmid-mediated resistance is the most important type, since it is transmissible, is usually highly stable, confers resistance to many different classes of antibiotics simultaneously, and often is associated with other characteristics that enable a microorganism to colonize and invade a susceptible host.

Mechanisms of Resistance

The basic mechanisms by which a microorganism can resist an antimicrobial agent are (1) to alter the receptor for the drug (the molecule on which it exerts its effect); (2) to decrease the amount of drug that reaches the receptor by altering entry or increasing removal of the drug; (3) to destroy or inactivate the drug; and (4) to develop resistant metabolic pathways. Bacteria can possess one or all of these mechanisms simultaneously.

Altered receptors

ß-Lactam Resistance. The ability to analyze changes in receptors for ß-lactams by competition experiments in which penicillin is inhibited from binding to penicillin-binding proteins has explained a number of cases of bacterial resistance to penicillins and cephalosporins. In 1977, *Streptococcus pneumoniae* strains resistant to penicillin G were encountered in South Africa. Plasmids were not the cause of the resistance. Penicillin-resistant *S pneumoniae* cells have altered penicillin-binding proteins, which bind penicillin less well. Resistance of *S pneumoniae* to penicillin has been increasing, and there are now relatively resistant isolates (minimal inhibitory concentration [MIC], 0.1 to 1 mg/ml) in many parts of the world.

Altered penicillin-binding proteins also explain the resistance of some *Staphylococcus aureus* strains to ß-lactamase-stable penicillins (the so-called methicillin-resistant strains). The ß-lactams induce synthesis of a new penicillin-binding protein, PBP2a, which does not bind any ß-lactam. The ß-lactam resistance of coagulase-negative staphylococci is also the result of altered penicillin-binding proteins. Staphylococcal organisms resistant to methicillin are resistant to all penicillins, cephalosporins, and carbapenems.

The resistance of group D streptococci to ß-lactam antibiotics appears to be the result of lower affinity of the penicillin-binding proteins for the penicillins. Enterococci are resistant to all cephalosporins because of failure to bind to the penicillin-binding proteins. One Gram-negative species for which resistance to ß-lactam antibiotics can be correlated with diminished affinity of the target enzymes is *N gonorrhoeae*.

Vancomycin Resistance. Certain transposable genetic elements encode special cell wall-synthesizing enzymes which change the structure of the normal D-Ala-D-Ala side chain in the peptidoglycan assembly pathway. The altered side chain (D-Ala-D-Lac) does not bind vancomycin and allows normal peptidoglycan polymerization to occur in the presence of the drug. Depending upon the nature of the vancomycin resistance gene, high-level resistance can occur to glycopeptides. Thus far, this type of resistance has been found in enterococci but not in multi-resistant isolates of *Staphylococcus aureus*.

Macrolide-lincomycin Resistance. Macrolide-lincomycin resistance in clinical isolates of staphylococci and streptococci has been recognized for several decades. The resistance is due to methylation of two adenine nucleotides in the 23S component of 50S RNA. This resistance is plasmid mediated, and the resistance is encoded on transposons. Resistance results from induction of an enzyme

that is normally repressed. The methylated RNA binds macrolidelincomycin-type drugs less well than unmethylated RNA does. Induction of resistance varies by species, and in most Gram-positive species erythromycin is a more effective inducer of resistance than is clindamycin. The plasmids that mediate macrolide-lincomycin resistance in streptococci and staphylococci have extensive structural similarity, indicating that these plasmids readily pass between these species.

Rifampin Resistance. The resistance of bacteria to rifampin is caused by an alternation of one amino acid in DNA-directed RNA polymerase, which results in reduced binding of rifampin. The degree of resistance is related to the degree to which the enzyme is changed, but does not correlate strictly with enzyme inhibition. This form of resistance occurs at a low level in any population of bacteria so that resistance develops by natural selection during a course of therapy. Naturally resistant organisms are more common among members of the Enterobacteriaceae, explaining why agents of urinary tract infections rapidly became resistant to rifampin. The resistance of *Neisseria meningitides* to rifampin appeared in closed military settings in which rifampin has been used for prophylaxis.

Sulfonamide-trimethoprim Resistance. Sulfonamide can be rendered ineffective by altered or new dihydropteroic synthetase that has poor affinity for sulfonamides and preferentially binds p-aminobenzoic acid. Sulfonamide resistance of this type can result from a point mutation or from acquisition of a plasmid that causes synthesis of the new enzyme. A most serious resistance problem is an increase in resistance to trimethoprim. This plasmid- and transposon-mediated resistance is due to production of an altered dihydrofolate reductase that has markedly reduced affinity for trimethoprim.

Quinolone Resistance. Resistance to quinolones can be caused by mutations in DNA gyrase subunits A or B, reduced outer membrane permeability in gram-negative cells, or to active efflux transporters found in many bacteria. The highest level of resistance to the newer fluoroquinolones is most frequently associated with chromosomal mutations, causing amino acid substitutions in a highly conserved region in the A subunit of DNA gyrase. Multiple-mechanisms of resistance can occur in a single isolate of bacteria, leading to a higher level of resistance to many fluoroauinolones.

Tetracycline Resistance. The uptake of tetracycline by members of the Enterobacteriaceae is biphasic. In an initial energy-independent rapid phase, tetracycline binds to cell surface layers and passes by diffusion through the outer layers of the cell. In the second, energy-dependent phase, tetracycline crosses the cytoplasmic membrane, probably by means of a proton-motive force. The precise transport system has not been identified.

Tetracycline resistance is common in both Gram-positive and Gram-negative bacteria. In most cases it is plasmid encoded and inducible; however, chromosomal, constitutive resistance is found in some organisms such as *Proteus* species. Many plasmid-encoded specified tetracycline resistance determinants have been found in enteric bacteria. The most common of these determinants, TetB, is also present in *H influenzae*. Tetracycline resistance in *Staphylococcus aureus* is due primarily to small multicopy plasmids; chromosomal resistance is rare. Tetracycline resistance is found on nonconjugative plasmids in *Streptococcus faecalis* and on the chromosome of *S pneumoniae*, *S agalactiae* (group B streptococci), and oral streptococci. *Clostridium* species such as *C difficile* harbor chromosomal genes for tetracycline resistance.

Basically, tetracycline resistance is due to a decrease in the levels of drug accumulation. Decreased uptake and increased efflux both probably participate. Resistant bacteria bind less tetracycline, and the tetracycline they do accumulate is lost by an energy-dependent process when they are in a drug-free milieu.

Plasmid-mediated resistance to tetracyclines can be partially overcome in Gram-positive species by modifying the tetracycline nucleus. Hence, achievable concentrations of minocycline and doxycycline, in particular, will inhibit some tetracycline-resistant streptococci such as *S pneumoniae*, and some *S aureus* strains. Molecular modification has not been successful in overcoming the tetracycline resistance of members of the Enterobacteriaceae or *Pseudomonas* or most *Bacteroides* species.

Tetracycline resistance is a major concern because it is located on plasmids near insertion sites, and these plasmids readily acquire other genetic information to enlarge the spectrum of resistance. The widespread use of tetracycline in animal feeds may be a factor in the extensive, worldwide resistance of members of the Enterobacteriaceae, particularly enteric species such as *Salmonella*, to tetracyclines and subsequently to many other drugs. Not only can tetracycline resistance move among members of the Enterobacteriaceae on plasmids, but plasmids mediating tetracycline resistance have moved between *S aureus*, *S epidermidis*, *S pyogenes*, *S pneumoniae*, and *S faecalis*.

Fosfomycin Resistance. Fosfomycin and fosmidomycin, which inhibit cell wall synthesis, enter bacteria by means of a glycerol-phosphate or glucose-6-phosphate transport system. Gram-positive bacteria in which the glucose-6-phosphate transport system is poorly developed do not take up these drugs in concentrations adequate to inhibit the cell wall synthesis. This resistance usually is chromosomal. The resistance of Gram-negative bacteria to these agents is related primarily to the presence in the population of some bacteria that can function without the transport system. Plasmids and transposons that transfer resistance to fosfomycin have been found in bacteria such as *Serratia marcescens*.

Aminoglycoside Resistance. In the most important form of aminoglycoside resistance, the compound is modified outside the cell and resistance is due partly to poor uptake of the altered compound. Also, all aminoglycosides have free amino and hydroxy groups that are essential for binding to ribosomal proteins. A number of enzymes can acetylate the amino groups and phosphorylate or adenylate the hydroxyl groups (Fig. 9). Other forms of resistance, such as altered binding site on 30S ribosomes, are much less common.

In members of the Enterobacteriaceae and in *Pseudomonas* species, the aminoglycosides pass through the cell wall via channels designed to admit cationic molecules to the periplasmic space. These channels, called porin channels, are lined by the porin protein. Aminoglycosides are then translocated across the cell membrane by an energy-dependent proton-motive force and, in the cytoplasm, bind to ribosomes located just below the membrane. Aminoglycosides bind only to ribosomes actively engaged in protein synthesis. Binding to the ribosomes induces a protein involved in the uptake of the aminoglycosides.

Bacteria may contain in the periplasmic space enzymes that acetylate, phosphorylate, or adenylate aminoglycosides to various degrees. It is not clear whether the enzymes are free in the periplasmic space or bound to the cytoplasmic membrane. The modified aminoglycosides do not bind well to ribosomes, and hence uptake is poor or absent (Fig. 16).

Aminoglycoside-modifying enzymes have been found in Gram-positive species such as *S aureus, S faecalis, S pyogenes,* and enzymes are particularly prevalent in members of the Enterobacteriaceae and *P aeruginosa. S pneumoniae.* These Many of the genes for aminoglycoside-modifying enzymes are carried on transposons

Anaerobic organisms such as *Bacteroides* species are resistant to aminoglycosides because they lack an oxygen-

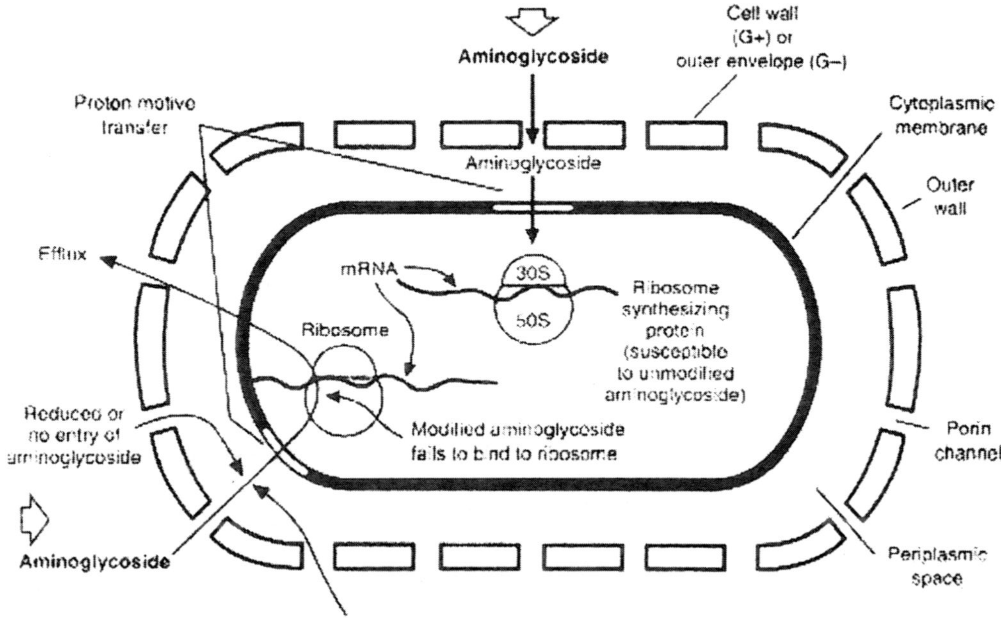

Figure 16: Diagrammatic representation of transfer and transfer reduction of aminoglycoside across the bacterial cell wall.

Contd . . .

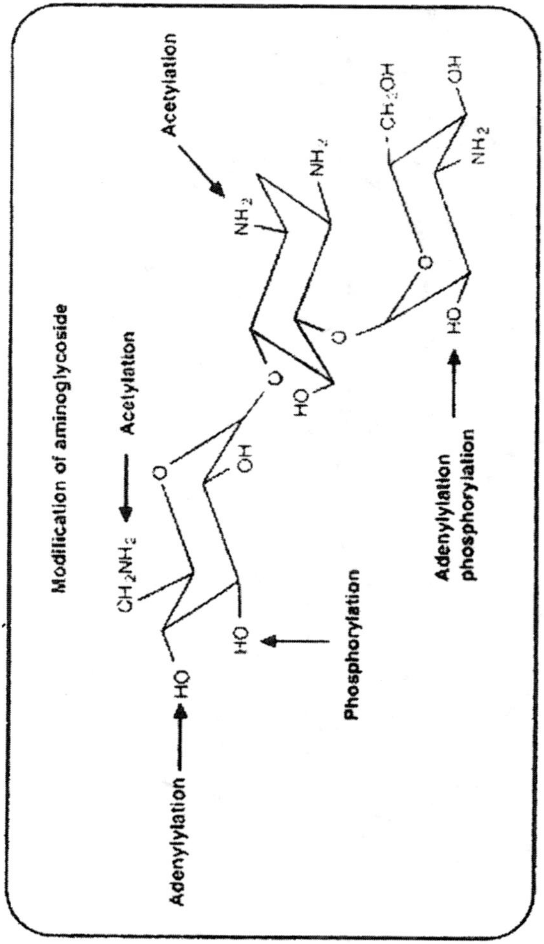
Modification of aminoglycoside
Acetylation
Acetylation
Adenylylation
Phosphorylation
Adenylylation
phosphorylation

Contd . . .

dependent transport system to move the drugs across the cytoplasmic membrane. Although most resistance of *S aureus* to aminoglycosides is due to aminoglycoside-modifying enzymes, small-colony variants of staphylococci also show resistance, which may be due to a defect in adenylate cyclase or in cyclic adenosine 5'-monophosphate (cAMP)binding proteins such that cells with a reduced growth rate do not transport aminoglycosides into the cytoplasm. Some members of the Enterobacteriaceae and *P aeruginosa* appear to be resistant because of altered porin channels, since these bacteria do not take up any drug and do not have aminoglycoside-inactivating enzymes.

Inactivation of a drug

Chloramphenicol Resistance. Many Gram-positive and Gram-negative bacteria, including some recently discovered *H influenzae* strains, are resistant to chloramphenicol because they possess the enzyme chloramphenicol transacetylate, which acetylates hydroxyl groups on the chloramphenicol structure. This enzyme, unlike the aminoglycoside-inactivating enzymes and ß-lactamases, is an intracellular enzyme of higher molecular weight and subunit structure. Acetylated chloramphenicol binds less well to the 50S ribosome.

ß-Lactam Resistance. The best-known mechanism of bacterial resistance is the resistance to ß-lactams, which is mediated by penicillinase enzymes. Resistance of *E coli* to penicillin was recognized in 1940, before sufficient penicillin was made to be clinically useful. In the 1940s, resistance of staphylococci was shown to be due to a penicillinase. As these enzymes also attack other ß-lactam compounds such as cephalosporins, carbapenems, and monobactams, they would be more appropriately designated ß-lactamases.

The most important activity of these enzymes is alteration of the ß-lactam nucleus (Fig. 17). ß-lactamases are widely distributed in nature and are usually classified on the basis of the principal compounds they destroy (e.g., as penicillinases or cephalosporinases) (Fig. 18). ß-Lactamases may be chromosomally or plasmid mediated, and they may be constitutive or inducible.

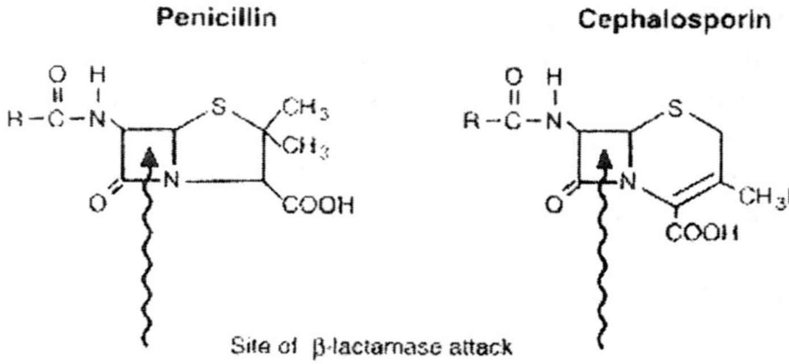

Figure 17: Site of ß-lactamase attack in penicillins and cephalosporins.

In Gram-positive species, ß-lactamases are primarily exoenzymes; that is, they are excreted into the milieu around the bacteria. Virtually all hospital isolates of staphylococci, both *S aureus* and *S epidermidis*, have ß-lactamases, and 50 to 80 percent of community-acquired staphylococcal isolates produce ß-lactamases. In Gram-negative species, both aerobic and anaerobic, ß-lactamases are contained in the periplasmic space, thus effectively protecting the penicillin-binding proteins.

Resistance of staphylococci to ß-lactams was soon overcome with the antistaphylococcal penicillins and the cephalosporins. Some strains of *S aureus* produce more ß-lactamase constitutively and can destroy some of the cephalosporins.

In 1974, *H influenzae* was shown to possess a plasmid mediated ß-lactamase. At present 10 to 35 percent of *H influenzae* strains in the United States produce ß-lactamases.

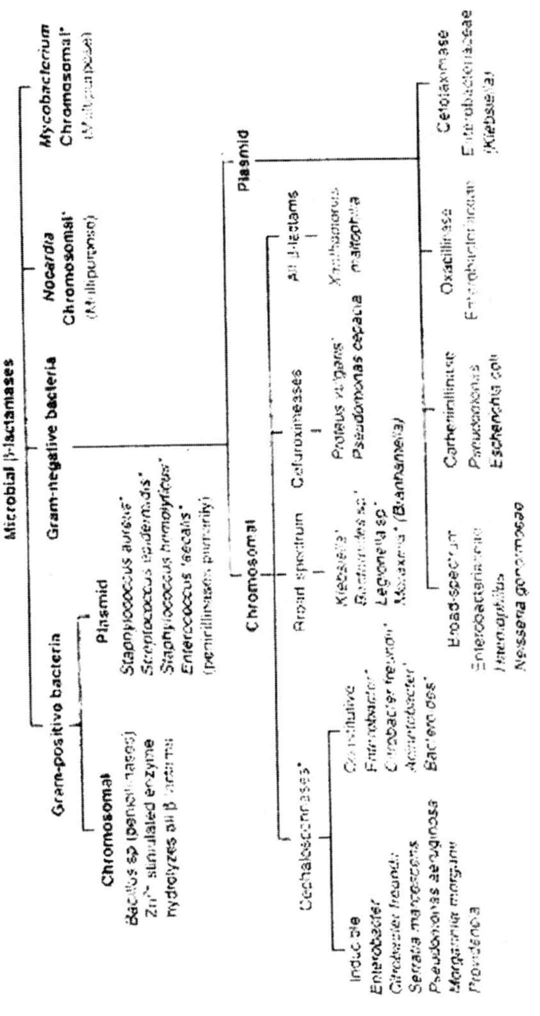

*Inhibited by clavulanate, sulbactam

Figure 18: β-Lactamase found in bacteria and their classification and synthesis, whether chromosomally or plasmid mediated.

The TnA transposon has become more widespread, and the resistance of *Haemophilus* species to penicillin G and ampicillin seems to be increasing yearly. The *Haemophilus* ß-lactamase is the same structurally as the enzyme found in *E coli, Salmonella, Shigella,* and *N gonorrhoeae*. The enzyme has generally been called the TEM enzyme after the initials of the Greek girl from whom an *E coli* strain containing a plasmid ß-lactamase was first isolated.

These enzymes are also called Richmond-Sykes class IIIa enzymes from a classification proposed by Richmond and Sykes in 1973. By far the most common plasmid ß-lactamase found in nature is TEM-1, which accounts for 75 to 80 percent of plasmid-mediated ß-lactamase resistance worldwide. Recently new ß-lactamases have been found that hydrolyze compounds such as inomethoxy cephalosporin, which were not destroyed by other plasmid-encoded ß-lactamases. The new ß-lactamases have an altered amino acid composition, which permits binding to the cephalosporin and subsequent hydrolysis. How common these new enzymes will become is unknown.

Chromosomally mediated ß-lactamases are present in many *Enterobacter, Citrobacter, Proteus-Providencia,* and *Pseudomonas* species. All *Klebsiella* species possess a ß-lactamase, which acts primarily as a penicillinase and is chromosomally mediated. Constitutively produced ß-lactamases are also present in many anaerobic species.

Table 3 lists the major ß-lactamases of clinical importance. ß-Lactamases vary in their ability to destroy penicillins and cephalosporins. ß-Lactamase activity is only one component of the ß-lactam resistance of Gram-negative bacteria, since resistance to ß-lactams is a combination of decreased entry, ß-lactamase stability and affinity of the compounds for penicillin-binding proteins.

Resistant Metabolic Pathway

No synthesis of a new type of cell wall resistant to ß-lactams has occurred, but some bacteria, particularly some streptococci, lack the hydrolytic enzymes necessary for forming a new cell wall, and so ß-lactams do not lyse these bacteria. An altered hydrolytic system thus converts a bactericidal antibiotic into a bacteriostatic agent. Whether such resistance occurs in Gram-negative species is not clear.

Some thymidine-requiring streptococci are not inhibited by trimethoprim and sulfonamides and so are not killed by these agents. These organisms are a rare cause of urinary tract infections. Other bacteria produce adequate deoxyribosylthymine 5'-monophosphate (DTMP) by alternative methods and, as a result. survive exposure to these folate inhibitors.

Certain *Candida* or *Cryptococcus* yeasts are resistant to flucytosine because they cannot convert it to its active component, fluorouracil. Other fungi can resist the polyenes and imidazoles because they synthesize membrane components by different metabolic mechanisms.

Antimicrobial Agents

Antibiotics are frequently used in combination for the following reasons: (1) to treat a life-threatening infection; (2) to prevent emergence of bacterial resistance; (3) to treat mixed infections of aerobic and anaerobic bacteria; (4) to enhance antibacterial activity (synergy); and (5) to use lower doses of a toxic drug. Combined treatment is reasonable when the precise agents of a serious infection are unknown. Use of two or more drugs to prevent the emergence of resistance is effective for tuberculosis and for therapy of some chronic infections.

The use of combinations to achieve synergy is more complicated. Synergy occurs when a combination of two drugs causes inhibition or killing when used at a fourfold-lower concentration than that of either component drug used separately (Fig. 19). However, indifference or antagonism may occur instead. Indifference means that the combined action is the same as with either component; antagonism refers to a reduction in the activity of one or both components in the presence of the other (Fig. 19).

Important examples of bacterial synergy include (1) combinations of anti-cell wall agents with aminoglycosides, (2) use of ß-lactamase inhibitors with ß-lactamase-susceptible antibiotics, and (3) combinations of drugs that act on sequential steps in bacterial metabolic or synthetic pathways. Examples of synergy that have proved clinically important are the combination of penicillin and streptomycin to treat *Enterococcus faecalis* endocarditis and the combination of carbenicillin and gentamicin to treat P aeruginosa infections.

Recently the ß-lactamase inhibitor clavulanic acid or sulbactam has been combined with amino penicillins to inhibit *S aureus, Klebsiella pneumoniae, H influenzae*, and anaerobic organisms such as *Bacteroides* species, all of which are resistant to amoxicillin or ampicillin when they contain ß-lactamases. The combination of sulfamethoxazole and trimethoprim attacks two parts of the folic acid cycle and synergistically inhibits many bacteria. Finally, combinations of two penicillins that affect different stages of cell wall synthesis in Gram-negative bacteria are synergistic. This is true for the combination of mecillinam (amdinocillin), which binds to PBP2 of bacteria, and penicillins or cephalosporins, which bind to PBP lb or 3.

Antagonism can occur when a bacteriostatic agent is combined with a bactericidal agent. The classic example has been the combination of chlortetracycline and penicillin in treatment of pneumococcal meningitis. This effect has not been explained from a molecular standpoint, and tetracyclines and penicillins or cephalosporins are used to treat mixed infections such as pelvic inflammatory disease due to *N gonorrhoeae* and *Chlamydia*. Some ß-lactam antibiotics can induce ß-lactamases that inactivate other ß-

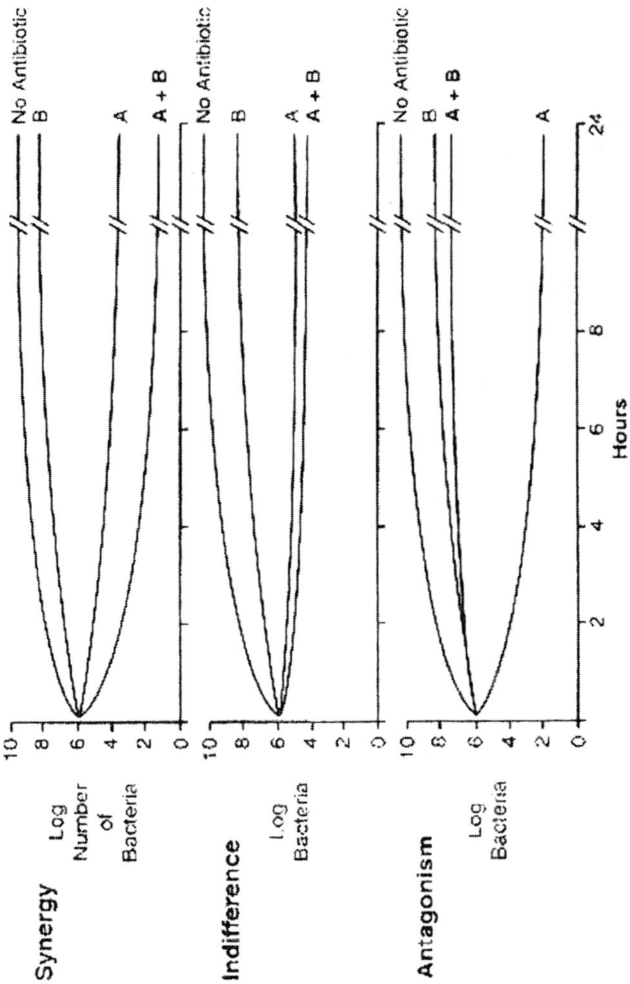

Figure 19: Example of how two antibiotics (A and B) may interact with synergy, indifference, or antagonism.

lactams, and antagonism can be shown in the test tube, but the relevance for clinical infections is not established.

Toxicology of Antimicrobial Agents

Antimicrobial agents can be directly toxic, can interact with other drugs to increase their toxicity, or can alter microbial flora to cause infection by organisms that are normally saprophytic. Allergic reactions can be caused by an agent, but penicillins can produce either immediate, IgE-mediated, or delayed hypersensitivity reactions. Cutaneous reactions have been reported with every class of antimicrobial agent. Hematologic reactions can range from the life-threatening blood dyscrasia that occurs in 1 in 60,000 individuals who receive chloramphenicol to hemolytic anemia due to sulfonamides in individuals who lack the enzyme glucose-6-phosphate dehydrogenase.

Depression of blood platelet activity has occurred with many agents. By altering the gastrointestinal flora, almost all antibiotics can cause overgrowth of *Clostridium difficile*, which produces a toxin that causes diarrhea and even pseudomembranous colitis. Alteration of intestinal flora by antibiotics can also result in overgrowth of *Candida* in the mouth, vagina, or gastrointestinal tract. Since a number of antibiotics are metabolized in the liver, damage to the liver can occur. This has been of particular concern with isoniazid, which is used to treat tuberculosis. Damage to the kidneys can follow the use of aminoglycosides. Neurologic toxicity is fortunately fairly uncommon, but the aminoglycosides can damage the auditory or vestibular apparatus if the dosage is not closely monitored.

Bacteria continue to evolve new mechanisms of resistance to old and to new antimicrobial agents. Some bacteria such as *P aeruginosa* are particularly adept at utilizing a number of different mechanisms simultaneously to become resistant to agents in virtually every class and those with such diverse sites of action as cell wall, protein biosynthesis, or DNA and RNA synthesis. Progress in medicine will keep patients alive who have nosocomial infections with resistant pathogens.

Mechanism to Reduce Bacterial Resistance

Proper selection of new antibiotics will be a major force in slowing the development of antimicrobial resistance. Proper hygiene practices will reduce plasmid transfer and the establishment of multiple drug-resistant bacteria in the hospital and will delay the appearance of such species in the community.

Table 4: Mechanism to reduce antibiotic resistance

1. Control, reduce, or cycle antibiotic usage
2. Improve hygiene in hospitals and among hospital personnel and reduce movement of patients to eliminate the dissemination of resistant organisms within hospitals
3. Discover or develop new antibiotics
4. Modify existing antibiotics chemically to produce compounds inert to known mechanisms of resistance
5. Develop inhibitors of antibiotic-modifying enzymes
6. Define agents that would "cure" resistance plasmids

Table 4 lists a number of mechanisms to prevent bacterial resistance. The health care provider must be continually alert to the appearance of antibiotic resistance within the hospital and community.

Bibliography

Alexander, Martin et al. "Microbial Technologies to Overcome Environmental Problems of Persistent Pollutants". *Nairobi: United Nations Environment Programme,* 1987. MAIN TD172.5 .E93 1983.

Baker, Kenneth Frank et al. *Ecology of Soil-bourne Plant Pathogens, Prelude to Biological Control.* Berkeley, CA: University of California Press, 1965. BOT QR111 .I55 1963.

Banfield, J. F., and K. H. Nealson, "Geomicoroblogy: Interactions Between Microbes and Minerals". *Reviews in Mineralogy,* Vol. 35. Mineral. Soc. Amer., Washington, DC., 1997

Brack, A. (Ed.), *The Molecular Origins of Life: Assembling Pieces of the Puzzle. Cambridge University Press, London,* 1998

Brock, T. D. *Milestones in Microbiology.* Prentice-Hall, Englewood Cliffs, NJ, 1961.

Dusenbery, David B. *Life at a Small Scale: the Behavior of Microbes.* New York: Scientific American Library, distributed by W.H. Freeman, 1996. MAIN QR41.2 .D87 1996.

Lengeler, J. W. et al. *Biology of Prokaryotes.* Blackwell Science. Stuttgart, 1999.

Li, Koibong and Leslie A. Lewis. *A Novel Approach to the Evolution of Microorganisms.* New York: Vantage Press, 1987. MAIN QR13 .L53 1987.

Lisitzin, A. P. Oceanic Sedimentation. American Geophysical Union. Washington, DC, 1996.

Lovley, D. R. (Ed.)., Environmental Microbe-Metal Interactions. ASM Press, Washington, DC, 2000.

Madigan, M. T., J. M. Martkinko, and J. Parker, *Brock Biology of Microorganisms,* 9th Ed. Prentice Hall. Upper Saddle River, NJ, 2000.

Monastersky, Richard. *Fossil Soil Has the Dirt on Early Microbes.* Science News Volume 153, p 151. Main Serials Q1 .S76, March 7, 1998.

Pelczar, Michael J. *Microbiology.* New York: McGraw-Hill, 1958. MAIN QR41 .P4 1958.

Raloff, Janet. *Plants Recruit Oil-Detoxifying Microbes.* Science News. Volume 148, August 5, 1995.

Witt, Steven C. *Biotechnology, Microbes and the Environment.* San Francisco, CA: Center for Science Information, 1990. PUBLIC QR100 .W57 1990; BIODIV QR100 .W57 1990.

Index